W9-CPN-318

Teen Finance Series

# Savings And Investment Information For Teens, Third Edition

# Savings And Investment Information For Teens, Third Edition

### Tips For A Successful Financial Life

### Including Facts About Economic Principles, Wealth Development, Bank Accounts, Stocks, Bonds, Mutual Funds, And Other Financial Tools

OMNIGRAPHICS
615 Griswold, Ste. 901
Detroit, MI 48226

Bibliographic Note
Because this page cannot legibly accommodate all the copyright notices, the Bibliographic Note portion of the Preface constitutes an extension of the copyright notice.

* * *

Omnigraphics
a part of Relevant Information
Keith Jones, *Managing Editor*

* * *

Library of Congress Cataloging-in-Publication Data

Names: Omnigraphics, Inc., issuing body.

Title: Savings and investment information for teens: tips for a successful financial life, including facts about economic principles, wealth development, bank accounts, stocks, bonds, mutual funds, and other financial tools.

Description: Third edition. | Detroit, MI: Omnigraphics, [2017] | Series: Teen finance series | Includes bibliographical references and index.

Identifiers: LCCN 2017007801 (print) | LCCN 2017012233 (ebook) | ISBN 9780780815544 (eBook) | ISBN 9780780815537 (hardcover: alk. paper)

Subjects: LCSH: Saving and investment. | Teenagers--Finance, Personal.

Classification: LCC HG4521 (ebook) | LCC HG4521 .S337 2017 (print) | DDC 339.4/30835--dc23

LC record available at https://lccn.loc.gov/2017007801

# Table Of Contents

# Part Three: Banks And Bonds

# Part Four: Stocks And Mutual Funds

# Part Five: If You Need More Information

# Preface

## About This Book

The financial services market offers today's consumers a wide variety of products, services, and providers to choose from to meet their financial needs. While this degree of choice provides a great number of options, it also requires that consumers be equipped with the information, knowledge, and skills to evaluate their options and identify those that best suit their needs and circumstances. This is particularly important for young adults who are looking to make important financial decisions that will shape the rest of their lives. Unfortunately, significant numbers of young Americans continue to demonstrate relatively low levels of financial literacy, and research indicates that the gap between the amount of financial responsibility given to them and their demonstrated ability to manage financial decisions is rapidly widening. Recent studies have shown many students do not understand the basic financial principles around saving and investing, and have difficulty applying financial decision-making skills to real life situations.

*Savings And Investment Information for Teens*, Third Edition, provides updated information to help young adults learn how to develop the habit of saving money and investing for the future. It explains how the economy works and how factors such as interest rates and inflation impact personal wealth. It offers practical suggestions for developing a financial plan, and it describes the risks and rewards associated with bank accounts, stocks, bonds, and mutual funds. The book concludes with a directory of resources for additional information for further reading.

## How To Use This Book

This book is divided into parts and chapters. Parts focus on broad areas of interest; chapters are devoted to single topics within a part.

*Part One: How The Economy Works* describes the basic principles that govern the functioning of the U.S. and global economies. It provides historical information about the use of money, explains the federal reserve system, the gross domestic process, and the economic factors that influence interest rates, inflation, and consumer prices.

*Part Two: Keys To Wealth Development* explains the need for financial literacy and capability among teens. It highlights the fundamental tools that can be used in saving money and making it grow. It discusses the benefits and risks of different types of investment choices and provides information on how to understand financial documents, and how to work with financial industry professionals. The part also includes cautions against common misunderstandings, frauds, and scams. It concludes with a chapter about the hazards associated with managing money in online environment.

*Part Three: Banks And Bonds* discusses the similarities and differences among banks, thrifts, and credit unions. The part describes the most common investment vehicles used in managing cash, including various types of savings accounts, certificates of deposit (CDs), and bonds. It discusses the benefits, risks, liquidity, and potential for generating returns associated with different savings instruments, and it offers an explanation about which types of accounts are insured by the Federal Deposit Insurance Corporation (FDIC).

*Part Four: Stocks And Mutual Funds* explains equity investments and the various ways people can own stocks as part of an investment portfolio, including owning individual stocks and purchasing different types of mutual funds. It also explains special risks associated with investing in foreign stocks, trading in microcap stocks, and day trading.

*Part Five: If You Need More Information* provides a directory of savings and investment organizations and suggestions for additional reading.

## Bibliographic Note

This volume contains documents and excerpts from publications issued by the following U.S. government agencies: Consumer Financial Protection Bureau (CFPB); Consumer.gov; Federal Deposit Insurance Corporation (FDIC); Federal Reserve Board (FRB); Federal Trade Commission (FTC); Library of Congress (LOC); U.S. Bureau of Economic Analysis (BEA); U.S. Bureau of Labor Statistics (BLS); U.S. Department of the Treasury; U.S. Securities and Exchange Commission (SEC); U.S. Small Business Administration (SBA); USA.gov; and Youth.gov.

It may also contain original material produced by Omnigraphics.

The photograph on the front cover is © wavebreakmedia/iStock.

# Part One
## How The Economy Works

# Chapter 1
# The History Of Money

At one time, if you wanted something that belonged to another person, you had offer him or her something of your own that was agreed to be of equal value. That's called trading, or the barter system, and it's been in place from the beginning of human history. Bartering depends on individuals possessing items with intrinsic value, that is, items that are worth something because they can be eaten or used, such as a cow or a tool, or items that are desired for their rarity and beauty, like an unusual rock or shiny piece of metal. Naturally occurring substances, like gold, silver, and gemstones became popular items for trade and remain highly prized today. But in various areas at different times in human history, everything from seashells to beads were considered valuable enough for barter.

## The Emergence Of Coins

Although the barter system worked well, and still works today for many purposes, it wasn't long before people realized that they needed something more portable than animals or large, bulky items in order to do business with others who lived some distance away. So coins—small, usually metal, objects that could be transported easily—first appeared, according to many experts, in what is now Turkey around 650 B.C.E. These early coins were made of electrum, a naturally occurring alloy of gold and silver, and were often struck with a hammer and die on one side to leave a unique mark, often identifying its origin or paying tribute to a god or a ruler.

Eventually, gold and silver coins became accepted as a standard unit of currency throughout the region and helped spur the scientific, cultural, and artistic development

"The History Of Money," © 2017 Omnigraphics.

of the Greek empire. Coins appeared in many other parts of the ancient world, as well, including China, Egypt, India, Persia, and Rome, most often made of gold and silver, as well as other metals, like copper and bronze. Part of the significance of coins was that they provided a monetary standard, a widely accepted unit of exchange that went beyond the usefulness of the metal itself. Gold, for example, would have little practical use for a person in ancient times. It's too soft for making tools or weapons. Yet gold and silver remain among the most valuable metals even today, because they are almost universally deemed as desirable, part because of their shiny appearance but also because of their relative scarcity.

# The Origins Of Paper Money

Experimentation with paper money is thought to have begun in China during the Tang Dynasty, around the year 900. The Chinese had invented paper itself around the first century B.C.E., and as their culture and economy advanced, merchants began signing paper notes of credit for trading purposes. In about 1024 these evolved into standardized promissory notes issued by the government that represented a quantity of copper, gold, or silver coins that were held in the treasury. But gradually the government started printing more paper notes than could be backed by real metal, which led to out-of-control inflation. In 1380, one standardized unit of currency, called a guan, was worth 1,000 copper coins, and by 1535 the guan was valued at about one-quarter of a copper coin. As a result, paper money was abolished in China.

The first paper money in Europe was printed in Sweden in the seventeenth century, amid a good deal of controversy. Merchants and government officials were concerned that this could mean the ruin of the country's financial system. As a result, each paper banknote was individually signed by at least 16 government officials certifying that it could be exchanged for gold or silver. When other European countries and merchants saw how well the Swedish system worked, the use of paper currency spread quickly. Governments, princes, and individual merchants began printing their own banknotes, and unfortunately they weren't as careful as Sweden in ensuring that the paper was backed by anything substantial. As a result, the value of banknotes was only as good as the reputation, and wealth, of the person or institution that issued it. Experiments continued, with banknotes falling in and out of favor as public skepticism ebbed and flowed from country to country, and it was not until the nineteenth century that the use of paper money became accepted in most places.

## Money Timeline

**~650 B.C.E.:** The barter system was the primary means of exchanging goods and services

**c. 650 B.C.E.:** The first known coins came into use in what is now Turkey

**c. 900:** The first experimentation with paper money is thought to have begun in China

**c. 1600:** Gold and silver coins from various countries came into use in North America

**1690:** First paper currency printed in America by the Massachusetts Bay Colony

**1776:** Continental Congress issues the first Continentals, paper money used to help finance the Revolutionary War

**1861:** Congress authorizes the U.S. Treasury to issue "greenbacks," paper money needed to help pay for the Civil War

**1914:** Congress passes the Federal Reserve Act, which officially puts the United States on the gold standard

**1933:** Congress ends the gold standard for individuals and businesses in the United States

**1973-1976:** The United States takes final steps to sever the ties between currency and gold

# History Of Money In The United States

Gold and silver coins from various countries were in use in North America from the time of the first European settlements in the early seventeenth century. The first paper currency printed in America was issued by the Massachusetts Bay Colony in 1690 to fund military expeditions during the French and Indian War. Other colonies began to follow suit, and the currency, known as bills of credit, was used for general exchange, as well as to support military and economic expeditions and to pay debts. Not surprisingly, as the colonies printed more and more bills, the bills began to lose value, and the resulting inflation caused the British Parliament to pass a series of Currency Acts to help regulate the printing and use of paper money in the colonies.

## Paper Money Helps Finance The Revolution

To help finance the Revolutionary War, the Continental Congress issued about $240 million in paper currency called Continentals, with the understanding that these could be redeemed for an agreed amount of gold or silver after the war. But the individual colonies continued to print bills of credit, and that practice, along with counterfeiting by the British to undermine the colonial monetary system, resulted in a serious devaluation of Continentals and runaway inflation. By 1781, Continentals were so worthless that they no one would accept them, and they were essentially finished as money. It was only with a loan from France in the form of specie (gold and silver coins) that the war was able to continue.

Because of these experiences, the delegates to the Constitutional Convention inserted a clause into the Constitution that forbade individual states from issuing bills of credit or to use any form of currency other than gold or silver coins. It also said that only Congress could coin money and regulate its value. The basic unit of currency in the new country was called the "dollar" and at the time it was deemed to be worth about 375 grains of silver.

Alexander Hamilton, the first secretary of the treasury, convinced Congress in 1791 to establish the Bank of the United States, a private institution whose initial function was to collect taxes and hold the country's money, but it soon began to issue banknotes, which were redeemable in precious metals. Other banks followed suit, and once again paper money began to flood the market. Some banks issued more bills than they could back with gold and silver, and bills of various amounts of perceived value were in circulation throughout the country. By 1860, thousands of banks were issuing bills, and the country's monetary system was becoming unstable.

## "Greenbacks" Are Issued During The Civil War

To meet the expense of the Civil War, in 1861 Congress authorized the U.S. Treasury to issue demand notes in denominations of $5, $10, and $20. Known as "greenbacks," these were bills that were not backed by gold or silver. They were largely untrusted, and their value soon dropped. After the war, the government wanted to re-establish monetary stability and agreed to exchange the greenbacks for gold on demand. This officially tied the value of the U.S. dollar to gold, and in 1914 Congress passed the Federal Reserve Act, which created the Federal Reserve System, the country's central banking system, which set limits on the amount of money that could be issued and mandated that every U.S. dollar had to be backed by 40 cents worth of gold in the treasury.

The **Federal Reserve** system is the central bank of the United States. It includes the Board of Governors in Washington, D.C., and 12 independent regional Reserve banks. This decentralized structure ensures that the economic conditions of all areas of the country are taken into account in the making of monetary policy.

## The Gold Standard

The official link between the dollar and the value of gold resulted in the United States remaining on the "gold standard" until 1933. In that year, as part of the initiative to bring the country out of the Great Depression, Congress passed a law ending the gold standard, prohibiting the private possession of most gold, and stating that people could no longer demand gold in exchange for their paper money. However, for the purposes of international trade, U.S. dollars could still be exchanged for gold at a rate fixed by the government until 1971, when the United States ended this practice. Then, in 1973 and 1976, additional steps were taken to completely sever the relationship between U.S. currency and gold. Today most countries do not tie their paper money to gold, silver, or other metals.

## What Does It Mean?

**Banknote:** Paper money; a country's currency, usually issued by its central bank

**Barter system:** The practice of trading goods or services for other goods or services, without the exchange of money

**Currency:** The metal or paper money used in any given country

**Devaluation:** A reduction in the official value of currency

**Demand note:** Paper money that has an agreed value but is not backed by gold or silver

**Gold standard:** A system in which a country's currency is tied to a fixed amount of gold

**Inflation:** An increase in the price of goods and services and subsequent reduction in the value of money

**Promissory note:** A document stating that one person will pay a certain amount of money to another

**Specie:** Money in the form of coins

**Striking a coin:** Placing a metal blank between one or two dies containing a reversed version of the image to appear on the finished coin and then striking it with a heavy hammer to imprint the image

## References

1. Cleveland, Don. "A History of Printed Money," International Bank Note Society, July 20, 2008.

2. "History of Money," HistoryWorld.net, n.d.

3. "History of Paper Money," Federal Reserve Bank of Atlanta, n.d.

4. "The History of American Currency," U.S. Currency Education Program, n.d.

5. Karasavvas, Theodoros. "Barter, Bills and Banknotes: The 5,000 Year History of Money," *Barter News Weekly*, December 2, 2016.

6. Skousen, W. Cleon. "The History of American Money," CMI Gold and Silver, n.d.

# Chapter 2
# The American Experience With Money

The first system of "money" in North America was not coins or bills but the exchange of commodities. For thousands of years, Native Americans used the barter system, trading goods like furs, tobacco, indigo, rice, wheat, and corn with each other and with neighboring tribes. Eventually they introduced the first actual money in North America, called wampum, composed of beads made from shells and strung together to exchange for food, tools, weapons, and other useful items. When European settlers began arriving, they too mostly used the barter system, but some also adopted wampum as a means of exchange.

The earliest gold and silver coins used by the settlers were from European countries, including Great Britain, Portugal, France, and Spain. The first coins actually produced in the English colonies were issued in the Massachusetts Bay Colony in 1652, and America's first paper currency was also printed there in 1690. Other colonies followed suit, and a variety of paper money came into use. To help finance the Revolutionary War, the Continental Congress issued about $240 million in paper currency called Continentals, which were supposed to be redeemable for an agreed amount of gold or silver after the war. This became the first paper currency issued by the United States government. Unfortunately, individual states continued to print their own money, which caused a great deal of confusion and resulted in Continentals becoming virtually worthless. To keep this from happening in the future, states were forbidden to issue paper money by the new U.S. Constitution.

"The American Experience With Money," © 2017 Omnigraphics.

## Timeline Of The Gold Standard In The United States

**1865:** After the Civil War, the government keeps its promise to exchange "greenbacks" for gold, tying the value of the U.S. dollar to gold.

**1879:** The United States adopts the gold standard, in which a standard amount of gold defines the value of U.S. currency, and the amount of gold for which currency can be redeemed.

**1900:** Congress passes the Gold Standard Act, officially establishing gold as the only standard for redeeming paper money.

**1913:** The Federal Reserve Act mandates that every U.S. dollar must be backed by 40 cents worth of gold in the treasury.

**1933:** In response to the Great Depression, Congress ends the gold standard, bans private ownership of gold, and declares that currency can no longer be exchanged for gold. (However, for the purposes of international trade, U.S. dollars could still be redeemed for gold.)

**1943:** Representatives from the United States and 43 other countries agree that all currency would be linked to the U.S. dollar, which was still redeemable in gold for international trade. At the time, the United States held about 75 percent of the world's gold reserves.

**1971:** President Richard Nixon announces that the United States would temporarily stop exchanging U.S. dollars for gold for purposes of international trade.

**1974:** President Gerald Ford signs a law that once again legalizes the private ownership of gold.

**1976:** The government redefines the U.S. dollar, officially severing all its links to gold, effectively removing the international monetary system from a gold standard. Today, very few countries tie their currency to gold, silver, or other metals.

# The Bank Of The United States

Alexander Hamilton, the first secretary of the U.S. Treasury, convinced Congress to establish the Bank of the United States. Part of the reason for its creation was to help pay off the debt from the American Revolution by holding, controlling, and disbursing the country's money. But it also issued a national currency (the dollar) that would be accepted in all states, created money by borrowing as needed, loaned money to the government, and eventually oversaw the regulation of private banks that were chartered by various states.

From the beginning, the bank was a major source of controversy in the new country. Hamilton and his Federalist Party, who believed in a strong, financially sound national government, were opposed by Thomas Jefferson and the Democratic-Republicans, who advocated for states' rights and a primarily agrarian economy. The debate centered on the two parties' different interpretations of the Constitution. The Preamble gave Congress the right to make laws that were "right and proper" in order to carry out its part in the governing of the nation. But the Tenth Amendment said that any powers not specifically granted to Congress were given to the individual states. Hamilton's party thought the Bank of the United States was necessary for the economic health of the country, while Jefferson's party felt it would give too much power to the federal government. In the end, President Washington was convinced by the Federalists, and signed the bank into law in 1791.

But that didn't end the controversy. The two factions kept the argument going and continued to make the Bank of the United an example of their political beliefs and their interpretations of the Constitution. The bitter debate resulted in the bank's charter failing to be renewed in 1811. It was revived in 1816, but the partisan factions wouldn't drop their feud over the issue. In the early 1830s, President Andrew Jackson and his Democratic Party took up opposition to the bank, while the new Whig Party, led by Henry Clay, decided to make its mark by defending the institution in what became known as the "Bank Wars" during the presidential campaign of 1832, in which Jackson defeated Clay. Jackson vetoed the renewal of the bank's charter amid strong opposition, but the veto held, and the bank dissolved after its charter ran out in 1836. It was re-chartered as a commercial bank in Pennsylvania, where it continued to operate until it failed in 1841.

# The United States Mint

In addition to urging Congress to create the Bank of the United States, Alexander Hamilton also championed the establishment of the United States Mint. On April 2, 1792, Congress passed the Coinage Act, which created the Mint and authorized construction of a building to house it in Philadelphia, the nation's capital at the time. The Act also specified the salary of the Mint's director, as well as those of other Mint employees. President Washington appointed David Rittenhouse, a highly regarded scientist, inventor, and mathematician, as the first director of the Mint, a position he held until 1795.

The Coinage Act mandated that coins produced by the Mint must bear the words "United States of America," "Liberty," and the year of coinage, but Rittenhouse believed the coins should also be works of art, and he personally consulted on the design. He hand-struck the first coins himself to test the Mint's new equipment and presented them to Washington as gift. Legend has it that those first "pattern" or sample coins were made from Martha Washington's silverware. The first coins authorized by Congress were made of copper (the half-cent, cent), silver (half-dime, dime, quarter, half-dollar, dollar), and gold (quarter-eagle, half-eagle, eagle), and the first ones to enter mass production were the copper half-cent and one-cent coins in 1793.

The Constitution did not specify the degree to which the federal government could become involved in the country's monetary system. It only specified that Congress could mint metal coins, set the percentage of precious metal in those coins, and officially determine the amount of precious metal of any foreign coins circulating in the United States.

But controversy soon erupted again. This time the issue was that the Mint was unable to supply enough coins to satisfy the country's need, in part because of a shortage of the metals needed for their production. Hamilton and other Federalists argued that the Mint should be closed and the Bank of the United States take over responsibility for minting coins, because it had better access to precious metals and could run the operation more efficiently. Congress took up the debate, but after several close votes the Mint remained open. In 1803, Elias Boudinot, then director of the Mint, submitted a report to Congress outlining his plan to improve efficiency and increase the Mint's production. A bill was passed that year authorizing the Mint's continued operations, and no serious challenge to its work has been mounted since that time. As more states joined the Union, more Mints were added throughout the country. Today the Mint operates facilities in Philadelphia, Denver, San Francisco, and West Point, New York, in addition to its headquarters in Washington, D.C.

## The Free Banking Era

The period from 1836, when the Bank of the United States was dissolved, to 1863 is sometimes called the Free Banking Era. During this time, there was no central federal bank, and the individual states ran their own banking systems. State-chartered banks were free to issue paper currency against their gold and silver reserves, and regulations about interest rates, loan terms, and the amount of coin or precious metal reserves they were required to maintain were set by the states, not by the federal government. In addition, some states passed free banking acts, which allowed banks to open and run like any other business, with almost no legislative oversight.

The result was chaos. Banks operated with less regulation than at any other time in U.S. history, with the result that almost anyone could open a bank, many were severely underfunded, and a lot of their currency became worthless. About half the banks failed, with many of them going out of business because they were unable to redeem their banknotes in specie (gold and silver coins), leaving depositors with loads of useless paper. Some of the problems were caused the inherent lack of regulation, some by crooks who opened banks and defrauded the public by intentionally issuing more currency than they ever planned to redeem, and others were simply the result of poor management by inexperienced business people.

The counterfeiting of American money goes back to the earliest European settlers who began dying common white shells to resemble the rarer blue-black shells used by native tribes as wampum. When copper, silver, and gold coins came into use, their designs became more and more elaborate in an attempt to foil counterfeiters. Early paper money proved even easier to fake than coins, so through the years its design and printing techniques have become increasingly sophisticated. Some of the latest bills employ anti-counterfeiting measures like watermarks, interwoven security threads, and even ink that changes color as the bill is held at different angles.

# National Banks

In the United States, a national bank is a commercial bank that is a member of the Federal Reserve System and the Federal Deposit Insurance Corporation (FDIC), which insures bank deposits against loss. These banks are chartered and overseen by the Office of the Comptroller of the Currency (OCC), part of the U.S. Treasury Department, and are required to have the word "national" or the letters "NA" (for national association) in their names. To become a national bank, a bank must prove the competence and experience of its senior managers and board of directors and must demonstrate its stability by having sufficient capital reserves to withstand a certain amount of economic fluctuation.

Currently there are more than 350 national banks in the United States. Some of the largest, with more than 1,000 locations, include familiar names like Bank of America, Citizens Bank, Chase, PNC Bank, Regions Bank, SunTrust, U.S. Bank, and Wells Fargo. But not all national banks have so many branches or subsidiaries around the country. Some operate in just one region, state, or city. Whatever their size, national banks manage the process for buying and selling U.S. Treasury bonds, handle daily transactions with their local Federal Reserve Bank, and perform many of the same functions as any other bank, including maintaining savings and checking accounts for customers.

## References

1. "About the United States Mint," USmint.gov, 2016.

2. "Bank of the United States," Encyclopaedia Britannica, September 12, 2016.

3. Flaherty, Edward. "A Brief History of Central Banking in the United States," Letrug.nl, n.d.

4. Hendrik, Rhab. "The Free Banking Era," ArticlesFactory.com, January 5, 2011.

5. Hill, Andrew T. "The First Bank of the United States," Federalreservehistory.org, December 4, 2015.

6. Hunt, Steve. "History of the United States Mint," SBCgold.com, September 17, 2015.

7. "Money Matters: The American Experience with Money," Federal Reserve Bank of Chicago, 1996.

8. Paige, Joseph. "Native American Money," Native American Cultural Center, 2006.

9. Sanches, Daniel. "The Free Banking Era: A Lesson for Today?" Federal Reserve Bank of Philadelphia, third quarter, 2016.

10. "What Are the Major National Banks of the United States?" Reference.com, n.d.

# Chapter 3
# The Federal Reserve System And How It Affects You

## Federal Reserve System

The Federal Reserve System, often referred to as the Federal Reserve or simply "the Fed," is the central bank of the United States. It was created by the Congress to provide the nation with a safer, more flexible, and more stable monetary and financial system. The Federal Reserve was created on December 23, 1913, when President Woodrow Wilson signed the Federal Reserve Act into law. The Federal Reserve's responsibilities fall into four general areas.

- Conducting the nation's monetary policy by influencing money and credit conditions in the economy in pursuit of full employment and stable prices.

- Supervising and regulating banks and other important financial institutions to ensure the safety and soundness of the nation's banking and financial system and to protect the credit rights of consumers.

- Maintaining the stability of the financial system and containing systemic risk that may arise in financial markets.

- Providing certain financial services to the U.S. government, U.S. financial institutions, and foreign official institutions, and playing a major role in operating and overseeing the nation's payments systems.

About This Chapter: Text beginning with the heading "Federal Reserve System" is excerpted from "Current FAQs: About The Fed," Federal Reserve Board (FRB), March 1, 2017; Text under the heading "Three Key System Entities Of Federal Reserve" is excerpted from "The Three Key System Entities," Federal Reserve Board (FRB), October 24, 2016; Text beginning with the heading "The Decentralized System Structure And Its Philosophy" is excerpted from "Structure Of The Federal Reserve System," Federal Reserve Board (FRB), January 19, 2017.

# Who Owns The Federal Reserve?

The Federal Reserve System is not "owned" by anyone. Although parts of the Federal Reserve System share some characteristics with private-sector entities, the Federal Reserve was established to serve the public interest.

The Federal Reserve derives its authority from the Congress, which created the System in 1913 with the enactment of the Federal Reserve Act.

The Board of Governors in Washington, D.C., is an agency of the federal government. The Board—appointed by the President and confirmed by the Senate—provides general guidance for the Federal Reserve System and oversees the 12 Reserve Banks. The Board reports to and is directly accountable to the Congress but, unlike many other public agencies, it is not funded by congressional appropriations. In addition, though the Congress sets the goals for monetary policy, decisions of the Board—and the Fed's monetary policy-setting body, the Federal Open Market Committee—about how to reach those goals do not require approval by the President or anyone else in the executive or legislative branches of government.

Some observers mistakenly consider the Federal Reserve to be a private entity because the Reserve Banks are organized similarly to private corporations. For instance, each of the 12 Reserve Banks operates within its own particular geographic area, or District, of the United States, and each is separately incorporated and has its own board of directors. Commercial banks that are members of the Federal Reserve System hold stock in their District's Reserve Bank. However, owning Reserve Bank stock is quite different from owning stock in a private company. The Reserve Banks are not operated for profit, and ownership of a certain amount of stock is, by law, a condition of membership in the System. In fact, the Reserve Banks are required by law to transfer net earnings to the U.S. Treasury, after providing for all necessary expenses of the Reserve Banks, legally required dividend payments, and maintaining a limited balance in a surplus fund.

# How Is The Federal Reserve System Structured?

The Federal Reserve System was designed to give it a broad perspective on the economy and on economic activity in all parts of the nation. It is a federal system, composed of a central, independent governmental agency—the Board of Governors—in Washington, D.C., and 12 regional Federal Reserve Banks, located in major cities throughout the nation. These components share responsibility for supervising and regulating certain financial institutions and activities; providing banking services to depository institutions and to the federal government;

and ensuring that consumers receive adequate information and fair treatment in their business with the banking system. The Federal Open Market Committee (FOMC) is the monetary policy making body of the Federal Reserve System.

# Three Key System Entities Of Federal Reserve

Three key Federal Reserve entities—the Federal Reserve Board of Governors (Board of Governors), the Federal Reserve Banks (Reserve Banks), and the Federal Open Market Committee (FOMC)—make decisions that help promote the health of the U.S. economy and the stability of the U.S. financial system.

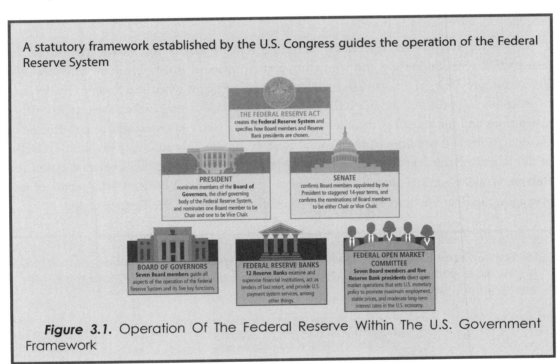

A statutory framework established by the U.S. Congress guides the operation of the Federal Reserve System

**Figure 3.1.** Operation Of The Federal Reserve Within The U.S. Government Framework

## The Federal Reserve Board

The Board of Governors—located in Washington, D.C.—is the governing body of the Federal Reserve System. It is run by seven members, or "governors," who are nominated by the President of the United States and confirmed in their positions by the U.S. Senate. The Board of Governors guides the operation of the Federal Reserve System to promote the goals and fulfill the responsibilities given to the Federal Reserve by the Federal Reserve Act.

All of the members of the Board serve on the FOMC (Federal Open Market Committee), which is the body within the Federal Reserve that sets monetary policy. Each member of the Board of Governors is appointed for a 14-year term; the terms are staggered so that one term expires on January 31 of each even-numbered year. After serving a full 14-year term, a Board member may not be reappointed. If a Board member leaves the Board before his or her term expires, however, the person nominated and confirmed to serve the remainder of the term may later be appointed to a full 14-year term.

The Chair and Vice Chair of the Board are also appointed by the President and confirmed by the Senate, but serve only four-year terms. They may be reappointed to additional four-year terms. The nominees to these posts must already be members of the Board or must be simultaneously appointed to the Board.

The Board oversees the operations of the 12 Reserve Banks and shares with them the responsibility for supervising and regulating certain financial institutions and activities. The Board also provides general guidance, direction, and oversight when the Reserve Banks lend to depository institutions and when the Reserve Banks provide financial services to depository institutions and the federal government. The Board also has broad oversight responsibility for the operations and activities of the Federal Reserve Banks. This authority includes oversight of the Reserve Banks' services to depository institutions, and to the U.S. Treasury, and of the Reserve Banks' examination and supervision of various financial institutions. As part of this oversight, the Board reviews and approves the budgets of each of the Reserve Banks.

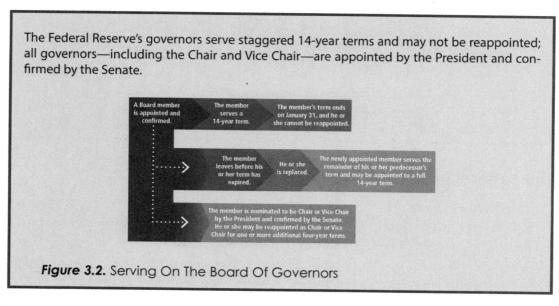

The Federal Reserve's governors serve staggered 14-year terms and may not be reappointed; all governors—including the Chair and Vice Chair—are appointed by the President and confirmed by the Senate.

**Figure 3.2.** Serving On The Board Of Governors

The Board also helps to ensure that the voices and concerns of consumers and communities are heard at the central bank by conducting consumer-focused supervision, research, and policy analysis, and, more generally, by promoting a fair and transparent consumer financial services market.

## The Federal Reserve Banks: Structure And Function

The 12 Federal Reserve Banks and their 24 Branches are the operating arms of the Federal Reserve System. Each Reserve Bank operates within its own particular geographic area, or district, of the United States.

Each Reserve Bank gathers data and other information about the businesses and the needs of local communities in its region. That information is then factored into monetary policy decisions by the FOMC and other decisions made by the Board of Governors.

The boards of directors of the Reserve Banks represent a cross-section of banking, commercial, agricultural, and industrial interests. Six of the nine members of each board of directors are chosen to represent the public interest; those six board directors nominate their Bank's president

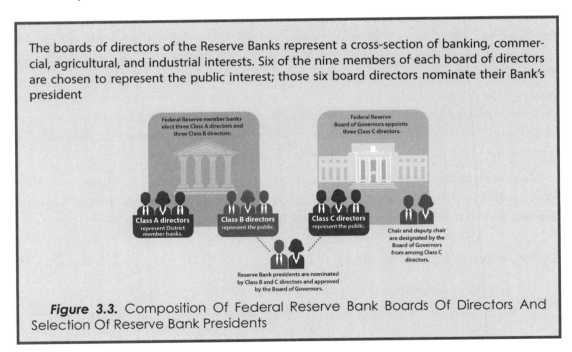

**Figure 3.3.** Composition Of Federal Reserve Bank Boards Of Directors And Selection Of Reserve Bank Presidents

## Reserve Bank Leadership

As set forth in the Federal Reserve Act, each Reserve Bank is subject to "the supervision and control of a board of directors." Much like the boards of directors of private corporations, Reserve Bank boards are responsible for overseeing their Bank's administration and governance, reviewing the Bank's budget and overall performance, overseeing the Bank's audit process, and developing broad strategic goals and directions. However, unlike private corporations, Reserve Banks are not operated in the interest of shareholders, but rather in the public interest.

Each year, the Board of Governors designates one chair and one deputy chair for each Reserve Bank board from among its Class C directors. The Federal Reserve Act requires that the chair of a Reserve Bank's board be a person of "tested banking experience," a term which has been interpreted as requiring familiarity with banking or financial services.

Each Reserve Bank board delegates responsibility for day-to-day operations to the president of that Reserve Bank and his or her staff. Reserve Bank presidents act as chief executive officers of their respective Banks and also serve, in rotation, as voting members of the FOMC. Presidents are nominated by a Bank's Class B and C directors and approved by the Board of Governors for five-year terms.

Reserve Bank Branches also have boards of directors. Pursuant to policy established by the Board of Governors, Branch boards must have either five or seven members. All Branch directors are appointed: the majority of directors on a Branch board are appointed by the Reserve Bank, and the remaining directors on the board are appointed by the Board of Governors. Each Branch board selects a chair from among those directors appointed by the Board of Governors. Unlike Reserve Bank directors, Branch directors are not divided into different classes. However, Branch directors must meet different eligibility requirements, depending on whether they are appointed by the Reserve Bank or the Board of Governors.

Reserve Bank and Branch directors are elected or appointed for staggered three-year terms. When a director does not serve a full term, his or her successor is elected or appointed to serve the unexpired portion of that term.

## Reserve Bank Responsibilities

The Reserve Banks carry out Federal Reserve core functions by:

1. Supervising and examining state member banks (state-chartered banks that have chosen to become members of the Federal Reserve System), bank and thrift holding companies, and nonbank financial institutions that have been designated as systemically important under authority delegated to them by the Board;

2. Lending to depository institutions to ensure liquidity in the financial system;

3. Providing key financial services that undergird the nation's payment system, including distributing the nation's currency and coin to depository institutions, clearing checks,

operating the FedWire and automated clearinghouse (ACH) systems, and serving as a bank for the U.S. Treasury; and

4. Examining certain financial institutions to ensure and enforce compliance with federal consumer protection and fair lending laws, while also promoting local community development.

In its role providing key financial services, the Reserve Bank acts, essentially, as a financial institution for the banks, thrifts, and credit unions in its District—that is, each Reserve Bank acts as a "bank for banks." In that capacity, it offers (and charges for) services to these depository institutions similar to those that ordinary banks provide their individual and business customers: the equivalent of checking accounts; loans; coin and currency; safekeeping services; and payment services (such as the processing of checks and the making of recurring and non-recurring small- and large-dollar payments) that help banks, and ultimately their customers, buy and sell goods, services, and securities.

In addition, through their leaders and their connections to, and interactions with, members of their local communities, Federal Reserve Banks provide the Federal Reserve System with a wealth of information on conditions in virtually every part of the nation—information that is vital to formulating a national monetary policy that will help to maintain the health of the economy and the stability of the nation's financial system.

## The Federal Open Market Committee (FOMC): Selection And Function

The FOMC is the body of the Federal Reserve System that sets national monetary policy. The FOMC makes all decisions regarding the conduct of open market operations, which affect the federal funds rate (the rate at which depository institutions lend to each other), the size and composition of the Federal Reserve's asset holdings, and communications with the public about the likely future course of monetary policy. Congress enacted legislation that created the FOMC as part of the Federal Reserve System in 1933 and 1935.

### FOMC Membership

The FOMC consists of 12 voting members—the 7 members of the Board of Governors; the president of the Federal Reserve Bank of New York; and 4 of the remaining 11 Reserve Bank presidents, who serve one-year terms on a rotating basis.

The Federal Open Market Committee's (FOMC) structure promotes the consideration of broad U.S. economic perspectives and the public interest in key monetary policy decisions made by the U.S. central bank.

FOMC

**Board of Governors**
(permanent FOMC participants)

**Federal Reserve Bank of New York president**
(permanent FOMC participant)

**Reserve Bank presidents**
(serve one-year terms on a rotating basis)

*Figure 3.4.* Composition Of The Federal Open Market Committee

All 12 of the Reserve Bank presidents attend FOMC meetings and participate in FOMC discussions, but only the presidents who are Committee members at the time may vote on policy decisions. By law, the FOMC determines its own internal organization and, by tradition, the FOMC elects the Chair of the Board of Governors as its chair and the president of the Federal Reserve Bank of New York as its vice chair. FOMC meetings are typically held eight times each year in Washington, D.C., and at other times as needed.

## FOMC Responsibilities

The FOMC is charged with overseeing "open market operations," the principal tool by which the Federal Reserve executes U.S. monetary policy. These operations affect the federal funds rate, which in turn influence overall monetary and credit conditions, aggregate demand, and the entire economy. The FOMC also directs operations undertaken by the Federal Reserve in foreign exchange markets and, in recent years, has authorized currency swap programs with foreign central banks.

## Other Significant Entities Contributing To Federal Reserve Functions

Two other groups play important roles in the Federal Reserve System's core functions:

1. Depository institutions—banks, thrifts, and credit unions; and

2. Federal Reserve System advisory committees, which make recommendations to the Board of Governors and to the Reserve Banks regarding the System's responsibilities.

## Depository Institutions

Depository institutions offer transaction, or checking, accounts to the public and may maintain accounts of their own at their local Federal Reserve Banks. Depository institutions are required to meet reserve requirements—that is, to keep a certain amount of cash on hand or in an account at a Reserve Bank based on the total balances in the checking accounts they hold.

Depository institutions that have higher balances in their Reserve Bank accounts than they need to meet reserve requirements may lend to other depository institutions that need those funds to satisfy their own reserve requirements. This rate influences interest rates, asset prices and wealth, exchange rates, and, thereby, aggregate demand in the economy. The FOMC sets a target for the federal funds rate at its meetings and authorizes actions called open market operations to achieve that target.

## Advisory Councils

Four advisory committees assist and advise the Board on matters of public policy.

- **Federal Advisory Council (FAC).** This council, established by the Federal Reserve Act, comprises 12 representatives of the banking industry. The FAC ordinarily meets with the Board four times a year, as required by law. Annually, each Reserve Bank chooses one person to represent its District on the FAC. FAC members customarily serve three one-year terms and elect their own officers.

- **Community Depository Institutions Advisory Council (CDIAC).** The CDIAC was originally established by the Board of Governors to obtain information and views from thrift institutions (savings and loan institutions and mutual savings banks) and credit unions. More recently, its membership has expanded to include community banks. Like the FAC, the CDIAC provides the Board of Governors with firsthand insight and information about the economy, lending conditions, and other issues.

- **Model Validation Council.** This council was established by the Board of Governors in 2012 to provide expert and independent advice on its process to rigorously assess the models used in stress tests of banking institutions. Stress tests are required under the Dodd-Frank Wall Street Reform and Consumer Protection Act. The council is intended to improve the quality of stress tests and thereby strengthen confidence in the stress-testing program

- **Community Advisory Council (CAC).** This council was formed by the Federal Reserve Board in 2015 to offer diverse perspectives on the economic circumstances and financial services needs of consumers and communities, with a particular focus on the concerns of low- and moderate-income populations. The CAC complements the FAC and CDIAC, whose members represent depository institutions. The CAC meets semiannually with members of the Board of Governors. The 15 CAC members serve staggered three-year terms and are selected by the Board through a public nomination process.

Federal Reserve Banks also have their own advisory committees. Perhaps the most important of these are committees that advise the Banks on agricultural, small business, and labor matters. The Federal Reserve Board solicits the views of each of these committees biannually.

# The Decentralized System Structure And Its Philosophy

In establishing the Federal Reserve System, the United States was divided geographically into 12 Districts, each with a separately incorporated Reserve Bank. District boundaries were based on prevailing trade regions that existed in 1913 and related economic considerations, so they do not necessarily coincide with state lines.

As originally envisioned, each of the 12 Reserve Banks was intended to operate independently from the other Reserve Banks. Variation was expected in discount rates—the interest rate that commercial banks were charged for borrowing funds from a Reserve Bank. The setting of a separately determined discount rate appropriate to each District was considered the most important tool of monetary policy at that time. The concept of national economic policy making was not well developed, and the impact of open market operations—purchases and sales of U.S. government securities—on policymaking was less significant.

As the nation's economy became more integrated and more complex, through advances in technology, communications, transportation, and financial services, the effective conduct of monetary policy began to require increased collaboration and coordination throughout the System. This was accomplished in part through revisions to the Federal Reserve Act in 1933 and 1935 that together created the modern-day Federal Open Market Committee (FOMC).

The Depository Institutions Deregulation and Monetary Control Act (DIDMCA) of 1980 (Monetary Control Act) introduced an even greater degree of coordination among Reserve Banks with respect to the pricing of financial services offered to depository institutions. There has also been a trend among Reserve Banks to centralize or consolidate many of their financial services and support functions and to standardize others. Reserve Banks have become more efficient by entering into intra-System service agreements that allocate responsibilities for services and functions that are national in scope among each of the 12 Reserve Banks.

# The U.S. Approach To Central Banking

The framers of the Federal Reserve Act purposely rejected the concept of a single central bank. Instead, they provided for a central banking "system" with three salient features:

1.  A central governing Board,

2.  A decentralized operating structure of 12 Reserve Banks, and

3.  A combination of public and private characteristics.

Although parts of the Federal Reserve System share some characteristics with private-sector entities, the Federal Reserve was established to serve the public interest.

There are three key entities in the Federal Reserve System: the Board of Governors, the Federal Reserve Banks (Reserve Banks), and the Federal Open Market Committee (FOMC). The Board of Governors, an agency of the federal government that reports to and is directly accountable to Congress, provides general guidance for the System and oversees the 12 Reserve Banks.

Within the System, certain responsibilities are shared between the Board of Governors in Washington, D.C., whose members are appointed by the President with the advice and consent of the Senate, and the Federal Reserve Banks and Branches, which constitute the System's operating presence around the country. While the Federal Reserve has frequent communication with executive branch and congressional officials, its decisions are made independently.

# Chapter 4

# Measuring The Economy: Gross Domestic Product (GDP) And National Income And Product Accounts (NIPAs)

The National Income And Product Accounts (NIPAs) are one of the three major elements of the U.S. national economic accounts. The NIPAs display the value and composition of national output and the distribution of incomes generated in its production.

The NIPAs provide information to help answer three basic questions.

1. What is the output of the economy—its size, its composition, and its use?

2. What are the sources and uses of national income?

3. What are the sources of saving, which provides for investment in future production?

The NIPA estimates are presented in a set of integrated accounts that show U.S. production, distribution, consumption, investment, and saving.

(*Source: "Concepts And Methods Of The U.S. National Income And Product Accounts," Bureau of Economic Analysis (BEA), U.S Department of Commerce.*)

## Measuring The Economy

How fast is the economy growing? Is it speeding up or slowing down? How does the trade deficit affect economic growth? What's happening to the pattern of spending on goods and

About This Chapter: This chapter includes text excerpted from "Measuring The Economy: A Primer On GDP And The National Income And Product Accounts," U.S. Bureau of Economic Analysis (BEA), December 2015.

services in the economy? To answer these types of questions about the economy, economists and policymakers turn to the national income and product accounts (NIPAs) produced by the Bureau of Economic Analysis (BEA).

---

## Origin Of National Income And Product Accounts (NIPAs)

The NIPAs trace their origin back to the 1930s, when the lack of comprehensive economic data hampered efforts to develop policies to combat the Great Depression. In response to this need, the U.S. Department of Commerce commissioned future Nobel Laureate Simon Kuznets to develop estimates of national income. He coordinated the work of a group of researchers at the National Bureau of Economic Research and of his staff at the Commerce Department, and initial estimates were presented in a 1934 report to the U.S. Senate, National Income, 1929–32.

As the United States transitioned to a wartime economy in the early 1940s, it became apparent that planning for the war effort required a measure of national production. Annual estimates of "gross national expenditure," which gradually evolved to gross national product (GNP), were introduced early in 1942 to complement the estimates of national income. The U.S. national income and product statistics were first presented as part of a complete and consistent double-entry accounting system in the summer of 1947. The accounts presented a framework for classifying and recording the economic transactions among major sectors: households, businesses, government, and international (termed "rest of the world"). This framework placed the GNP statistics in the broader context of the economy as a whole and provided a more complete picture of how the economy works.

Since then, the national accounts have continued to expand in response to demands for better and more detailed information on the U.S. economy. At the end of 1999, the Commerce Department named the invention and ongoing development of the NIPAs and its marquee measure GDP as "its greatest achievement of the century."

(*Source: "Concepts And Methods Of The U.S. National Income And Product Accounts," Bureau of Economic Analysis (BEA), U.S Department of Commerce.*)

---

The NIPAs are a set of economic accounts that provide information on the value and composition of output produced in the United States during a given period and on the types and uses of the income generated by that production. Featured in the NIPAs is gross domestic product (GDP), which measures the value of the goods and services produced by the U.S. economy in a given time period.

GDP is one of the most comprehensive and closely watched economic statistics: It is used by the White House and Congress to prepare the Federal budget, by the Federal Reserve to formulate monetary policy, by Wall Street as an indicator of economic activity, and by the business community to prepare forecasts of economic performance that provide the basis for production, investment, and employment planning. But to fully understand an economy's performance, one must ask not only "What is GDP?" (or "What is the value of the economy's output?"), but other questions such as: "How much of the increase in GDP is the result of inflation and how much is an increase in real output?" "Who is producing the output of the economy?" "What output are they producing?" "What income is generated as a result of that production?" and "How is that income used (to consume more output, to invest, or to save for future consumption or investment)?" Thus, while GDP is the featured measure of the economy's output, it is only one summary measure.

The answers to the follow-up questions are found by looking at other measures found in the NIPAs; these include personal income, corporate profits, and government spending. Because the economy is so complex, the NIPAs simplify the information by organizing it in a way that illustrates the processes taking place.

# The Circular Flow Of Income And Expenditures

To better understand the economy and the NIPAs, consider a simple economy consisting solely of businesses and individuals, as reflected in the circular flow diagram below:

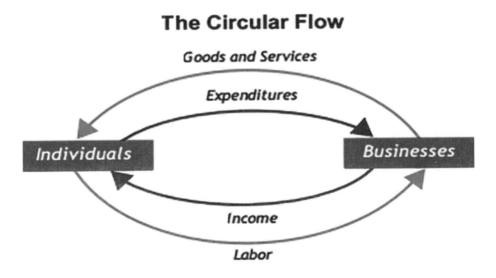

*Figure 4.1.* Circular Flow Of Income And Expenditures

In this simple economy, individuals provide the labor that enables businesses to produce goods and services. These activities are represented by the outer lines that read 'Good and Services' and 'Labor' in the figure above. Alternatively, one can think of these transactions in terms of the monetary flows that occur. Businesses provide individuals with income (in the form of compensation) in exchange for their labor. That income is, in turn, spent on the goods and services businesses produce. These activities are represented by the inner lines in the figure above.

## Economic Concepts In The NIPAs

The circular flow diagram illustrates the interdependence of the "flows," or activities, that occur in the economy, such as the production of goods and services (or the "output" of the economy) and the income generated from that production. The circular flow also illustrates the equality between the income earned from production and the value of goods and services produced. Of course, the total economy is much more complicated than the illustration above. An economy involves interactions between not only individuals and businesses, but also Federal, state, and local governments and residents of the rest of the world. Also not shown in this simple illustration of the economy are other aspects of economic activity such as investment in capital (produced—or fixed—assets such as structures, equipment, research and development, and software), flows of financial capital (such as stocks, bonds, and bank deposits), and the contributions of these flows to the accumulation of fixed assets. The NIPAs provide a framework for presenting actual measures of these economic flows.

## Output

The featured measure of output in the NIPAs is GDP. GDP measures the market value of the goods, services, and structures produced by the nation's economy in a particular period. While GDP is used as an indicator of economic activity, it is not a measure of well-being (for example, it does not account for rates of poverty, crime, or literacy). The following are several points to keep in mind when considering the output of the economy

1. **GDP includes market production and some non-market production.** GDP is composed of goods and services that are produced for sale in the "market"—the generic term referring to the forum for economic transactions—and of non-market goods and services—those that are not sold in the market, such as the defense services provided by the federal government, the education services provided by local governments, the emergency housing or health care services provided by nonprofit institutions serving households (such as the Red Cross), and the housing services provided by and for persons who own and live in their home (referred to as "owner-occupants"). However,

not all productive activity is included in GDP. Some activities, such as the care of one's own children, unpaid volunteer work for charities, and illegal activities, are not included because data are not available to accurately measure their value.

2. **Whenever possible, GDP is valued at market prices.** The NIPAs value market goods and services using prices set by the market. This approach provides a common unit of measurement (dollars) that facilitates comparisons of the various goods and services that make up economic activity. Using market values also facilitates the analysis of the impacts on the economy of events such as the implementation of government programs or the occurrence of natural disasters. In some cases, market prices do not fully reflect the value of a good or service, and may include some types of services where an actual exchange has not occurred. In these cases, the value of the good or service produced is "imputed" from similar market transactions. Imputations measure the value of goods and services that are not fully reflected in market prices. Examples of imputed measures in the NIPAs include the value of compensation-in-kind (such as meals provided by employers) and the value of owner-occupied housing. In cases where there are no similar market transactions available to impute a value of the goods or service being produced, the output of these services is valued by estimating the costs (such as employee compensation and purchases of materials and supplies) of producing the good or service.

3. **GDP is a measure of current production, not sales.** In the NIPAs, the measure of output refers to output produced in that period, regardless of when that output is sold. For example, an automaker may produce a car in one period and sell it in a later period. In the first period, the production of the car is recorded in GDP as an addition to inventories, a component of private enterprise investment. In the later period, the sale of the car is recorded twice, both as a consumer expenditure and as a withdrawal from inventories. As no new production took place, GDP is not affected.

4. **GDP is equal to the value of goods and services for "final" users.** The measurement of GDP captures the value of products that are consumed and not used in a later stage of production, those that are sold, given away, or otherwise transferred to foreign residents, those that are used to produce other goods and that last more than a year, and those that may be inventoried for future consumption. When considering the production process for the entire economy, the value of intermediate products—that is, goods and services that are used as inputs in the production process (and will not contribute to future production)—is excluded, so that the measure of output is an

unduplicated total. For example, consider a simple economy with one product, bread, which is produced in three stages:

i.   Wheat is grown, harvested, and sold for $1 by a farmer (for simplification, it is assumed the wheat is produced using no intermediate products);

ii.  The wheat is used by a miller to produce flour, which is sold for $3; and

iii. The flour is used by a baker to produce bread, which is sold to a consumer for $7.

This information is summarized in Table 4.1. Intermediate Product, Income And Sales

**Table 4.1.** Intermediate Product, Income And Sales

|  | Intermediate Product | Income | Sales |
|---|---|---|---|
| **Farmer, Wheat** | $0.00 | $1.00 | $1.00 |
| **Miller, Flour** | $1.00 | $2.00 | $3.00 |
| **Baker, Bread** | $3.00 | $4.00 | $7.00 |
| **Total** | $4.00 | $7.00 | $11.00 |

When the miller purchases $1 worth of wheat from the farmer to produce flour and then sells the flour to the baker for $3, the $3 the miller charges for the flour includes the $1 price of the wheat (an intermediate product) plus the $2 value added by his own resources (in this example, his labor). When the baker makes the flour into bread and sells the bread to a consumer for $7, the $7 the baker charges includes the $3 value of the flour (an intermediate product) and the $4 value added by his own resources. The value of the ultimate product—the bread—is the price paid by the consumer ($7); the bread is recognized as the ultimate product because it is eaten by the consumer and not used in another production process. If the total sales of the wheat, the flour, and the bread were all included, the aggregate value ($1 + $3 + $7, or $11) would overstate the value of production by triple-counting the value of the wheat and double-counting the value of the flour.

5.   **GDP can be measured in three different ways.** The nature of economic activity reflected in the circular flow diagram suggests two ways to measure GDP. First, GDP can be measured as the sum of expenditures, or purchases, by final users. This is known as the expenditures approach (and is illustrated by the formula familiar to students of economics: GDP = Consumption + Investment + Government spending + eXports – iMports) and is used to identify the final goods and services purchased by persons, businesses, governments, and foreigners. Second, because the market price of a good or service will reflect all of the incomes earned and costs incurred in production,

GDP can also be measured as the sum of these charges. This is known as the income approach and is used to examine the purchasing power of households and the financial status of business income. In addition, GDP can also be measured either as total sales less the value of intermediate inputs or as the sum of the "value added" at each stage of the production process. The value-added approach to measuring GDP is central to the U.S. industry accounts and is used to analyze the industrial composition of U.S. output.

These three approaches can be illustrated using the information from Table 4.2

**Table 4.2.** Intermediate Product, Income-Value Added And Sales-Total Output

|  | **Intermediate Product** | **Income = Value Added** | **Sales = Total Output** |
|---|---|---|---|
| **Farmer, Wheat** | $0.00 | $1.00 | $1.00 |
| **Miller, Flour** | $1.00 | $2.00 | $3.00 |
| **Baker, Bread** | $3.00 | $4.00 | $7.00* |
| **Total** | $4.00 | $7.00* | $11.00 |

*Output (sum of final expenditures)=Total income earned from production Value added=Total output–Total intermediate products

- As demonstrated in point 4 above, GDP can be derived as the sum of final expenditures for bread, which is the $7 spent by consumers

- It can be derived as the sum of the incomes earned in the production of bread—that is, as the sum of the $1 earned by the farmer for his labor, the $2 earned by the miller for his labor, and the $4 earned by the baker for his labor.

- It can be derived as the value added, or total output less intermediate products, across all industries—that is, the $1 of output by the farmer, plus the $3 of output by the miller, plus the $7 of output by the baker minus the $0 of intermediate inputs by the farmer, minus the $1 of intermediate inputs by the miller, minus the $3 of intermediate inputs by the baker ($11 – $4 = $7).

6. **GDP captures output produced in the United States.** GDP is a measure of the goods, services, and structures produced by labor and property located within the United States (in the NIPAs, the United States comprises the 50 states and the District of Columbia (D.C.)). Thus, GDP includes the output of U.S. offices or establishments of foreign companies located in the United States, and it excludes the output of foreign offices or establishments of U.S. companies located outside the United States. This treatment aligns GDP with other key U.S. statistics associated with the domestic economy, such as population and employment.

7. **GDP is a "gross" measure.** GDP reflects production in a given time period, regardless of whether that production is used for consumption, for investment in new fixed assets or inventories, or for replacing depreciated fixed assets. Economic depreciation, or the consumption of fixed capital (CFC), is a measure of the amount that would need to be "set aside" to cover the physical deterioration, normal obsolescence, and accidental damage (except that caused by a catastrophic event) of existing fixed assets. Subtracting CFC from GDP leaves "net domestic product," which is a measure of current production that excludes the investment that is necessary to replace existing fixed assets as they wear out or become obsolete. Thus, net domestic product is a measure that indicates how much of the Nation's output is available for consumption or for adding to the Nation's wealth.

---

The NIPAs feature some of the most closely watched economic statistics that influence the decisions made by government officials, business persons, and households. Foremost among these estimates is GDP, the most widely recognized measure of the nation's production. In particular, the quarterly estimates of inflation-adjusted GDP provide the most comprehensive picture of current economic conditions in the United States. Other key NIPA estimates include the monthly estimates of personal income and outlays, which provide current information on consumer income, spending, and saving, and the quarterly estimates of corporate profits, which provide an economic measure of U.S. corporate financial performance.

(*Source: "Concepts And Methods Of The U.S. National Income And Product Accounts," Bureau of Economic Analysis (BEA), U.S Department of Commerce.*)

---

# Income

In addition to GDP, which is measured using the final expenditures approach, the NIPAs also present gross domestic income (GDI), which is GDP measured using the income approach. As noted above, this approach measures output as the sum of the incomes accruing to the owners of the factors of production (capital and labor) and to governments. In other words, as the circular flow diagram suggests, income is equal to product (GDI is equal to GDP).

The NIPAs also include other measures of income. Two of these are gross national income (GNI) and personal income. GNI, the most comprehensive measure of a nation's income, is calculated as GDI plus income receipts from the rest of the world less income payments to the rest of the world. As such, it is a measure of income from production that accrues to U.S. residents, regardless of where that productive activity is located. Its companion production measure is gross national product (GNP). Personal income is the income received by persons from participation in production (including compensation, proprietors' income, and interest and dividend income) and from transfers from government and businesses. Personal income is closely monitored both as an indicator of economic activity and as a predictor of future spending. It is important to note that the income measures in the NIPAs do not include gains or losses resulting from changes in the prices of assets (that is, capital gains or losses), because a change in the price of an asset does not represent income from production.

# NIPA Sectors

From the NIPAs, one can determine who demands the goods and services that are produced, or one can examine who supplies the output being produced. Three major types of producers (or sectors) are recognized:

**Businesses.** This sector engages in the production and sale of goods and services for profit, or at least for a price that approximates the costs of production. The sector comprises all for-profit corporate and non-corporate private entities and certain other entities, including mutual financial institutions, private non-insured pension funds, cooperatives, nonprofit organizations that primarily serve businesses, Federal Reserve banks, federally sponsored credit agencies, and government enterprises. Government enterprises are government agencies—such as the U.S. Postal Service (USPS) or state government-run utilities—that cover a substantial portion of their operating costs by selling goods and services to the public.

**Households and institutions.** This sector engages in the production of household services—that is, the housing services provided to homeowners, the goods and services provided by nonprofit institutions, and the compensation paid to domestic workers. The sector consists of households (families and unrelated individuals) and nonprofit institutions servings households (such as Goodwill Industries International).

**General governments.** This sector receives revenues from taxes and other sources and uses these revenues to provide public goods and services, such as education and defense, and transfer payments, such as social security or Medicaid benefits. The sector includes Federal, state, and local government agencies, except for government enterprises. In addition, various measures are shown for subsets of these sectors (or subsectors). For example, separate measures are available for farm businesses, nonfarm businesses, corporations, non-corporate businesses, households, nonprofit institutions serving households, Federal Government, state and local governments, and pension plans.

# Chapter 5

# Small Businesses And Corporations In The U.S. Economy

## Small Businesses

> ### What Is Small Businesses' Share Of Net New Jobs?
>
> Small firms accounted for 64 percent of the net new jobs created between 1993 and 2011 (or 11.8 million of the 18.5 million net new jobs). Since the latest recession, from mid-2009 to 2011, small firms, led by the larger ones in the category (20-499 employees), accounted for 67 percent of the net new jobs.
>
> *(Source: "Advocacy: The Voice Of Small Business In Government," Small Business Administration (SBA); Bureau of Labor Statistics (BLS); Business Employment Dynamics (BED).)*

You may take it for granted that your company is a "small business." The distinction is important if you wish to register for government contracting as a small business. To be a small business, you must adhere to industry size standards established by the U.S. Small Business Administration. As you register as a government contractor in the System for Award Management (SAM), you will also self-certify your business as small.

The U.S. Small Business Administration (SBA), for most industries, defines a "small business" either in terms of the average number of employees over the past 12 months, or average

---

About This Chapter: Text under the heading "Small Businesses" is excerpted from "Qualifying As A Small Business," U.S. Small Business Administration (SBA), March 2016; Text under the heading "Corporation" is excerpted from "Starting And Managing," U.S. Small Business Administration (SBA), February 2, 2017; Text under the heading "Different Types Of Business Structures" is excerpted from "Starting And Managing," U.S. Small Business Administration (SBA), February 18, 2017.

annual receipts over the past three years. In addition, SBA defines a U.S. small business as a concern that:

- Is organized for profit

- Has a place of business in the United States

- Operates primarily within the United States or makes a significant contribution to the U.S. economy through payment of taxes or use of American products, materials or labor

- Is independently owned and operated

- Is not dominant in its field on a national basis

The business may be a sole proprietorship, partnership, corporation, or any other legal form. In determining what constitutes a small business, the definition will vary to reflect industry differences, such as size standards.

## Small Business Sustainability

Small businesses can have a huge impact on national sustainability. Implementing sustainable business practices can help small businesses save money, meet consumer demand, and contribute to the sustainability of the Nation. Greening your small business can lead to positive recognition from customers, employees, regulators, and the media. Green businesses often experience benefits for brand image, customer loyalty, community relations, and appeal to socially responsible investors and portfolio managers.

(*Source: "Starting And Managing," U.S. Small Business Administration (SBA).*)

## Size Standards

Because all federal agencies must use SBA size standards for contracts identified as small business, you need to select North American Industry Classification System (NAICS) codes that best describe your business and then determine if the business meet size standards for the selected NAICS codes. Once you have determined you are indeed a small business, you can then certify your business as small by registering as a government contractor.

## What Are The Small Business Size Standards?*

Your business might be eligible for programs that are reserved for small business concerns. To qualify, your business must satisfy SBA's definition of a business concern, along with the size standards for small business.

SBA has established numerical definitions, or "size standards," for all for-profit industries. Size standards represent the largest size that a business (including its subsidiaries and affiliates) may be to remain classified as a small business concern. These size standards apply to SBA's financial assistance and to its other programs, as well as to Federal government procurement programs when there is a benefit available to qualifying as a small business concern. Also, the Small Business Act states that unless specifically authorized by statute, no federal department or agency may prescribe a size standard for categorizing a business concern as a small business concern, unless such proposed size standard meets certain criteria and is approved by the Administrator of SBA.

Based on the analyses of relevant industry, program and other factors, SBA's Size Standards Division makes recommendations to the Administrator for developing or revising size standards. The Small Business Act authorizes the SBA's Administrator to establish small business size standards. In general, SBA, for each industry, examines the following primary factors in developing or revising the size standard.

- Industry structure
- Federal procurement—small business share in federal contracts SBA also considers the following secondary factors
- Technological change
- Competing products from other industries
- Industry growth trends
- History of the activity in the industry
- Impacts on SBA programs

SBA also considers public comments on proposed rules before issuing any final rule.

*Text excerpted from "Contracting," U.S. Small Business Administration (SBA), February 2, 2017.*

## Small Businesses Comprise What Share Of The U.S. Economy?

Small businesses make up:

- 99.7 percent of U.S. employer firms,
- 64 percent of net new private-sector jobs,

- 49.2 percent of private-sector employment,
- 42.9 percent of private-sector payroll,
- 46 percent of private-sector output,
- 43 percent of high-tech employment,
- 98 percent of firms exporting goods, and
- 33 percent of exporting value.

*(Source: "Advocacy: The Voice Of Small Business In Government," Small Business Administration (SBA); U.S. Census Bureau; Bureau of Labor Statistics (BLS); Business Employment Dynamics (BED).)*

## Small Businesses And The U.S. Economy[†]

Entrepreneurship plays a vital role in the growth of the U.S. economy. As the primary source for information on the nation's labor market, the U.S. Bureau of Labor Statistics (BLS) collects data on new businesses and job creation. The following highlights from data series produced by BLS Business Employment Dynamics (BED) program provide insight on the contribution of young and small businesses to the overall number of businesses and jobs in the economy.

Small businesses are typically the entry point for entrepreneurs as they develop ideas and build a customer base before deciding whether to expand. Of the nine size classes in the BED series, the six smallest (249 employees or smaller) have seen their shares of private sector employment decrease since the early 1990s, while the three largest size classes (250 or more employees) have seen their shares of total employment increase.

New business establishments make an important contribution to the economy; however, it is inevitable that some of these establishments will eventually fail. Survival rates for establishments vary by industry. The health care and social assistance industry, for example, consistently ranks among the industries with the highest survival rates over time, while construction ranks among the lowest.

[†]*Text excerpted from "Entrepreneurship And The U.S. Economy," Bureau Of Labor Statistics (BLS), April 28, 2016.*

# Corporation

A corporation (sometimes referred to as a C corporation) is an independent legal entity owned by shareholders. This means that the corporation itself, not the shareholders that own it, is held legally liable for the actions and debts the business incurs.

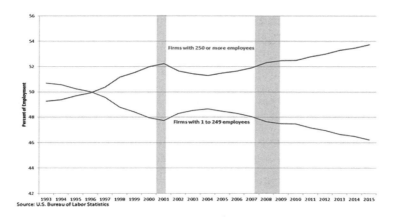

**Figure 5.1.** Percent Distribution Of Private Sector Employment By Size Of Firm, 1993–2015

Corporations are more complex than other business structures because they tend to have costly administrative fees and complex tax and legal requirements. Because of these issues, corporations are generally suggested for established, larger companies with multiple employees.

For businesses in that position, corporations offer the ability to sell ownership shares in the business through stock offerings. "Going public" through an initial public offering (IPO) is a major selling point in attracting investment capital and high quality employees.

## Forming A Corporation

A corporation is formed under the laws of the state in which it is registered. To form a corporation you'll need to establish your business name and register your legal name with your state government. If you choose to operate under a name different than the officially registered name, you'll most likely have to file a fictitious name (also known as an assumed name, trade name, or DBA name, short for "doing business as"). State laws vary, but generally corporations must include a corporate designation (Corporation, Incorporated, Limited) at the end of the business name.

To register your business as a corporation, you need to file certain documents, typically articles of incorporation, with your state's Secretary of State office. Some states require corporations to establish directors and issue stock certificates to initial shareholders in the registration process. Contact your state business entity registration office to find out about specific filing requirements in the state where you form your business.

Once your business is registered, you must obtain business licenses and permits. Regulations vary by industry, state and locality.

## Corporation Taxes

Corporations are required to pay federal, state, and in some cases, local taxes. Most businesses must register with the IRS and state and local revenue agencies, and receive a tax ID number or permit. Unlike sole proprietors and partnerships, corporations pay income tax on their profits. In some cases, corporations are taxed twice—first, when the company makes a profit, and again when dividends are paid to shareholders on their personal tax returns.

## Advantages Of A Corporation

- **Limited liability.** When it comes to taking responsibility for business debts and actions of a corporation, shareholders' personal assets are protected. Shareholders can generally only be held accountable for their investment in stock of the company.

- **Ability to generate capital.** Corporations have an advantage when it comes to raising capital for their business—the ability to raise funds through the sale of stock.

- **Corporate tax treatment.** Corporations file taxes separately from their owners. Owners of a corporation only pay taxes on corporate profits paid to them in the form of salaries, bonuses, and dividends, while any additional profits are awarded a corporate tax rate, which is usually lower than a personal income tax rate.

- **Attractive to potential employees.** Corporations are generally able to attract and hire high-quality and motivated employees because they offer competitive benefits and the potential for partial ownership through stock options.

## Disadvantages Of A Corporation

- **Time and money.** Corporations are costly and time-consuming ventures to start and operate. Incorporating requires start-up, operating and tax costs that most other structures do not require.

- **Double taxing.** In some cases, corporations are taxed twice—first, when the company makes a profit, and again when dividends are paid to shareholders.

- **Additional paperwork.** Because corporations are highly regulated by federal, state, and in some cases local agencies, there are increased paperwork and record-keeping burdens associated with this entity.

# Different Types Of Business Structures

## Sole Proprietorship

A sole proprietorship is the simplest and most common structure chosen to start a business. It is an unincorporated business owned and run by one individual with no distinction between the business and the owner. You are entitled to all profits and are responsible for all your business's debts, losses, and liabilities.

### Forming A Sole Proprietorship

No formal action is required to form a sole proprietorship. If you are the only owner, this status automatically comes from your business activities. In fact, you may already own one without knowing it. If you are a freelance graphic designer, for example, you are a sole proprietor.

But like all businesses, you need to obtain the necessary licenses and permits. Regulations vary by industry, state and locality.

If you choose to operate under a name different than your own, you will most likely have to file a fictitious name (also known as an assumed name, trade name, or DBA name, short for "doing business as").

## Partnership

A partnership is a single business where two or more people share ownership. Each partner contributes to all aspects of the business, including money, property, labor or skill. In return, each partner shares in the profits and losses of the business.

Because partnerships entail more than one person in the decision-making process, it's important to discuss a wide variety of issues up front and develop a legal partnership agreement. This agreement should document how future business decisions will be made, including how the partners will divide profits, resolve disputes, change ownership (bring in new partners or buy out current partners) and how to dissolve the partnership. Although partnership agreements are not legally required, they are strongly recommended and it is considered extremely risky to operate without one.

### Types Of Partnerships

There are three general types of partnership arrangements:

- **General Partnerships** assume that profits, liability and management duties are divided equally among partners. If you opt for an unequal distribution, the percentages assigned to each partner must be documented in the partnership agreement.

- **Limited Partnerships** (also known as a partnership with limited liability) are more complex than general partnerships. Limited partnerships allow partners to have limited liability as well as limited input with management decisions. These limits depend on the extent of each partner's investment percentage. Limited partnerships are attractive to investors of short-term projects.

- **Joint Ventures** act as general partnership, but for only a limited period of time or for a single project. Partners in a joint venture can be recognized as an ongoing partnership if they continue the venture, but they must file as such.

## Limited Liability Company

A limited liability company (LLC) is a hybrid type of legal structure that provides the limited liability features of a corporation and the tax efficiencies and operational flexibility of a partnership. The "owners" of an LLC are referred to as "members." Depending on the state, the members can consist of a single individual (one owner), two or more individuals, corporations or other LLCs.

Unlike shareholders in a corporation, LLCs are not taxed as a separate business entity. Instead, all profits and losses are "passed through" the business to each member of the LLC. LLC members report profits and losses on their personal federal tax returns, just like the owners of a partnership would.

## Cooperative

A cooperative is a business or organization owned by and operated for the benefit of those using its services. Profits and earnings generated by the cooperative are distributed among the members, also known as user-owners.

Typically, an elected board of directors and officers run the cooperative while regular members have voting power to control the direction of the cooperative. Members can become part of the cooperative by purchasing shares, though the amount of shares they hold does not affect the weight of their vote. Cooperatives are common in the healthcare, retail, agriculture, art and restaurant industries.

## S Corporation

An S corporation (also referred to as an S corp) is a special type of corporation created through an IRS tax election. An eligible domestic corporation can avoid double taxation (once to the corporation and again to the shareholders) by electing to be treated as an S corporation.

An S corp is a corporation with the Subchapter S designation from the IRS. What makes the S corp different from a traditional corporation (C corp) is that profits and losses can pass through to your personal tax return. Consequently, the business is not taxed itself. Only the shareholders are taxed. There is an important caveat, however: any shareholder who works for the company must pay him or herself "reasonable compensation." Basically, the shareholder must be paid fair market value, or the Internal Revenue Service (IRS) might reclassify any additional corporate earnings as "wages."

# Chapter 6

# Strong Dollar, Weak Dollar: Foreign Exchange Rates And The U.S. Economy

## Foreign Currency Exchange Rates, Quotes, And Pricing

A foreign currency exchange rate is a price that represents how much it costs to buy the currency of one country using the currency of another country. Currency traders buy and sell currencies through forex transactions based on how they expect currency exchange rates will fluctuate. When the value of one currency rises relative to another, traders will earn profits if they purchased the appreciating currency, or suffer losses if they sold the appreciating currency. As discussed below, there are also other factors that can reduce a trader's profits even if that trader "picked" the right currency.

Currencies are identified by three-letter abbreviations. For example, USD is the designation for the U.S. dollar, EUR is the designation for the Euro, GBP is the designation for the British pound, and JPY is the designation for the Japanese yen.

Forex transactions are quoted in pairs of currencies (e.g., GBP/USD) because you are purchasing one currency with another currency. Sometimes purchases and sales are done

About This Chapter: Text under the heading "Foreign Currency Exchange Rates, Quotes, And Pricing" is excerpted from "Forex: Foreign Currency Transactions," U.S. Securities and Exchange Commission (SEC), October 1, 2013; Text under the heading "How Does The Foreign Exchange Value Of The Dollar Relate To Federal Reserve Policy?" is excerpted from "Current FAQs: Economy, Jobs, And Prices," Federal Reserve Board (FRB), August 24, 2016; Text under the heading "Effects Of A Stronger Dollar On U.S. Activity And Inflation" is excerpted from "The Transmission Of Exchange Rate Changes To Output And Inflation," Federal Reserve Board (FRB), November 12, 2015; Text under the heading "Dollar Depreciation" is excerpted from "How Do The Effects Of Dollar Depreciation Show Up In The GDP Accounts?" U.S. Bureau of Economic Analysis (BEA), August 7, 2016.

relative to the U.S. dollar, similar to the way that many stocks and bonds are priced in U.S. dollars. For example, you might buy Euros using U.S. dollars. In other types of forex transactions, one foreign currency might be purchased using another foreign currency. An example of this would be to buy Euros using British pounds—that is, trading both the Euro and the pound in a single transaction. For investors whose local currency is the U.S. dollar (i.e., investors who mostly hold assets denominated in U.S. dollars), the first example generally represents a single, positive bet on the Euro (an expectation that the Euro will rise in value), whereas the second example represents a positive bet on the Euro and a negative bet on the British pound (an expectation that the Euro will rise in value relative to the British pound).

There are different quoting conventions for exchange rates depending on the currency, the market, and sometimes even the system that is displaying the quote. For some investors, these differences can be a source of confusion and might even lead to placing unintended trades.

For example, it is often the case that the Euro exchange rates are quoted in terms of U.S. dollars. A quote for EUR of 1.4123 then means that 1,000 Euros can be bought for approximately 1,412 U.S. dollars. In contrast, Japanese yen are often quoted in terms of the number of yen that can be purchased with a single U.S. dollar. A quote for JPY of 79.1515 then means that 1,000 U.S. dollars can be bought for approximately 79,152 yen. In these examples, if you bought the Euro and the EUR quote increases from 1.4123 to 1.5123, you would be making money. But if you bought the yen and the JPY quote increases from 79.1515 to 89.1515, you would actually be losing money because, in this example, the yen would be depreciating relative to the U.S. dollar (i.e., it would take more yen to buy a single U.S. dollar).

Before you attempt to trade currencies, you should have a firm understanding of currency quoting conventions, how forex transactions are priced, and the mathematical formulae required to convert one currency into another.

Currency exchange rates are usually quoted using a pair of prices representing a "bid" and an "ask." Similar to the manner in which stocks might be quoted, the "ask" is a price that represents how much you will need to spend in order to purchase a currency, and the "bid" is a price that represents the (lower) amount that you will receive if you sell the currency. The difference between the bid and ask prices is known as the "bid-ask spread," and it represents an inherent cost of trading—the wider the bid-ask spread, the more it costs to buy and sell a given currency, apart from any other commissions or transaction charges.

Generally speaking, there are three ways to trade foreign currency exchange rates:

1. **On an exchange that is regulated by the Commodity Futures Trading Commission (CFTC).** An example of such an exchange is the Chicago Mercantile Exchange, which offers currency futures and options on currency futures products. Exchange-traded currency futures and options provide traders with contracts of a set unit size, a fixed expiration date, and centralized clearing. In centralized clearing, a clearing corporation acts as single counterparty to every transaction and guarantees the completion and credit worthiness of all transactions.

2. **On an exchange that is regulated by the U.S. Securities and Exchange Commission (SEC).** An example of such an exchange is the National Association of Securities Dealers Automated Quotations (NASDAQ), Option Market Index (OMX), PHLX (formerly the Philadelphia Stock Exchange), which offers options on currencies (i.e., the right but not the obligation to buy or sell a currency at a specific rate within a specified time). Exchange-traded options on currencies also provide investors with contracts of a set unit size, a fixed expiration date, and centralized clearing.

3. **In the off-exchange market.** In the off-exchange market (sometimes called the over-the-counter, or OTC, market), an individual investor trades directly with a counterparty, such as a forex broker or dealer; there is no exchange or central clearinghouse. Instead, the trading generally is conducted by telephone or through electronic communications networks (ECNs). In this case, the investor relies entirely on the counterparty to receive funds or to be able to trade out of a position.

---

Individual investors who are considering participating in the foreign currency exchange (or "forex") market need to understand fully the market and its unique characteristics. Forex trading can be very risky and is not appropriate for all investors.

It is common in most forex trading strategies to employ leverage. Leverage entails using a relatively small amount of capital to buy currency worth many times the value of that capital. Leverage magnifies minor fluctuations in currency markets in order to increase potential gains and losses. By using leverage to trade forex, you risk losing all of your initial capital and may lose even more money than the amount of your initial capital. You should carefully consider your own financial situation, consult a financial adviser knowledgeable in forex trading, and investigate any firms offering to trade forex for you before making any investment decisions.

(*Source: "Foreign Currency Exchange (Forex) Trading For Individual Investors," U.S. Securities and Exchange Commission (SEC).*)

---

# How Does The Foreign Exchange Value Of The Dollar Relate To Federal Reserve Policy?

The U.S. Department of the Treasury is the lead agency setting U.S. international economic policy, including policies regarding the dollar. The value of the dollar is determined in foreign exchange markets, and neither the U.S. Treasury nor the Federal Reserve targets a level for the exchange rate. Nonetheless, movements in the exchange value of the dollar represent an important consideration for monetary policy—such movements exert influence on U.S. economic activity and prices and constitute one of the ways the effects of monetary policy reach the broader economy. Accordingly, while U.S. monetary policy does not aim for a particular level of the dollar, policymakers take into account the effects of the dollar on prices and economic activity in the United States.

# Effects Of A Stronger Dollar On U.S. Activity And Inflation

An appreciation of the dollar reduces U.S. exports because it causes the relative price of U.S. goods to rise in foreign markets; for example, the price in yen of a U.S.-made pair of jeans will rise.

A stronger dollar makes foreign goods cheaper for U.S. consumers and hence boosts U.S. real imports. Nevertheless, an extensive literature has found that the degree of pass-through of exchange rate changes to U.S. import prices is low, as foreign exporters prefer to keep the dollar price of the goods they sell in the U.S. market relatively constant. For example, a typical estimate is that an appreciation of the dollar of 10 percent causes U.S. non-oil import prices to fall only about 3 percent after a year and only slightly more thereafter. The low exchange rate pass-through helps account for the more modest estimated response of U.S. real imports to a 10 percent exchange rate appreciation, which indicates that real imports rise only about 3-3/4 percent after three years.

# Dollar Depreciation

When the dollar depreciates against major foreign currencies, one generally expects to see current-dollar exports increase, as U.S. produced goods become cheaper abroad. The effect on current-dollar imports is more ambiguous: Depreciation increases the dollar cost of a given volume of imports, but the volume may decline to the extent that domestic goods and services are substituted for imports in response to the increase in the relative cost of purchases from abroad. Assuming that the export stimulus effect and the volume effect on imports together outweigh the import-cost effect, dollar depreciation would be expected to lead to an improvement in U.S. competitiveness, an improvement in net exports, and a corresponding increase in GDP.

The price and quantity effects that move in opposite directions as a result of U.S. dollar depreciation are often difficult to identify separately from movements due to other market forces. For example, dollar depreciation against oil-producing nations' currencies would result in an increase in the price of imported petroleum and a likely decrease in the quantity of petroleum imported—the magnitude of the response would be determined by the product's elasticity (responsiveness to price change). However, other developments in the economy may also affect the demand for petroleum, such as cyclical fluctuations or changes in fuel economy, to a degree that often cannot be readily determined. In addition, the separate effects may be difficult to identify because the foreign supplier may not fully pass through the costs associated with dollar deprecation or the domestic seller of the imported product may absorb some of these costs.

> The relative strength of the U.S. economy means that its currency, the dollar, is the most powerful in the world. The U.S. dollar is used in most international transactions and so anything that happens with the U.S. economy will affect international finances in a substantial way.

# Chapter 7
# What Determines Interest Rates?

## Why Do Interest Rates Matter?

Interest rates matter in many different ways that affect the U.S. economy. One way that interest rates matter is they influence borrowing costs. Lower interest rates, for example, would encourage more people to obtain a mortgage for a new home or to borrow money for an automobile or for home improvement. Lower rates also would encourage businesses to borrow funds to invest in expansion such as purchasing new equipment, updating plants, or hiring more workers. Higher interest rates would restrain such borrowing by consumers and businesses. The Fed seeks to set interest rates to help set the backdrop for promoting the conditions that achieve the mandate set by the Congress—namely, maximum sustainable employment, low and stable inflation, and moderate long-term interest rates.

## Supply And Demand

As with any other price in our market economy, interest rates are determined by the forces of supply and demand, in this case, the supply of and demand for credit. If the supply of credit from lenders rises relative to the demand from borrowers, the price (interest rate) will tend to fall as lenders compete to find use for their funds. If the demand rises relative to the supply, the interest rate will tend to rise as borrowers compete for increasingly scarce funds.

About This Chapter: Text beginning with the heading "Why Do Interest Rates Matter?" is excerpted from "Current FAQs," Federal Reserve Board (FRB), March 2, 2017; Text under the heading "Monetary Policy, Fiscal Policy, And Interest Rates" is excerpted from "What Is The Difference Between Monetary Policy And Fiscal Policy, And How Are They Related?" Federal Reserve Board (FRB), September 9, 2016.

The principal source of the demand for credit comes from our desire for current spending and investment opportunities. The principal source of the supply of credit comes from savings, or the willingness of people, firms, and governments to delay spending. Depository institutions such as banks, thrifts, and credit unions, as well as the Federal Reserve, play important roles in influencing the supply of credit.

*(Source: "Points Of Interest: What Determines Interest Rates?" Education Resources Information Center (ERIC).)*

# Moderate Long-Term Interest Rates

The Federal Reserve works to promote a strong U.S. economy. The Congress has directed the Fed to conduct the nation's monetary policy to support three specific goals: maximum sustainable employment, stable prices, and moderate long-term interest rates. These goals are sometimes referred to as the Fed's "mandate."

Maximum sustainable employment is the highest level of employment that the economy can sustain while maintaining a stable inflation rate.

Prices are considered stable when consumers and businesses don't have to worry about rising or falling prices when making plans, or when borrowing or lending for long periods. When prices are stable, long-term interest rates remain at moderate levels, so the goals of price stability and moderate long-term interest rates go together.

The Fed seeks to achieve its monetary policy mandate by influencing interest rates and general financial conditions. For example, by keeping policy interest rates low, the Fed makes homes more affordable for consumers and makes it cheaper for businesses to invest, expand, and hire. And by raising policy interest rates when inflation pressures are building, the Fed helps to cool the economy and preserve price stability.

## Interest Rate Predictions

The level of interest rates influences people's behavior by affecting economic decisions that determine the well-being of the nation: how much people are willing to save, and how much businesses are willing to invest.

With so many important decisions based on the level of interest rates, it is not surprising that people want to know which way rates are going to move. However, with so many diverse elements influencing rates, it is also not surprising that people are not able to predict the direction of these movements precisely.

Even though we are not able to predict accurately and consistently how interest rates will move, these movements are clearly not random. To the contrary, they are strictly controlled by the most calculating master of all—the economic forces of the market.

*(Source: "Points Of Interest: What Determines Interest Rates?" Education Resources Information Center (ERIC).)*

# Monetary Policy, Fiscal Policy, And Interest Rates

Monetary policy is a term used to refer to the actions of central banks to achieve macroeconomic policy objectives such as price stability, full employment, and stable economic growth. In the United States, the Congress established maximum employment and price stability as the macroeconomic objectives for the Federal Reserve; they are sometimes referred to as the Federal Reserve's dual mandate. Apart from these overarching objectives, the Congress determined that operational conduct of monetary policy should be free from political influence. As a result, the Federal Reserve is an independent agency of the federal government. Fiscal policy is a broad term used to refer to the tax and spending policies of the federal government. Fiscal policy decisions are determined by the Congress and the Administration; the Federal Reserve plays no role in determining fiscal policy.

The Federal Reserve uses a variety of policy tools to foster its statutory objectives of maximum employment and price stability. One of its main policy tools is the target for the federal funds rate (the rate that banks charge each other for short-term loans), a key short-term interest rate. The Federal Reserve's control over the federal funds rate gives it the ability to influence the general level of short-term market interest rates. By adjusting the level of short-term interest rates in response to changes in the economic outlook, the Federal Reserve can influence longer-term interest rates and key asset prices. These changes in financial conditions then affect the spending decisions of households and businesses.

Another key policy tool that the Federal Reserve has employed since the financial crisis is "forward guidance" about the path of the federal funds rate. Since December 2008, the Federal Reserve's target for the federal funds rate has been between 0 and 1/4 percent—effectively, as low as it can go. Through forward guidance, the Federal Open Market Committee provides an indication to households, businesses, and investors about the stance of monetary policy expected to prevail in the future, given the current economic outlook. By providing information about how long the Committee expects to keep the target for the federal funds rate exceptionally low, the forward guidance can put downward pressure on longer-term interest rates and thereby lower the cost of credit for households and businesses, and also help improve broader financial conditions.

## Price Of Credit

To understand the economic forces that drive (and sometimes are driven by) interest rates, we first need to define interest rates. An interest rate is a price, and like any other price, it relates to a transaction or the transfer of a good or service between a buyer and a seller. This special type of transaction is a loan or credit transaction, involving a supplier of surplus funds, i.e., a lender or saver, and a demander of surplus funds, i.e., a borrower.

In a loan transaction, the borrower receives funds to use for a period of time, and the lender receives the borrower's promise to pay at some time in the future. The borrower receives the benefit of the immediate use of funds. The lender, on the other hand, gives up the immediate use of funds, forgoing any current goods or services those funds could purchase. In other words, lenders loan funds they have saved—surplus funds they do not need for purchasing goods or services today.

Because these lenders/savers sacrifice the immediate use of funds, they ask for compensation in addition to the repayment of the funds loaned. This compensation is interest, the price the borrower must pay for the immediate use of the lender's funds. Put more simply, interest rates are the price of credit.

*(Source: "Points Of Interest: What Determines Interest Rates?" Education Resources Information Center (ERIC).)*

The monetary policy making body within the Federal Reserve System is the Federal Open Market Committee (FOMC). The FOMC currently has eight scheduled meetings per year, during which it reviews economic and financial developments and determines the appropriate stance of monetary policy. In reviewing the economic outlook, the FOMC considers how the current and projected paths for fiscal policy might affect key macroeconomic variables such as gross domestic product growth, employment, and inflation. In this way, fiscal policy has an indirect effect on the conduct of monetary policy through its influence on the aggregate economy and the economic outlook. For example, if federal tax and spending programs are projected to boost economic growth, the Federal Reserve would assess how those programs would affect its key macroeconomic objectives—maximum employment and price stability—and make appropriate adjustments to its monetary policy tools.

# Chapter 8
# Inflation And The Consumer Price Index (CPI)

## What Is Inflation?

Inflation occurs when the prices of goods and services increase over time. Inflation cannot be measured by an increase in the cost of one product or service, or even several products or services. Rather, inflation is a general increase in the overall price level of the goods and services in the economy.

Federal Reserve policymakers evaluate changes in inflation by monitoring several different price indexes. A price index measures changes in the price of a group of goods and services. The Fed considers several price indexes because different indexes track different products and services, and because indexes are calculated differently. Therefore, various indexes can send diverse signals about inflation.

> **Inflation:** Inflation can be defined as the overall general upward price movement of goods and services in an economy. BLS has various indexes that measure different aspects of inflation.
>
> (*Source: "Overview Of BLS Statistics On Inflation And Prices," Bureau of Labor Statistics (BLS), U.S. Department of Labor(DOL).*)

---

About This Chapter: Text under the heading "What Is Inflation?" is excerpted from "Current FAQs: Economy, Jobs, And Prices," Federal Reserve Board (FRB), September 9, 2016; Text under the heading "What Is Consumer Price Index (CPI)?" is excerpted from "Consumer Price Index," U.S. Bureau Of Labor Statistics (BLS), U.S. Department of Labor (DOL), February 1, 2017.

## How Does The Federal Reserve Evaluate Changes In The Rate Of Inflation?

The Fed often emphasizes the price inflation measure for personal consumption expenditures (PCE), produced by the Department of Commerce, largely because the PCE index covers a wide range of household spending. However, the Fed closely tracks other inflation measures as well, including the consumer price indexes and producer price indexes issued by the U.S. Department of Labor (DOL).

When evaluating the rate of inflation, Federal Reserve policymakers also take the following steps:

- First, because inflation numbers can vary erratically from month to month, policymakers generally consider average inflation over longer periods of time, ranging from a few months to a year or longer.

- Second, policymakers routinely examine the subcategories that make up a broad price index to help determine if a rise in inflation can be attributed to price changes that are likely to be temporary or unique events. Since the Fed's policy works with a lag, it must make policy based on its best forecast of inflation. Therefore, the Fed must try to determine if an inflation development is likely to persist or not.

- Finally, policymakers examine a variety of "core" inflation measures to help identify inflation trends. The most common type of core inflation measures excludes items that tend to go up and down in price dramatically or often, like food and energy items. For those items, a large price change in one period does not necessarily tend to be followed by another large change in the same direction in the following period. Although food and energy make up an important part of the budget for most households—and policymakers ultimately seek to stabilize overall consumer prices—core inflation measures that leave out items with volatile prices can be useful in assessing inflation trends.

# What Is Consumer Price Index (CPI)?

The Consumer Price Index (CPI) is a measure of the average change over time in the prices paid by urban consumers for a market basket of consumer goods and services.

## How Is The CPI Used?

The CPI affects nearly all Americans because of the many ways it is used. Following are major uses:

- As an economic indicator.

- As a deflator of other economic series.

- As a means of adjusting dollar values.

## Whose Buying Habits Does The CPI Reflect?

The CPI reflects spending patterns for each of two population groups: all urban consumers and urban wage earners and clerical workers. The all urban consumer group represents about 89 percent of the total U.S. population. It is based on the expenditures of almost all residents of urban or metropolitan areas, including professionals, the self-employed, the poor, the unemployed, and retired people, as well as urban wage earners and clerical workers. Not included in the CPI are the spending patterns of people living in rural nonmetropolitan areas, farm families, people in the Armed Forces, and those in institutions, such as prisons and mental hospitals. Consumer inflation for all urban consumers is measured by two indexes, namely, the Consumer Price Index for All Urban Consumers (CPI-U) and the Chained Consumer Price Index for All Urban Consumers (C-CPI-U).

The Consumer Price Index for Urban Wage Earners and Clerical Workers (CPI-W) is based on the expenditures of households included in the CPI-U definition that also meet two requirements: more than one-half of the household's income must come from clerical or wage occupations, and at least one of the household's earners must have been employed for at least 37 weeks during the previous 12 months. The CPI-W population represents about 28 percent of the total U.S. population and is a subset, or part, of the CPI-U population.

## Is The CPI A Cost-Of-Living Index?

The CPI frequently is called a cost-of-living index, but it differs in important ways from a complete cost-of-living measure. U.S. Bureau of Labor Statistics (BLS) has for some time used a cost-of-living framework in making practical decisions about questions that arise in constructing the CPI. A cost-of-living index is a conceptual measurement goal, however, and not a straightforward alternative to the CPI. A cost-of-living index would measure changes over time in the amount that consumers need to spend to reach a certain utility level or standard of living. Both the CPI and a cost-of-living index would reflect changes in the prices of goods and services, such as food and clothing, that are directly purchased in the marketplace; but a complete cost-of-living index would go beyond this role to also take into account changes in other governmental or environmental factors that affect consumers' well-being. It is very difficult to determine the proper treatment of public goods, such as safety and education, and other broad concerns, such as health, water quality, and crime, that would constitute a complete cost-of-living framework.

## Does The CPI Measure My Experience With Price Change?

Not necessarily. It is important to understand that BLS bases the market baskets and pricing procedures for the CPI-U and CPI-W populations on the experience of the relevant average household, not of any specific family or individual. It is unlikely that your experience will correspond precisely with either the national indexes or the indexes for specific cities or regions.

## How Is The CPI Market Basket Determined?

The CPI market basket is developed from detailed expenditure information provided by families and individuals on what they actually bought. For the current CPI, this information was collected from the Consumer Expenditure Surveys for 2013 and 2014. In each of those years, about 7,000 families from around the country provided information each quarter on their spending habits in the interview survey. To collect information on frequently purchased items, such as food and personal care products, another 7,000 families in each of these years kept diaries listing everything they bought during a 2-week period.

Over the 2 year period, then, expenditure information came from approximately 28,000 weekly diaries and 60,000 quarterly interviews used to determine the importance, or weight, of the more than 200 item categories in the CPI index structure.

## What Goods And Services Does The CPI Cover?

The CPI represents all goods and services purchased for consumption by the reference population (U or W) BLS has classified all expenditure items into more than 200 categories, arranged into eight major groups. Major groups and examples of categories in each are as follows:

- Food and Beverages (breakfast cereal, milk, coffee, chicken, wine, full service meals, snacks)

- Housing (rent of primary residence, owners' equivalent rent, fuel oil, bedroom furniture)

- Apparel (men's shirts and sweaters, women's dresses, jewelry)

- Transportation (new vehicles, airline fares, gasoline, motor vehicle insurance)

- Medical Care (prescription drugs and medical supplies, physicians' services, eyeglasses and eye care, hospital services)

- Recreation (televisions, toys, pets and pet products, sports equipment, admissions);

- Education and Communication (college tuition, postage, telephone services, computer software and accessories);

- Other goods and services (tobacco and smoking products, haircuts and other personal services, funeral expenses).

Also included within these major groups are various government-charged user fees, such as water and sewerage charges, auto registration fees, and vehicle tolls. In addition, the CPI includes taxes (such as sales and excise taxes) that are directly associated with the prices of specific goods and services. However, the CPI excludes taxes (such as income and Social Security taxes) not directly associated with the purchase of consumer goods and services.

The CPI does not include investment items, such as stocks, bonds, real estate, and life insurance. (These items relate to savings and not to day-to-day consumption expenses.)

For each of the more than 200 item categories, using scientific statistical procedures, the Bureau has chosen samples of several hundred specific items within selected business establishments frequented by consumers to represent the thousands of varieties available in the marketplace. For example, in a given supermarket, the Bureau may choose a plastic bag of golden delicious apples, U.S. extra fancy grade, weighing 4.4 pounds to represent the Apples category.

## Consumer Price Index

**Consumer Price Index (CPI) program** produces monthly data on changes in the prices paid by urban consumers for a representative basket of goods and services. There are separate indexes for two groups or populations of consumers:

**CPI for All Urban Consumers (CPI-U)** is the index most often reported by the national media.

**CPI for Urban Wage Earners and Clerical Workers (CPI-W)** is the index most often used for wage escalation agreements.

**CPI Inflation Calculator** allows users to calculate the value of current dollars in an earlier period, or to calculate the current value of dollar amounts from years ago.

**Consumer price indexes** often are used to escalate or adjust payments for rents, wages, alimony, child support and other obligations that may be affected by changes in the cost of living. There is a fact sheet explaining how to use the CPI for escalating contracts.

An additional price index called the **Chained Consumer Price Index (C-CPI-U)** is also available. This measure is designed to be a closer approximation to a "cost-of-living" index than the CPI-U or CPI-W.

**Producer Price Indexes (PPIs)** are a family of indexes that measure changes in the selling prices received by domestic producers of goods and services. They formerly were referred to as Wholesale Price Indexes. When the PPIs are released, the news media will most often report the percentage change in the index for Finished Goods.

(*Source: "Overview Of BLS Statistics On Inflation And Prices," Bureau of Labor Statistics (BLS), U.S. Department of Labor(DOL).*)

## How Are CPI Prices Collected And Reviewed?

Each month, BLS data collectors called economic assistants visit or call thousands of retail stores, service establishments, rental units, and doctors' offices, all over the United States, to obtain information on the prices of the thousands of items used to track and measure price changes in the CPI. These economic assistants record the prices of about 80,000 items each month, representing a scientifically selected sample of the prices paid by consumers for goods and services purchased.

During each call or visit, the economic assistant collects price data on a specific good or service that was precisely defined during an earlier visit. If the selected item is available, the economic assistant records its price. If the selected item is no longer available, or if there have been changes in the quality or quantity (for example, eggs sold in packages of ten when they previously were sold by the dozen) of the good or service since the last time prices were collected, the economic assistant selects a new item or records the quality change in the current item.

The recorded information is sent to the national office of BLS, where commodity specialists who have detailed knowledge about the particular goods or services priced review the data. These specialists check the data for accuracy and consistency and make any necessary corrections or adjustments, which can range from an adjustment for a change in the size or quantity of a packaged item to more complex adjustments based upon statistical analysis of the value of an item's features or quality. Thus, commodity specialists strive to prevent changes in the quality of items from affecting the CPI's measurement of price change.

## How Is The CPI Calculated?

The CPI is a product of a series of interrelated samples. First, using data from the 1990 Census of Population, BLS selected the urban areas from which data on prices were collected and chose the housing units within each area that were eligible for use in the shelter component of the CPI. The Census of Population also provided data on the number of consumers represented by each area selected as a CPI price collection area. Next, another sample (of about 14,500 families each year) served as the basis for a Point-of-Purchase Survey that identified the places where households purchased various types of goods and services.

## How Are Taxes Treated In The CPI?

Certain taxes are included in the CPI, namely, taxes that are directly associated with the purchase of specific goods and services (such as sales and excise taxes). Government user fees are also included in the CPI. For example, toll charges and parking fees are included in the transportation category, and an entry fee to a national park would be included as part of the admissions index. In addition, property taxes should be reflected indirectly in the BLS method of measuring the cost of the flow of services provided by shelter, which we called owners' equivalent rent, to the extent that these taxes influence rental values. Taxes not directly associated with specific purchases, such as income and Social Security taxes, are excluded, as are the government services paid for through those taxes.

For certain purposes, one might want to define price indexes to include, rather than exclude, income taxes. Such indexes would provide an answer to a question different from the one to which the present CPI is relevant, and would be appropriate for different uses.

## How Do I Read Or Interpret An Index?

An index is a tool that simplifies the measurement of movements in a numerical series. Most of the specific CPI indexes have a 1982-84 reference base. That is, BLS sets the average index level (representing the average price level)-for the 36-month period covering the years 1982, 1983, and 1984-equal to 100. BLS then measures changes in relation to that figure. An index of 110, for example, means there has been a 10-percent increase in price since the reference period; similarly, an index of 90 means a 10-percent decrease. Movements of the index from one date to another can be expressed as changes in index points (simply, the difference between index levels), but it is more useful to express the movements as percent changes. This is because index points are affected by the level of the index in relation to its reference period, while percent changes are not.

In the table that follows, Item A increased by half as many index points as Item B between Year I and Year II. Yet, because of different starting indexes, both items had the same percent change; that is, prices advanced at the same rate. By contrast, Items B and C show the same change in index points, but the percent change is greater for Item C because of its lower starting index value.

**Table 8.1.** Change In Index

|  | Item A | Item B | Item C |
|---|---|---|---|
| **Year I** | 112.5 | 225 | 110 |
| **Year II** | 121.5 | 243 | 128 |
| **Change in index points** | 9 | 18 | 18 |
| **Percent change** | 9.0/112.500 x 100 = 8.0 | 18.0/225.000 x 100 = 8.0 | 18.0/110.000 x 100 = 16.4 |

## Is The CPI The Best Measure Of Inflation?

Inflation has been defined as a process of continuously rising prices or equivalently, of a continuously falling value of money.

Various indexes have been devised to measure different aspects of inflation. The CPI measures inflation as experienced by consumers in their day-to-day living expenses; the Producer Price Index (PPI) measures inflation at earlier stages of the production process; the Employment Cost Index (ECI) measures it in the labor market; the BLS International Price Program (IPP) measures it for imports and exports; and the Gross Domestic Product Deflator (GDP Deflator) measures inflation experienced by both consumers themselves as well as governments and other institutions providing goods and services to consumers. Finally, there are specialized measures, such as measures of interest rates.

The "best" measure of inflation for a given application depends on the intended use of the data. The CPI is generally the best measure for adjusting payments to consumers when the intent is to allow consumers to purchase at today's prices, a market basket of goods and services equivalent to one that they could purchase in an earlier period.

## Which Index Is The "Official CPI" Reported In The Media?

The broadest and most comprehensive CPI is called the All Items Consumer Price Index for All Urban Consumers (CPI-U) for the U.S. City Average, 1982–84 = 100.

In addition to the All Items CPI, BLS publishes thousands of other consumer price indexes. One such index is called "All items less food and energy." Some users of CPI data use this index because food and energy prices are relatively volatile, and these users want to focus on what they perceive to be the "core" or "underlying" rate of inflation.

When CPI data are reported, these data can be reported on a not seasonally adjusted basis as well as a seasonally adjusted basis. Often, the media will report some, or all, of the following:

- Index level, not seasonally adjusted. (for example, May 2008 = 216.632).

- 12-month percent change, not seasonally adjusted. (for example, May 2007 to May 2008 = 4.2 percent).

- 1-month percent change on a seasonally adjusted basis. (for example, from April 2008 to May 2008 = 0.6 percent).

- Annual rate of percent change so far this year (for example, from December 2007 to May 2008 if the rate of increase over the first 5 months of the year continued for the full year, after the removal of seasonal influences, the rise would be 4.0 percent).

- Annual rate based on the latest seasonally adjusted 1-month change. For example, if the rate from April 2008 to May 2008 continued for a full 12 months, then the rise, compounded, would be 8.1 percent. A statutory framework established by the U.S. Congress guides the operation of the Federal Reserve System

# Part Two
## Keys To Wealth Development

# Chapter 9
# Financial Literacy And Capability

Financial capability and literacy is "the capacity, based on knowledge, skills, and access, to manage financial resources effectively." This set of skills can help youth achieve financial well-being, which happens when they can fully meet current and ongoing financial obligations, feel secure in their financial future, and are capable of making decisions that allow them to enjoy life. Financial education is how youth can learn these skills through a variety of resources and programming.

Today's youth face a financial marketplace that is more complex than the one faced by previous generations. A study found that millennials have greater financial concerns than older generations:

- 55 percent of millennials with student debt worry that they will not be able to pay off their debt, and

- almost 50 percent are concerned that they have too much debt in general (i.e., credit cards).

Financial capability is knowing how to spend wisely, manage credit, and plan for the future. Financial capability is an effective way to help youth, no matter their circumstances, avoid common financial vulnerabilities and build economic stability. Youth should be educated about

About This Chapter: Text in this chapter begins with excerpts from "Financial Literacy," Youth.gov, November 19, 2016; Text under the heading "Money Management: Five Ways To Cut Spending" is excerpted from "Start Smart: Money Management For Teens," Federal Deposit Insurance Corporation (FDIC), June 12, 2014; Text under the heading "How To Ace Your First Test Managing Real Money In The Real World" is excerpted from "Money Tips For All Ages," Federal Deposit Insurance Corporation (FDIC), June 12, 2014; Text under the heading "Tips For Teaching Young People About Money" is excerpted from "Tips For Teaching Young People About Money," Federal Deposit Insurance Corporation (FDIC), June 10, 2014.

finances early in life and at pivotal points in their development and financial lives. Having a higher financial literacy early in life is associated with:

- less credit card debt,

- higher savings rates, and

- fewer personal bankruptcies.

As they approach high school graduation, students and their caregivers will make important decisions about whether to pursue higher education and if so, how to face the reality of paying for it. Additionally, youth who do not attend college or trade school directly after high school will more quickly face financial responsibilities as adults. These early choices can have a long-lasting impact on their financial well-being.

As the country continues to emerge from the aftermath of the financial crisis, Americans are, on average, experiencing less financial stress and improved satisfaction with their financial condition. However, large segments of society continue to face financial difficulties. The financial difficulties of individuals and families can dramatically affect the financial health of local communities, and it is clear the financial well-being of individuals and families is fundamental to national financial stability. In the United States, nearly one in five households reports spending more than they earn in income (not including the purchase of a new home, car, or other big outlays). Nearly half of all households are not able to pay for an unexpected $400 expense without having to borrow money or sell something, and over half worry about running out of money in retirement.

The understanding, skills, tools, and resources to make informed financial decisions are important for attaining and maintaining financial health and security. Supporting the financial capability of Americans can take many forms, from providing timely, relevant and actionable information, to supporting the development of effective financial skills and habits, to creating an environment where it is easier for people to make and follow through on money decisions that serve their life goals. In the years ahead some work will need to be responsive to trends shaping Americans' financial security, including inequality of financial status; increasing diversity; longevity and the need for long-term financial security; and the power of technology.

*(Source: "Promoting Financial Success In The United States: National Strategy For Financial Literacy—2016 Update," MyMoney.gov, Financial Literacy and Education Commission (FLEC).)*

# Money Management: Five Ways To Cut Spending

Do you want to find ways to stretch your money, so it goes farther and is there when you really need it? Here are some suggestions for knowing how much money you have, how much you need for expenditures, and how to reach your goals by cutting back on what you spend.

1. **Practice self-control**: To avoid making a quick decision to buy something just because you saw it featured on display or on sale:

   - Make a shopping list before you leave home and stick to it.

   - Before you go shopping, set a spending limit (say, $5 or $10) for "impulse buys"—items you didn't plan to buy but that got your attention anyway. If you are tempted to spend more than your limit, wait a few hours or a few days and think it over.

   - Limit the amount of cash you take with you. The less cash you carry, the less you can spend and the less you lose if you misplace your wallet.

2. **Research before you buy**: To be sure you are getting a good value, especially with a big purchase, look into the quality and the reputation of the product or service you're considering. Read "reviews" in magazines or respected websites. Talk to knowledgeable people you trust. Check other stores or go online and compare prices. Look at similar items. This is known as "comparison shopping," and it can lead to tremendous savings and better quality purchases. And if you're sure you know what you want, take advantage of store coupons and mail-in "rebates."

3. **Keep track of your spending**: This helps you set and stick to limits, what many people refer to as budgeting. "Maintaining a budget may sound scary or complicated, but it can be as simple as having a notebook and writing down what you buy each month," said Janet Kincaid, Federal Deposit Insurance Corporation (FDIC) Senior Consumer Affairs Officer." Any system that helps you know how much you are spending each month is a good thing."

   Also pay attention to small amounts of money you spend. "A snack here and a magazine there can quickly add up," said Paul Horwitz, an FDIC Community Affairs Specialist. He suggested that, for a few weeks, you write down every purchase in a small notebook. "You'll probably be amazed at how much you spend without even thinking."

4. **Think "used" instead of "new."**: Borrow things (from the library or friends) that you don't have to own. Pick up used games, DVDs and music at "second-hand" stores around town.

5. **Take good care of what you buy**: It's expensive to replace things. Think about it: Do you really want to buy the same thing twice?

## Manage Finances And Save Money

To help you manage your money and reach your saving goals:

**Create a Budget**

A budget is your plan for how you will spend money over a set period of time. It shows how much money you make and how you spend your money. Creating a budget can help you:

- Pay your bills on time.
- Save for unplanned expenses in the future.

**Consider Ways to Save**

Saving money involves looking for deals and buying the items you need at the best price, using coupons or by shopping around. Check out MyMoney.gov's spending tips for ideas. You can also set up a saving plan to help you save for emergencies and for short term and long term goals. MyMoney.gov offers tips on saving, including helping you achieve your saving goals.

**Invest in Long Term Goals**

You can save for long term goals, such as retirement and college education, by investing.

*(Source: "Saving And Investing," USA.Gov, U.S. General Services Administration (GSA).)*

# How To Ace Your First Test Managing Real Money In The Real World

As a teen, you're beginning to make some grown-up decisions about how to save and spend your money. That's why learning the right ways to manage money—right from the start—is important. Here are suggestions.

- **Save some money before you're tempted to spend it.** When you get cash for your birthday or from a job, automatically put a portion of it—at least 10 percent, but possibly more—into a savings or investment account. This strategy is what financial advisors call "paying yourself first." Making this a habit can gradually turn small sums of money into big amounts that can help pay for really important purchases in the future.

Also put your spare change to use. When you empty your pockets at the end of the day, consider putting some of that loose change into a jar or any other container, and then about once a month put that money into a savings account at the bank.

"Spare change can add up quickly," said Luke W. Reynolds, Chief of the FDIC's Community Affairs Outreach Section. "But don't let that money sit around your house month after month, earning no interest and at risk of being lost or stolen."

If you need some help sorting and counting your change, he said, find out if your bank has a coin machine you can use for free. If not, the bank may give you coin wrappers.

Some supermarkets and other non-banking companies have self-service machines that quickly turn coins into cash, but expect to pay a significant fee for the service, often close to 10 cents for every dollar counted, plus you still have to take the cash to the bank to deposit it into your savings account.

- **Keep track of your spending.** A good way to take control of your money is to decide on maximum amounts you aim to spend each week or each month for certain expenses, such as entertainment and snack food. This task is commonly known as "budgeting" your money or developing a "spending plan." And to help manage your money, it's worth keeping a list of your expenses for about a month, so you have a better idea of where your dollars and cents are going.

---

## Fair Credit Reporting Act (FCRA)

The Fair Credit Reporting Act (FCRA) requires each of the nationwide consumer reporting companies—Equifax, Experian, and TransUnion—to provide you with a free copy of your credit report, at your request, once every 12 months. You can see your credit report at annualcreditreport.com External link or order a copy by calling 1-877-322-8228.

Remember: only annualcreditreport.com can give you the free annual credit report you are entitled to by law. Other websites that claim to offer "free credit reports," "free credit scores," or "free credit monitoring" are not part of the legally mandated free annual credit report program.

*(Source: "Money Matters," Office on Women's Health (OWH), U.S. Department of Health and Human Services (HHS).)*

---

"If you find you're spending more than you intended, you may need to reduce your spending or increase your income," Reynolds added. "It's all about setting goals for yourself and then making the right choices with your money to help you achieve those goals."

**Consider a part-time or summer job.** Whether it's babysitting, lawn mowing or a job in a "real" business, working outside of your home can provide you with income, new skills and references that can be useful after high school or college. Before accepting any job, ask your parents for their permission and advice.

- **Think before you buy.** Many teens make quick and costly decisions to buy the latest clothes or electronics without considering whether they are getting a good value.

"A $200 pair of shoes hawked by a celebrity gets you to the same destination at the same speed as a $50 pair," said Reynolds. "Before you buy something, especially a big purchase, ask yourself if you really need or just want the item, if you've done enough research and comparison-shopping, and if you can truly afford the purchase without having to cut back on spending for something else."

- **Be careful with cards.** Under most state laws, you must be at least 18 years old to obtain your own credit card and be held responsible for repaying the debt. If you're under 18, though, you may be able to qualify for a credit card as long as a parent or other adult agrees to repay your debts if you fail to do so.

  An alternative to a credit card is a debit card, which automatically deducts purchases from your savings or checking account. Credit cards and debit cards offer convenience, but they also come with costs and risks that must be taken seriously.

- **Protect yourself from crooks who target teens.** Even if you're too young to have a checking account or credit card, a criminal who learns your name, address and Social Security number (SSN) may be able to obtain a new credit card using your name to make purchases.

  One of the most important things you can do to protect against identity theft is to be very suspicious of requests for your name, Social Security number, passwords or bank or credit card information that come to you in an e-mail or an Internet advertisement, no matter how legitimate they may seem.

"Teens are very comfortable using e-mail and the Internet, but they need to be aware that criminals can be hiding at the other end of the computer screen," said Michael Benardo, manager of the FDIC's financial crimes section. These types of fraudulent requests can also come by phone, text message or in the mail.

- **Be smart about college.** If you're planning to go to college, learn about your options for saving or borrowing money for what could be a major expense—from tuition to books, fees and housing. Also consider the costs when you search for a school. Otherwise, when you graduate, your college debts could be high and may limit your options when it comes to a career path or where you can afford to live.

# Tips For Teaching Young People About Money

Here are ways that parents, guardians or even grandparents can teach money-management skills to youngsters.

- **Help children open their first bank accounts.** Discuss how to comparison-shop by looking at key aspects, such as the minimum balance requirements and the interest rate, expressed as the Annual Percentage Yield (APY), at several local financial institutions,

## Other Money Matters

As you get older, you'll have to take on responsibility for other important items, too. Some of these items include:

- Car insurance
- 401K (a savings plan for your retirement)
- Homeowner's insurance
- Federal and state taxes

A good way to learn about these issues is by taking a personal finance class at your school, community college, or local community center.

*(Source: "Money Matters," Office on Women's Health (OWH), U.S. Department of Health and Human Services (HHS).)*

suggested Lekeshia Frasure, Acting Chief of the FDIC's Outreach and Program Development Section. "Then guide your child in selecting and opening the right account for his or her needs," she said.

Many banks offer special savings accounts for students with features that may include a low minimum-balance requirement and certain fees waived.

- **Encourage young people to save money for future goals.** Explain the importance of setting money aside for short-term and long-term goals. For a young adult or teen, short-term savings can include money for fun, such as concert tickets, as well as "emergency" savings for unforeseen expenses including car repairs. Suggest that your child put at least 10 percent of any gifts, allowance or earnings into savings, and consider making your own matching contributions as an incentive.

- **Consider giving an allowance—even to a young adult.** The best systems encourage youngsters to decide in advance how much they should put into savings (which reinforces the concept of "pay yourself first," before they are tempted to spend the money), how much should go into the spending pile and how much should be set aside to share with others (for charity, birthdays or holiday gifts).

"An allowance can be one of the best ways to teach children about money management and the trade-offs we face in life, especially if you don't give them more money if they run out of their allowance early," said Irma Matias, an FDIC Community Affairs Specialist. Likewise, once your child is old enough, encourage him or her to get a part-time or summer job.

- **Try to set a good example with your own money management.** For instance, keep track of your debit card, ATM and other account transactions, and discuss with your child why doing so will help you track your current balance and avoid costly overdraft fees.

- **Help your kids develop a healthy skepticism of unsolicited offers and inquiries.** Young consumers are among the victims of scams and rip-offs, and even babies are targets for identity thieves wanting to use personal information to commit fraud. Information for parents on protecting children's personal information from identity theft is at the Federal Trade Commission's Web page on children's privacy (www.ftc.gov/bcp/ menus/consumer/data/child.shtm).

- **Talk with young people about money.** "Use any opportunity to engage in a conversation about financial choices and decisions," said Luke W. Reynolds, Acting Associate Director of the FDIC's Division of Depositor and Consumer Protection. "For example, teach children how to critically analyze ads because special offers often are not the great deal they appear to be."

# Chapter 10
# Develop A Financial Plan

---

## Drawing A Personal Financial Roadmap

Before you make any investing decision, sit down and take an honest look at your entire financial situation—especially if you've never made a financial plan before.

The first step to successful investing is figuring out your goals and risk tolerance—either on your own or with the help of a financial professional. There is no guarantee that you'll make money from your investments. But if you get the facts about saving and investing and follow through with an intelligent plan, you should be able to gain financial security over the years and enjoy the benefits of managing your money.

*(Source: "Financial Navigating In The Current Economy: Ten Things To Consider Before You Make Investing Decisions," U.S. Securities and Exchange Commission (SEC).)*

---

## Define Your Goals

Knowing how to secure your financial well-being is one of the most important things you can do for yourself. You don't have to be a genius to do it. You just need to know a few basics, form a plan, and be ready to stick to it.

To end up where you want to be, you need a financial plan. Ask yourself what you want. List your most important goals first. Decide how many years you have to meet each specific goal, because when you save or invest, you'll need to find an option that fits your time frame. Here are some tools to help you decide how much you'll need to save for various needs.

---

About This Chapter: This chapter includes text excerpted from "Define Your Goals," Investor.gov, U.S. Securities and Exchange Commission (SEC), August 25, 2016.

- The Ballpark Estimate, created by the American Savings Education Council (ASEC), can help you calculate what you'll need to save each year for retirement.

- The Financial Industry Regulatory Authority (FINRA) has a college savings calculator.

# Figure Out Your Finances

Take an honest look at your entire financial situation—what you own and what you owe. This is a "net worth statement." On one side, list what you own. These are your "assets." On the other side, list what you owe. These are your "liabilities" or debts. Subtract your liabilities from your assets. If your assets are larger than your liabilities, you have a "positive" net worth. If your liabilities are larger than your assets, you have a "negative" net worth.

You'll want to update your "net worth statement" every year to keep track of how you are doing. Don't be discouraged if you have a negative net worth—following a financial plan will help you turn it into positive net worth.

The next step is to keep track of your income and expenses. Write down what you and others in your family earn and spend each month, and include a category for savings and investing. If you are spending all your income, and never have money to save or invest, start by cutting back on expenses. When you watch where you spend your money, you will be surprised how small everyday expenses can add up. Many people get into the habit of saving and investing by paying themselves first. An easy way to do this is to have your bank automatically deposit money from your paycheck into a savings or investment account.

# Small Savings Add Up To Big Money

How much does a daily candy bar cost? Would you believe $465.84? Or more?

If you buy a candy bar every day for $1, it adds up to $365 a year. If you saved that $365 and put it into an investment that earns 5% a year, it would grow to $465.84 by the end of five years, and by the end of 30 years, to $1,577.50. That's the power of "compounding."

With compound interest, you earn interest on the money you save and on the interest that money earns. Over time, even a small amount saved can add up to big money.

If you buy on impulse, make a rule that you'll always wait 24 hours before buying anything. You may lose your desire to buy it after a day. Also, try emptying your pockets at the end of each day and putting spare change aside. You'll be surprised how quickly those nickels and dimes add up.

# Pay Off Credit Cards Or Other High Interest Debt

No investment strategy pays off as well as, or with less risk than, eliminating high interest debt. Most credit cards charge high interest rates—as much as 18% or more—if you don't pay off your balance in full each month. If you owe money on your credit cards, the wisest thing you can do is pay off the balance in full as quickly as possible. Virtually no investment will give you returns to match an 18% interest rate on your credit card. That's why you're better off eliminating all credit card debt before investing. Once you've paid off your credit cards, you can budget your money and begin to save and invest.

Here are some tips for avoiding credit card debt:

## Put Away The Plastic

- Don't use a credit card unless you know you'll have the money to pay the bill when it arrives.

## Know What You Owe

- It's easy to forget how much you've charged on your credit card. Every time you use a credit card, track how much you have spent and figure out how much you'll have to pay that month. If you know you won't be able to pay your balance in full, try to figure out how much you can pay each month and how long it'll take to pay the balance in full.

## Pay Off The Card With The Highest Rate

- If you've got unpaid balances on several credit cards, you should first pay down the card that charges the highest rate. Pay as much as you can toward that debt each month until your balance is once again zero, while still paying the minimum on your other cards. The same advice goes for any other high-interest debt (about 8% or above), which does not offer any tax advantages.

# Save For A Rainy Day

Savings are usually put into safe places that allow you access to your money at any time. Examples include savings accounts, checking accounts, and certificates of deposit. Your money may be insured by the Federal Deposit Insurance Corporation (FDIC) or National Credit Union Administration (NCUA). But there's a tradeoff between security and availability; your money earns a low interest rate.

Most smart investors put enough money in savings to cover an emergency, like sudden unemployment. Some make sure they have up to six months of their income in savings so that they know it will absolutely be there for them when they need it.

But how "safe" is a savings account if the interest it earns doesn't keep up with inflation? Let's say you save a dollar when it can buy a loaf of bread. But years later when you withdraw that dollar plus the interest you earned, it might only be able to buy half a loaf. That is why many people put some of their money in savings, but look to investing so they can earn more over longer periods of time.

# Understand What It Means To Invest

When investing, you have a greater chance of losing your money than when you save. Unlike FDIC-insured deposits, the money you invest in securities, mutual funds, and other similar investments are not federally insured. You could lose your "principal," which is the amount you've invested. That's true even if you purchase your investments through a bank. But when you invest, you also have the opportunity to earn more money. On the other hand, investing involves taking on some degree of risk.

# Diversify Your Investments

Diversification can be neatly summed up as, "Don't put all your eggs in one basket." The idea is that if one investment loses money, the other investments will make up for those losses. Diversification can't guarantee that your investments won't suffer if the market drops. But it can improve the chances that you won't lose money, or that if you do, it won't be as much as if you weren't diversified.

---

## Consider Dollar Cost Averaging

Through the investment strategy known as "dollar cost averaging," you can protect yourself from the risk of investing all of your money at the wrong time by following a consistent pattern of adding new money to your investment over a long period of time. By making regular investments with the same amount of money each time, you will buy more of an investment when its price is low and less of the investment when its price is high. Individuals that typically make a lump-sum contribution to an individual retirement account either at the end of the calendar year or in early April may want to consider "dollar cost averaging" as an investment strategy, especially in a volatile market.

*(Source: "Financial Navigating In The Current Economy: Ten Things to Consider Before You Make Investing Decisions," U.S. Securities and Exchange Commission (SEC).)*

---

# Gauge Your Risk Tolerance

What are the best saving and investment products for you? The answer depends on when you will need the money, your goals, and whether you will be able to sleep at night if you purchase a risky investment (one where you could lose your principal).

For instance, if you are saving for retirement, and you have 35 years before you retire, you may want to consider riskier investment products, knowing that if you stick to only the "savings" products or to less risky investment products, your money will grow too slowly. Or, given inflation and taxes, you may lose the purchasing power of your money. A frequent mistake people make is putting money they will not need for a very long time in investments that pay a low amount of interest.

On the other hand, if you are saving for a short-term goal, five years or less, you don't want to choose risky investments, because when it's time to sell, you may have to take a loss.

# Learn About Investment Options

While the SEC (U.S. Securities and Exchange Commission) cannot recommend any particular investment product, a vast array of investment products exists, including stocks and stock mutual funds, corporate and municipal bonds, annuities, exchange-traded funds, money market funds, and U.S. Treasury securities.

Stocks, bonds, and mutual funds are the most common asset categories. These are among the asset categories you would likely choose from when investing in a retirement savings program or a college savings plan. Other asset categories include real estate, precious metals and other commodities, and private equity. Some investors may include these asset categories within a portfolio. Investments in these asset categories typically have category-specific risks.

Before you make any investment, understand the risks of the investment and make sure the risks are appropriate for you. You'll also want to understand the fees associated with the buying, selling, and holding the investment.

# Chapter 11
# Savings And Investing

## Getting Started In Saving And Investing

The thought of starting a savings or investment account can be overwhelming, but it doesn't have to be. No matter how much or how little money you have, you can get started planning your financial future today with just a few basic steps. The important thing is to begin by thinking about what you want to achieve, and then learn about the opportunities that are available to you.

## Step One: Make A Plan

Every successful investor or savings account holder started out with one thing in common—they made a financial plan and they were prepared to stick to it. Every savings plan is different, because each person is different and has different goals in life. There is no wrong way to make a financial plan, and your plan doesn't have to stay the same forever. Your financial plan can change as your life changes, and there is no reason to wait for the perfect moment to begin. In fact, the sooner you make your financial plan, the better off you will be in the long run.

Here are some things to consider when thinking about your financial plan:

- What are your financial goals?

- How much money do you want to save, and why?

- Your savings goals can be anything that is important to you. For example: Are you saving to buy a car? Pay for college?

---

Make a list of your financial goals and then put them in order of importance. Include an estimate of the amount of money needed to reach each goal. Then think about how much time you will have to meet each specific goal. For example, in order to buy a car, how many months will you be able to save for that purchase? Knowing how much money you will need, and when you will need it, are the most important factors that will influence your savings and investment plan. Divide the amount of money you need by the number of weeks until the money is needed to determine how much money you will need to save each week in order to meet your goal. Online savings calculators can also help you figure how much money you will need to save each week or month in order to meet your goal. You can find a wealth of information about savings and investment, including savings calculators and links to other resources online at www.investor.gov.

---

**Quick Tip**

Getting started with saving and investing is as easy as 1–2–3!

1. Make a financial plan. What are your goals?
2. Understand your current financial status, including income, expenses, and debt.
3. Start saving and investing as soon as you've paid off your debts.

---

# Step Two: Know Your Financial Status

The second step in getting started in saving and investing is understanding your current financial situation. To do this, you will need to know how much money you owe to others and how much money you currently have. There are worksheets and calculators available online to help you with this step.

Once you have listed all of your debts and all of the money you currently have, you can then move on to examining your current income and expenses. Begin by listing all of your expenses, either monthly or weekly. Then write down how much money you earn. If your income is greater than your expenses, you can begin saving immediately. If your expenses are greater than your income, you will have to do some additional calculations in order to being saving or investing.

When expenses are greater than income, you will need to find ways to reduce your expenses. You can begin this process by writing down how you spend your money. What kinds of things do you buy each day, each week, or each month? Take note of where your money is going. Once you start paying close attention to your spending habits, you might be surprised to see how quickly small everyday purchases add up over time. The next step is to identify where you might be able to cut back on expenses. For example, instead of buying coffee from a coffee shop every day, you could save money by making coffee at home. If you find that you buy lunch fairly often, you might be able to reduce that expense by bringing your own lunch from home instead. There are many ways to cut back on unnecessary expenses, and each person will find different ways to save according to their own priorities.

Once you have found some ways to reduce your expenses, your first priority should be to pay off any existing debts. This is especially important for high-interest debts such as credit card balances. After you have paid those debts, you can start using that money for savings and investments.

# Step Three: Start Saving And Investing

When you are ready to begin saving and investing your money, you will need to learn about the different opportunities that are available to you. Saving and investing are two different ways to manage your money. The basic difference between saving and investing is the amount of risk involved.

A savings account is usually considered the safest place to keep your money. With savings accounts, you can generally access your money at any time, for any reason, whenever you need it. Savings account products include bank savings accounts, checking accounts, and credit union accounts. After you have paid off credit cards or other high-interest debts, some financial advisors recommend building a savings account containing the equivalent of up to six months of regular expenses. This amount is recommended because it can be used in case of an emergency, period of unemployment, or other financial need.

An investment is a way to manage money over a longer period of time. Unlike savings accounts, investments may not be as easy to access and there may be fees associated with withdrawing money. The longer-term commitment of an investment, such as in stocks, securities, and mutual funds, also comes with benefits and risks. When you make an investment, you give your money to a company or other enterprise such as a bank, hoping that the organization will be successful and pay you back with more money than you initially invested. The main benefit is that investments generally provide the opportunity to earn greater interest on the money you invest. Interest is the dividend that is paid when, for example, a stock that you purchased increases in value during the time that you own that stock. The main risk of certain investments is that there is a greater chance of losing some of the money you invested, for example, when a stock that you purchased decreases in value during the time that you own it. You will need to understand the relative benefits and risks associated with savings accounts and investments that you consider. You will also need to decide how much risk you are comfortable with in order to make the best investment decisions to meet your overall goals.

A recent study in which 8,000 teens were surveyed showed that 38 percent reported that they're actively saving money and 22 percent said they are saving more than they did the previous year. Fifty-seven percent of teens said they are saving money for new clothes while 36 percent are socking away cash to buy a car.

## References

1. "Saving and Investing: A Roadmap to Your Financial Security through Saving and Investing," Office of Investor Education and Advocacy (OIEA), U.S. Securities and Exchange Commission (SEC), June 2011.

2. "Saving and Investing," The Money Advice Service, n.d.

3. "The Facts on Saving and Investing," Office of Investor Education and Assistance, U.S. Securities and Exchange Commission (SEC), n.d.

# Chapter 12
# Risk Tolerance

## What Is Risk?

All investments involve some degree of risk. In finance, risk refers to the degree of uncertainty and/or potential financial loss inherent in an investment decision. In general, as investment risks rise, investors seek higher returns to compensate themselves for taking such risks.

Every saving and investment product has different risks and returns. Differences include: how readily investors can get their money when they need it, how fast their money will grow, and how safe their money will be. In this chapter, a number of risks investors face will be discussed. They include:

## Business Risk

With a stock, you are purchasing a piece of ownership in a company. With a bond, you are loaning money to a company. Returns from both of these investments require that that the company stays in business. If a company goes bankrupt and its assets are liquidated, common stockholders are the last in line to share in the proceeds. If there are assets, the company's bondholders will be paid first, then holders of preferred stock. If you are a common stockholder, you get whatever is left, which may be nothing.

If you are purchasing an annuity make sure you consider the financial strength of the insurance company issuing the annuity. You want to be sure that the company will still be around, and financially sound, during your payout phase.

About This Chapter: Text under the heading "What Is Risk?" is excerpted from "Introduction To Investing," Investor.gov, U.S. Securities and Exchange Commission (SEC), December 3, 2016; Text under the heading "Assessing Your Risk Tolerance" is excerpted from "Assessing Your Risk Tolerance," Investor.gov, U.S. Securities and Exchange Commission (SEC), December 3, 2016.

## Volatility Risk

Even when companies aren't in danger of failing, their stock price may fluctuate up or down. Large company stocks as a group, for example, have lost money on average about one out of every three years. Market fluctuations can be unnerving to some investors. A stock's price can be affected by factors inside the company, such as a faulty product, or by events the company has no control over, such as political or market events.

---

## Risk Tolerance

What are the best saving and investing products for you? The answer depends on when you will need the money, your goals, and if you will be able to sleep at night if you purchase a risky investment where you could lose your principal.

For instance, if you are saving for retirement, and you have 35 years before you retire, you may want to consider riskier investment products, knowing that if you stick to only the "savings" products or to less risky investment products, your money will grow too slowly—or given inflation or taxes, you may lose the purchasing power of your money. A frequent mistake people make is putting money they will not need for a very long time in investments that pay a low amount of interest.

On the other hand, if you are saving for a short-term goal, five years or less, you don't want to choose risky investments, because when it's time to sell, you may have to take a loss. Since investments often move up and down in value rapidly, you want to make sure that you can wait and sell at the best possible time.

*(Source: "Determine Your Risk Tolerance," U.S. Securities and Exchange Commission (SEC).)*

---

## Inflation Risk

Inflation is a general upward movement of prices. Inflation reduces purchasing power, which is a risk for investors receiving a fixed rate of interest. The principal concern for individuals investing in cash equivalents is that inflation will erode returns.

## Interest Rate Risk

Interest rate changes can affect a bond's value. If bonds are held to maturity the investor will receive the face value, plus interest. If sold before maturity, the bond may be worth more or less than the face value. Rising interest rates will make newly issued bonds more appealing to investors because the newer bonds will have a higher rate of interest than older ones. To sell an older bond with a lower interest rate, you might have to sell it at a discount.

## Liquidity Risk

This refers to the risk that investors won't find a market for their securities, potentially preventing them from buying or selling when they want. This can be the case with the more complicated investment products. It may also be the case with products that charge a penalty for early withdrawal or liquidation such as a certificate of deposit (CD).

## Are There Any Guarantees?

**The Federal Deposit Insurance Corporation (FDIC)**: Savings accounts, insured money market accounts, and certificates of deposit (CDs) are generally viewed as safe because they are federally insured by FDIC. This independent agency of the federal government insures your money up to $250,000 per insured bank. It is important to note that the total is per depositor not per account. But there's a tradeoff between security and availability; your money earns a low interest rate.

The FDIC insures deposits only. It does not insure securities, mutual funds, or similar types of investments that banks and thrift institutions may offer.

**The National Credit Union Administration (NCUA)**: The National Credit Union Share Insurance Fund (NCUSIF) is the federal fund created by Congress in 1970 to insure credit union member's deposits in federally insured credit unions. The Dodd-Frank Act permanently established NCUA's standard maximum share insurance amount at $250,000. NCUSIF is backed by the full faith and credit of the U.S. Government.

**Securities Investors Protection Corporation (SIPC)**: Securities you own, including mutual funds that are held for your account by a broker, or a bank's brokerage subsidiary, are not insured against loss in value. The value of your investments can go up or down depending on the demand for them in the market. The Securities Investors Protection Corporation (SIPC), a non government entity, replaces missing stocks and other securities in customer accounts held by SIPC member firm up to $500,000, including up to $250,000 in cash, if the firm fails.

# Assessing Your Risk Tolerance

When it comes to investing, risk and reward go hand in hand. The phrase "no pain, no gain"—comes close to summing up the relationship between risk and reward. Don't let anyone tell you otherwise: all investments involve some degree of risk. If you plan to buy securities—such as stocks, bonds, or mutual funds—it's important that you understand that you could lose some or all of the money you invest.

The reward for taking on risk is the potential for a greater investment return. If you have a financial goal with a long time horizon, you may make more money by carefully investing in higher risk assets, such as stocks or bonds, than if limit yourself to less risky assets. On the other hand, lower risk cash investments may be appropriate for short-term financial goals.

An aggressive investor, or one with a high risk tolerance, is willing to risk losing money to get potentially better results. A conservative investor, or one with a low risk tolerance, favors investments that maintain his or her original investment.

Many investment websites offer free online questionnaires to help you assess your risk tolerance. Some of the websites will even estimate asset allocations based on responses to the questionnaires. While the suggested asset allocations may be a useful starting point, keep in mind that the results may be biased towards financial products or services sold by companies or individuals sponsoring the websites.

# Chapter 13
# Advice For Investing Wisely

Starting young is the first important piece of advice for a beginning investor. The earlier you start to invest, the more money you'll accumulate. You'll also learn more about the investment process and develop good saving and money-management habits. But what is investing, and how does it differ from simply putting money in a savings account?

## Saving Versus Investing

Opening a savings account may be considered a type of investing, but simple bank accounts generally pay such a low rate of interest that they may not even keep up with inflation. They certainly have their place, and everyone should have one, but they're considered a poor choice from an investment perspective. Here are some differences:

- **Risk.** Practically speaking, the only real risk with a savings account is that inflation will outpace the interest you earn. That's because when you put your money in a savings account it's insured by the government up to $250,000. Most investments—especially those with high potential rewards—entail some risk, meaning you could possibly lose all the money you invested.

- **Availability of funds.** All or part of the money in a basic savings account can be withdrawn at any time with no notice at all. Many times, when money is invested, you're committed to leaving it there for a certain period of time. If there's a way to withdraw it before the agreed time period, could be a penalty involved.

- **Return on investment.** The amount of money you make on an investment is sometimes called your return. With a savings account the return—the interest the bank pays you—is very low. Investments are designed to give you a better return than bank interest. And higher-risk investments have the potential to earn a great deal more.

- **Philosophy.** The bottom line is that savings accounts are generally intended to provide you with cash on hand for emergencies or to accumulate money for a specific purpose. So you might open a bank account to save money for a car or for school. But investments aren't meant to hold money; their purpose is to make money for you. They can support long-range goals, such as starting a business in the future, ensuring a comfortable retirement, or, for some people, earning a living through further investment.

> There are no dumb questions! Ask a lot of questions of your bank representative, financial planner, mutual fund manager, and everyone else who will have a hand in helping manage your investments. The most important thing is for you to have the information you need to make good financial decisions.

# Types Of Investments

There are so many different kinds of investments that it's virtually impossible to cover them all. But many of them won't be of interest to young investors, and most are variations of a few major types. These include:

- **Certificates of deposit.** A certificate of deposit (CD) is a no-risk investment that could be considered one step above a savings account. You can get it from the same bank where you have your checking or savings account, and your money is insured by the government. The difference is that you agree to leave your funds in the CD for a certain length of time, from a few months to several years, and withdrawing it early means you'll likely pay a penalty. In exchange, CDs pay a slightly higher rate of interest than a savings account, and the longer you leave your money, the higher the rate will usually be.

- **Bonds.** When you purchase a bond, you're loaning money to a government or business for an agreed amount of time. During that period, the bond-issuer pays a set amount of interest, and when the bond comes due, or matures, the issuer repays the initial amount invested. There are several kinds, including U.S. Savings Bonds issued by the federal government; municipal bonds issued by states, counties or municipalities; and corporate bonds, issued by companies. Most bonds are considered fairly low-risk investments.

- **Stocks.** Buying stock gives you a share of ownership in a company, which means the value of your investment can rise and fall with the fortunes of that company. If the company does well, it might pay you dividends—part of its profits that it pays to stockholders, usually on a quarterly basis—and when you sell your stock its value could be much higher than what you paid for it. But if the company does badly, or fails entirely, you could lose all or part of your investment.

- **Mutual funds.** These are pools of money from many investors that are managed by an expert or team of experts. They're designed for people who don't want to pick and choose their own investments and would rather leave the details to professionals. Although some mutual funds concentrate on one specific type of investment, most of them invest in a variety of stocks, bonds, and other financial instruments. As with stocks, there are no guarantees, but the fact that mutual funds entail a variety of investments can make them a more stable choice.

- **Money market funds.** Actually a type of mutual fund, these are distinctive in that, although they're not foolproof or guaranteed, they are considered low-risk investments. They get their name from the fact that they primarily invest in cash, short-term government bonds, and other safe and very liquid (easily converted to cash) instruments. Their goal is to pay investors a modest rate of interest while retaining the value of the initial investment.

> Investing isn't a get-rich-quick scheme, or at least it shouldn't be. Smart investors—and those without a lot of extra money to lose—are in it for the long haul. The plan should be to build an investment portfolio in a carefully planned way and within your own limits of risk tolerance.

# How To Get Started Investing Wisely

It's never too early to start investing but it's important to be smart about it. Investment scams are one of the most popular ways to bilk unsuspecting (or even very experienced) people out of their money. In addition to illegal activity, there are a lot of ways to lose money on investments. Even people with years of experience lose money every year through unwise investment choices. But here are some ways to be smart and minimize risk:

- **Begin with a savings account.** True, a savings account isn't a great investment in itself, but it's a good way to start putting together enough money to invest. However, don't get to a target point—say $200 or $500—and move it all into an investment. A smarter plan is to retain some cash on hand for emergencies and only invest a portion of your total savings.

Although teens don't have as many financial responsibilities as adults, most teens want to know more about money and how to manage it. Learning to manage your money now will mean more in your pocket later. Whether you get money from an allowance, gifts, or a job, it is never too early to learn the basics about spending, saving, and investing. In many communities, banks and credit unions offer special accounts for teens. Teens looking to open a checking and savings account can avoid hurdles by going to the credit union or bank where their parents have an account.

**Savings account**: If you're serious about saving, keeping your money in a shoebox isn't going to cut it. It's time to start a savings account. This account should be separate from your checking account. Look for a bank that offers a higher interest rate (that's the money the bank pays you to keep your cash with them) and also make sure they don't charge a lot of service fees.

**Checking account**: There are several types of checking accounts. The basic type is mainly used to pay bills and to get cash via a debit (ATM) card to keep on hand for daily expenses. Keep in mind, some checking accounts require a minimum balance to avoid monthly fees.

Thankfully, most banks offer fee-free banking for teens. Many banks also offer bonus interest if you make more than one deposit a month and no withdrawals. Most teens under the age of 16 need parental or guardian consent to open a bank account.

*(Source: "Money Matters," Office on Women's Health (OWH), U.S. Department of Health and Human Services (HHS).)*

- **Start small.** A good way to get started investing is to purchase a certificate of deposit from the bank where you have a savings and checking account. There's always a minimum amount to get a CD, and higher amounts mean a better interest rate, but some banks offer CDs for as little as $100, so you might need to shop around if your bank's minimum is more than you can afford. As you compare CDs, pay attention to interest rates and also any fees that some banks charge.

- **Take the next step.** The next logical move could be to step up to a low-risk investment, such as government bonds. These have a stated interest rate and time frame for return, so they're a known quantity. You might not get rich from low-risk investments, but you're almost certain to make money. Most of these types of bonds have higher minimums than CDs, usually $1,000 and up.

- **Move up to mutual funds.** It might be fun and interesting to buy individual stocks, but that kind of investing takes a lot of research and experience if you want to minimize your risk and make money. A wiser route for a beginning investor is to rely on the experts who manage mutual funds to pick stocks, bonds, and other investments for you.

In addition to professional management, mutual funds give you the advantage of investing in a diversity of industries, regions, and products, which helps minimize the risk of having all your eggs in one basket.

- **Diversify.** This is one you'll hear a lot as you read and talk about investing. The temptation might be to buy stock in the latest tech startup that has a really cool game app, but that kind of investment carries a huge amount of risk in exchange for the possibility of a big payoff. A diversified portfolio (your collection of investments) protects you from a downturn in any given industry or company by offsetting losses in one area with gains in others. One of the biggest mistakes new investors make is not diversifying enough. It's important not only to put your money into different companies, but different kinds of companies, as well as a mix of stocks, bonds, and other investments.

- **Work with an expert.** As a novice investor, it's important for you to get reliable, unbiased advice. Some banks offer free investment advice for customers, so that might be a good place to start. Bear in mind, though, that the bank is likely to represent its own investment choices, so it's not completely unbiased. A good option is to consult a financial planner recommended by an experienced friend or relative. Some advisers charge fees only when they make a transaction for you—buying or selling stock, for example—while others charge fees to manage your account whether your money is moved around or not. So consider those fees when deciding on an adviser.

- **Research.** Whether you're deciding where, when, or how to invest your money, it's critical to do your homework. Professional money managers and experienced investors spend the majority of their time doing research and planning. You're probably not going to dig deep into industry trends and historical stock performance at first, but you should do some basic investigation and comparison before turning you money over to anyone. Even if a trusted friend recommends a financial planner, look up that person online, check reviews from clients, and find out if the adviser has a good track record. You can do the same with mutual funds or bonds. There's lot of information on the Web that can help you make smart decisions.

Finally, it's important at the early stage of investing set realistic expectations. The initial goal should be to make a bit more money than you'd get from interest in a savings account. As you add to your savings, you can shift more money into investments. And that, along with money being made on the investments themselves, will result in a healthy profit that can go a long way toward building wealth for the future.

The U.S. Securities and Exchange Commission (SEC) website has a lot of great investment advice, as well as information about specific investments, financial planners, and investment companies. For more information, go to: https://www.sec.gov/investment.

## References

1.  "Beginners' Guide to Investing," U.S. Securities and Exchange Commission (SEC), December 2, 2009.

2.  Folger, Jean. "Teaching Financial Literacy to Teens: Investing," Investopedia.com, n.d.

3.  "Invest Wisely: Advice from Your Securities Industry Regulators," U.S. Securities and Exchange Commission (SEC), August 1, 2007.

4.  "Teens Guide to Investing," Teensguidetomoney.com, n.d.

# Chapter 14

# Defining Asset Allocation, Diversification, And Rebalancing

## What Is Asset Allocation?

Asset allocation involves dividing your investments among different assets, such as stocks, bonds, and cash. The asset allocation decision is a personal one. The allocation that works best for you changes at different times in your life, depending on how long you have to invest and your ability to tolerate risk.

Factors to consider include your:

- **Time Horizon.** Your time horizon is the number of months, years, or decades you need to invest to achieve your financial goal. Investors with a longer time horizon may feel comfortable taking on riskier or more volatile investments. Those with a shorter time horizon may prefer to take on less risk.

- **Risk Tolerance.** Risk tolerance is your ability and willingness to lose some or all of your original investment in exchange for potentially greater returns.

Asset allocation is important because it has major impact on whether you will meet your financial goal. If you don't include enough risk in your portfolio, your investments may not earn a large enough return to meet your goal. For example, if you are saving for a long-term goal, such as retirement or college, most financial experts agree that you will likely need to include at least some stock or stock mutual funds in your portfolio.

*(Source: "Financial Navigating In The Current Economy: Ten Things To Consider Before You Make Investing Decisions," U.S. Securities and Exchange Commission (SEC).)*

---

About This Chapter: This chapter includes text excerpted from "Asset Allocation," Investor.gov, U.S. Securities and Exchange Commission (SEC), December 3, 2016.

# What Is Diversification?

The practice of spreading money among different investments to reduce risk is known as diversification. Diversification is a strategy that can be neatly summed up as "Don't put all your eggs in one basket."

One way to diversify is to allocate your investments among different kinds of assets. Historically, stocks, bonds, and cash have not moved up and down at the same time. Factors that may cause one asset class to perform poorly may improve returns for another asset class. People invest in various asset classes in the hope that if one is losing money, the others make up for those losses.

You'll also be better diversified if you spread your investments within each asset class. That means holding a number of different stocks or bonds, and investing in different industry sectors, such as consumer goods, healthcare, and technology. That way, if one sector is doing poorly, you may offset it with other holdings in sectors that are doing well.

Some investors find it easier to diversify by owning mutual funds. A mutual fund is a company that pools money from many investors and invests the money in stocks, bonds, and other financial products. Mutual funds make it easy for investors to own a small portion of many investments. A total stock market index fund, for example, owns stock in thousands of companies, providing a lot of diversification for one investment.

A mutual fund won't necessarily provide diversification, especially if it focuses on only one industry sector. If you invest in narrowly focused mutual funds, you may need to invest in several to be diversified. As you add more investments to your portfolio, you'll likely pay additional fees and expenses, which will lower your investment returns. So you'll need to consider these costs when deciding the best way to diversify your portfolio.

## Lifecycle Funds

To accommodate investors who prefer to use one investment to save for a particular investment goal, such as retirement, some mutual fund companies have begun offering a product known as a "lifecycle fund." A lifecycle fund is a diversified mutual fund that automatically shifts towards a more conservative mix of investments as it approaches a particular year in the future, known as its "target date." A lifecycle fund investor picks a fund with the right target date based on his or her particular investment goal. The managers of the fund then make all decisions about asset allocation, diversification, and rebalancing. It's easy to identify a lifecycle fund because its name will likely refer to its target date. For example, you might see lifecycle funds with names like "Portfolio 2015," "Retirement Fund 2030," or "Target 2045."

*(Source: "Financial Navigating In The Current Economy: Ten Things To Consider Before You Make Investing Decisions," U.S. Securities and Exchange Commission (SEC).)*

# What Is Rebalancing?

Rebalancing is what investors do to bring their portfolio back to its original asset allocation mix. Rebalancing is needed because over time, some investments will grow faster than others. This may push your holdings out of alignment with your investment goals. By rebalancing, you will ensure that your portfolio does not overweight a particular asset category, and you'll return your portfolio to a comfortable level of risk.

For example, you might start with 60 percent of your portfolio invested in stocks, but see that rise to 80 percent due to market gains. To re-establish your original asset allocation mix, you'll either need to sell some of your stocks or invest in other asset categories.

There are three ways you can rebalance your portfolio:

- You can sell investments where your holdings are over weighted and use the proceeds to buy investments for underweighted asset categories.

- You can buy new investments for underweighted asset categories.

- If you are continuing to add to your investments, you can alter your contributions so that more goes to underweighted asset categories until your portfolio is back into balance.

Before you rebalance your portfolio, you should consider whether the method of rebalancing you decide to use would entail transaction fees or tax consequences. Your financial professional or tax adviser can help you identify ways that you can minimize these potential costs.

Some financial experts advise rebalancing at regular intervals, such as every six or 12 months. Others recommend rebalancing when your holdings of an asset class increase or decrease more than a certain pre-set percentage. In either case, rebalancing tends to work best when done on a relatively infrequent basis.

Shifting money away from an asset class when it is doing well in favor of an asset category that is doing poorly may not be easy. But it can be a wise move. By cutting back on current "winners" and adding more current "losers," rebalancing forces you to buy low and sell high.

# Chapter 15
# A Beginner's Guide To Financial Statements

If you can read a nutrition label or a baseball box score, you can learn to read basic financial statements. If you can follow a recipe or apply for a loan, you can learn basic accounting. The basics aren't difficult and they aren't rocket science.

This chapter is designed to help you gain a basic understanding of how to read financial statements. Just as a CPR (Cardiopulmonary resuscitation) class teaches you how to perform the basics of cardiopulmonary resuscitation, this chapter will explain how to read the basic parts of a financial statement. It will not train you to be an accountant (just as a CPR course will not make you a cardiac doctor), but it should give you the confidence to be able to look at a set of financial statements and make sense of them. Let's begin by looking at what financial statements do.

## "Show Me The Money!"

We all remember Cuba Gooding Jr.'s immortal line from the movie Jerry Maguire, "Show me the money!" Well, that's what financial statements do. They show you the money. They show you where a company's money came from, where it went, and where it is now.

There are four main financial statements. They are:

1. balance sheets;

2. income statements;


---

About This Chapter: Text in this chapter begins with excerpts from "Beginners' Guide To Financial Statements," U.S. Securities and Exchange Commission (SEC), January 31, 2014; Text under the heading "Corporate Reports, How To Get" is excerpted from "Corporate Reports, How To Get," U.S. Securities and Exchange Commission (SEC), July 23, 2010.

3.  cash flow statements; and

4.  statements of shareholders' equity.

Balance sheets show what a company owns and what it owes at a fixed point in time. Income statements show how much money a company made and spent over a period of time. Cash flow statements show the exchange of money between a company and the outside world also over a period of time. The fourth financial statement, called a "statement of shareholders' equity," shows changes in the interests of the company's shareholders over time. Let's look at each of the first three financial statements in more detail.

# Balance Sheets

A balance sheet provides detailed information about a company's assets, liabilities and shareholders' equity.

Assets are things that a company owns that have value. This typically means they can either be sold or used by the company to make products or provide services that can be sold. Assets include physical property, such as plants, trucks, equipment and inventory. It also includes things that can't be touched but nevertheless exist and have value, such as trademarks and patents. And cash itself is an asset. So are investments a company makes.

Liabilities are amounts of money that a company owes to others. This can include all kinds of obligations, like money borrowed from a bank to launch a new product, rent for use of a building, money owed to suppliers for materials, payroll a company owes to its employees, environmental cleanup costs, or taxes owed to the government. Liabilities also include obligations to provide goods or services to customers in the future.

Shareholders' equity is sometimes called capital or net worth. It's the money that would be left if a company sold all of its assets and paid off all of its liabilities. This leftover money belongs to the shareholders, or the owners, of the company.

The following formula summarizes what a balance sheet shows:

Assets = Liabilities + Shareholders' Equity

A company's assets have to equal, or "balance," the sum of its liabilities and shareholders' equity.

A company's balance sheet is set up like the basic accounting equation shown above. On the left side of the balance sheet, companies list their assets. On the right side, they list their liabilities and shareholders' equity. Sometimes balance sheets show assets at the top, followed by liabilities, with shareholders' equity at the bottom.

Assets are generally listed based on how quickly they will be converted into cash. Current assets are things a company expects to convert to cash within one year. A good example is inventory. Most companies expect to sell their inventory for cash within one year. Noncurrent assets are things a company does not expect to convert to cash within one year or that would take longer than one year to sell. Noncurrent assets include fixed assets. Fixed assets are those assets used to operate the business but that are not available for sale, such as trucks, office furniture and other property.

Liabilities are generally listed based on their due dates. Liabilities are said to be either current or long-term. Current liabilities are obligations a company expects to pay off within the year. Long-term liabilities are obligations due more than one year away.

Shareholders' equity is the amount owns invested in the company's stock plus or minus the company's earnings or losses since inception. Sometimes companies distribute earnings, instead of retaining them. These distributions are called dividends.

A balance sheet shows a snapshot of a company's assets, liabilities and shareholders' equity at the end of the reporting period. It does not show the flows into and out of the accounts during the period.

---

**Profit and loss statement**: A profit and loss statement, also referred to as an income statement, enables you to project sales and expenses and typically covers a period of a few months to a year.

To determine net profit, subtract total operating expenses from gross profit. (Gross profit – total operating expenses = net profit.) Remember that gross profit is calculated as total sales minus the cost of goods sold. Costs of goods sold include things like raw materials, inventory and payroll taxes. Make sure to also factor in overhead costs such repairs, utilities, insurance and legal fees into your operating expenses to ensure your net profit is accurate.

*(Source: "3 Essential Financial Statements For Your Small Business," U.S. Small Business Administration (SBA).)*

---

# Income Statements

An income statement is a report that shows how much revenue a company earned over a specific time period (usually for a year or some portion of a year). An income statement also shows the costs and expenses associated with earning that revenue. The literal "bottom line" of the statement usually shows the company's net earnings or losses. This tells you how much the company earned or lost over the period.

Income statements also report earnings per share (or "EPS"). This calculation tells you how much money shareholders would receive if the company decided to distribute all of the net earnings for the period. (Companies almost never distribute all of their earnings. Usually they reinvest them in the business.)

To understand how income statements are set up, think of them as a set of stairs. You start at the top with the total amount of sales made during the accounting period. Then you go down, one step at a time. At each step, you make a deduction for certain costs or other operating expenses associated with earning the revenue. At the bottom of the stairs, after deducting all of the expenses, you learn how much the company actually earned or lost during the accounting period. People often call this "the bottom line."

At the top of the income statement is the total amount of money brought in from sales of products or services. This top line is often referred to as gross revenues or sales. It's called "gross" because expenses have not been deducted from it yet. So the number is "gross" or unrefined.

The next line is money the company doesn't expect to collect on certain sales. This could be due, for example, to sales discounts or merchandise returns.

When you subtract the returns and allowances from the gross revenues, you arrive at the company's net revenues. It's called "net" because, if you can imagine a net, these revenues are left in the net after the deductions for returns and allowances have come out.

Moving down the stairs from the net revenue line, there are several lines that represent various kinds of operating expenses. Although these lines can be reported in various orders, the next line after net revenues typically shows the costs of the sales. This number tells you the amount of money the company spent to produce the goods or services it sold during the accounting period.

The next line subtracts the costs of sales from the net revenues to arrive at a subtotal called "gross profit" or sometimes "gross margin." It's considered "gross" because there are certain expenses that haven't been deducted from it yet.

The next section deals with operating expenses. These are expenses that go toward supporting a company's operations for a given period—for example, salaries of administrative personnel and costs of researching new products. Marketing expenses are another example. Operating expenses are different from "costs of sales," which were deducted above, because operating expenses cannot be linked directly to the production of the products or services being sold.

Depreciation is also deducted from gross profit. Depreciation takes into account the wear and tear on some assets, such as machinery, tools and furniture, which are used over the long term. Companies spread the cost of these assets over the periods they are used. This process of spreading these costs is called depreciation or amortization. The "charge" for using these assets during the period is a fraction of the original cost of the assets.

After all operating expenses are deducted from gross profit, you arrive at operating profit before interest and income tax expenses. This is often called "income from operations."

Next companies must account for interest income and interest expense. Interest income is the money companies make from keeping their cash in interest-bearing savings accounts, money market funds and the like. On the other hand, interest expense is the money companies paid in interest for money they borrow. Some income statements show interest income and interest expense separately. Some income statements combine the two numbers. The interest income and expense are then added or subtracted from the operating profits to arrive at operating profit before income tax.

Finally, income tax is deducted and you arrive at the bottom line: net profit or net losses. (Net profit is also called net income or net earnings.) This tells you how much the company actually earned or lost during the accounting period. Did the company make a profit or did it lose money?

## Earnings Per Share (EPS)

Most income statements include a calculation of earnings per share or EPS. This calculation tells you how much money shareholders would receive for each share of stock they own if the company distributed all of its net income for the period. To calculate EPS, you take the total net income and divide it by the number of outstanding shares of the company.

# Cash Flow Statements

Cash flow statements report a company's inflows and outflows of cash. This is important because a company needs to have enough cash on hand to pay its expenses and purchase assets. While an income statement can tell you whether a company made a profit, a cash flow statement can tell you whether the company generated cash.

A cash flow statement shows changes over time rather than absolute dollar amounts at a point in time. It uses and reorders the information from a company's balance sheet and income statement.

The bottom line of the cash flow statement shows the net increase or decrease in cash for the period. Generally, cash flow statements are divided into three main parts. Each part reviews the cash flow from one of three types of activities:

1. operating activities;

2. investing activities; and

3. financing activities.

## Operating Activities

The first part of a cash flow statement analyzes a company's cash flow from net income or losses. For most companies, this section of the cash flow statement reconciles the net income (as shown on the income statement) to the actual cash the company received from or used in its operating activities. To do this, it adjusts net income for any non-cash items (such as adding back depreciation expenses) and adjusts for any cash that was used or provided by other operating assets and liabilities.

## Investing Activities

The second part of a cash flow statement shows the cash flow from all investing activities, which generally include purchases or sales of long-term assets, such as property, plant and equipment, as well as investment securities. If a company buys a piece of machinery, the cash flow statement would reflect this activity as a cash outflow from investing activities because it used cash. If the company decided to sell off some investments from an investment portfolio, the proceeds from the sales would show up as a cash inflow from investing activities because it provided cash.

## Financing Activities

The third part of a cash flow statement shows the cash flow from all financing activities. Typical sources of cash flow include cash raised by selling stocks and bonds or borrowing from banks. Likewise, paying back a bank loan would show up as a use of cash flow.

# Read The Footnotes

A horse called "Read The Footnotes" ran in the 2004 Kentucky Derby. He finished seventh, but if he had won, it would have been a victory for financial literacy proponents everywhere. It's so important to read the footnotes. The footnotes to financial statements are packed with information. Here are some of the highlights:

- **Significant accounting policies and practices:** Companies are required to disclose the accounting policies that are most important to the portrayal of the company's financial condition and results. These often require management's most difficult, subjective or complex judgments.

- **Income taxes:** The footnotes provide detailed information about the company's current and deferred income taxes. The information is broken down by level—federal, state, local and/or foreign, and the main items that affect the company's effective tax rate are described.

- **Pension plans and other retirement programs:** The footnotes discuss the company's pension plans and other retirement or post-employment benefit programs. The notes contain specific information about the assets and costs of these programs, and indicate whether and by how much the plans are over- or under-funded.

- **Stock options:** The notes also contain information about stock options granted to officers and employees, including the method of accounting for stock-based compensation and the effect of the method on reported results.

# Read The Management's Discussion And Analysis (MD&A) Of Financial Condition And Results Of Operations

You can find a narrative explanation of a company's financial performance in a section of the quarterly or annual report entitled, "Management's Discussion and Analysis of Financial Condition and Results of Operations." MD&A is management's opportunity to provide investors with its view of the financial performance and condition of the company. It's management's opportunity to tell investors what the financial statements show and do not show, as well as important trends and risks that have shaped the past or are reasonably likely to shape the company's future.

The SEC's rules governing MD&A require disclosure about trends, events or uncertainties known to management that would have a material impact on reported financial information. The purpose of MD&A is to provide investors with information that the company's management believes to be necessary to an understanding of its financial condition, changes in financial condition and results of operations. It is intended to help investors to see the company through the eyes of management. It is also intended to provide context for the financial statements and information about the company's earnings and cash flows.

# Financial Statement Ratios And Calculations

You've probably heard people banter around phrases like "P/E ratio," "current ratio" and "operating margin." But what do these terms mean and why don't they show up on financial statements? Listed below are just some of the many ratios that investors calculate from information on financial statements and then use to evaluate a company. As a general rule, desirable ratios vary by industry.

Debt-to-Equity Ratio = Total Liabilities / Shareholders' Equity

If a company has a debt-to-equity ratio of 2 to 1, it means that the company has two dollars of debt to every one dollar shareholders invest in the company. In other words, the company is taking on debt at twice the rate that its owners are investing in the company.

Inventory Turnover Ratio = Cost of Sales / Average Inventory for the Period

If a company has an inventory turnover ratio of 2 to 1, it means that the company's inventory turned over twice in the reporting period.

Operating Margin = Income from Operations / Net Revenues

Operating margin is usually expressed as a percentage. It shows, for each dollar of sales, what percentage was profit.

P/E Ratio = Price per share / Earnings per share

If a company's stock is selling at $20 per share and the company is earning $2 per share, then the company's P/E Ratio is 10 to 1. The company's stock is selling at 10 times its earnings.

Working Capital = Current Assets − Current Liabilities

- **Debt-to-equity ratio** compares a company's total debt to shareholders' equity. Both of these numbers can be found on a company's balance sheet. To calculate debt-to-equity ratio, you divide a company's total liabilities by its shareholder equity, or

- **Inventory turnover** ratio compares a company's cost of sales on its income statement with its average inventory balance for the period. To calculate the average inventory balance for the period, look at the inventory numbers listed on the balance sheet. Take the balance listed for the period of the report and add it to the balance listed for the previous comparable period, and then divide by two. (Remember that balance sheets are snapshots in time. So the inventory balance for the previous period is the beginning balance for the current period, and the inventory balance for the current period is the ending balance.) To calculate the inventory turnover ratio, you divide a company's cost of sales (just below the net revenues on the income statement) by the average inventory for the period, or

- **Operating margin** compares a company's operating income to net revenues. Both of these numbers can be found on a company's income statement. To calculate operating margin, you divide a company's income from operations (before interest and income tax expenses) by its net revenues, or

- **P/E ratio** compares a company's common stock price with its earnings per share. To calculate a company's P/E ratio, you divide a company's stock price by its earnings per share, or

- **Working capital** is the money leftover if a company paid its current liabilities (that is, its debts due within one-year of the date of the balance sheet) from its current assets.

## Bringing It All Together

Although this chapter discusses each financial statement separately, keep in mind that they are all related. The changes in assets and liabilities that you see on the balance sheet are also reflected in the revenues and expenses that you see on the income statement, which result in the company's gains or losses. Cash flows provide more information about cash assets listed on a balance sheet and are related, but not equivalent, to net income shown on the income statement. And so on. No one financial statement tells the complete story. But combined, they provide very powerful information for investors. And information is the investor's best tool when it comes to investing wisely.

## How To Get Corporate Reports

You'll find this information in the company's quarterly reports on Form 10-Q, annual reports (with audited financial statements) on Form 10-K, and periodic reports of significant events on Form 8-K.

It's usually easy to find information about large companies from the companies themselves, newspapers, brokerage firms, and the SEC. By contrast, it can be extremely difficult to find information about small companies. Generally, smaller companies only have to file reports with the SEC if they have $10 million or more in assets and 500 or more shareholders, or list their securities on an exchange or Nasdaq.

You can get corporate reports from the following sources:

- **The SEC**: You can find out whether a company files by using the SEC's database known as EDGAR. To obtain copies of public filings you may access How to Request Public Documents.

- **The company**: Ask the company if it is registered with the SEC and files reports with them. That information may be listed on its website. Check out new or smaller companies thoroughly because many frauds involve these types of companies. SEC's brochures on Internet fraud and microcap companies provide valuable information you shouldn't miss.

- **Other government regulators**: Banks do not have to file reports with the SEC, but file with banking regulators. Visit their websites: Federal Reserve System's National Information Center of Banking Information, the Office of the Comptroller of the Currency, or the Federal Deposit Insurance Corporation.

## Other Types Of Information

To find out whether a company has been cleared to sell its securities in a particular state and whether it is in good standing, you can contact the following:

- **Your state securities regulator**: Contact the North American Securities Administrators Association to get the name and phone number of your state securities regulator to see if the company has been cleared to sell securities in your state and to find out about the people behind the company.

- **The Secretary of State where the company is incorporated**: You can find out whether the company is a corporation in good standing and has filed annual reports with the state through the secretary of state where the company is incorporated. Check the National Association of Secretaries of State's website for a list of most secretaries of state.

You can find general financial information about companies from the following reference books and commercial databases. The SEC cannot recommend or endorse any particular research firm, its personnel, or its products. But there are a number of resources you may consult:

- *Bloomberg News Service* and *Lexis/Nexis* provide news stories about a company. *Dun & Bradstreet, Moody's, Hoover's Profiles*, and *Standard & Poor's Corporate Profiles* provide financial data about companies. These and other sources are available in many public libraries or law and business school libraries.

## Bankruptcies

If you have questions about what happens when a company declares bankruptcy, you can get information from SEC's brochure on bankruptcy.

## Old Stock Certificates

If you have an old stock certificate, read about the resources you can check to see whether the certificate has value.

# Chapter 16

# Working With Financial Professionals

## Personal Financial Advisors

Personal financial advisors are professionals who help people decide how to manage their money in the best way. There are many different types of financial advisors, including investment managers, stock brokers, bankers, insurance brokers, tax preparers, tax attorneys, and so on.

Some common services provided by personal financial advisors include:

- Helping people identify and prioritize financial goals.

- Helping people learn about various types of financial services that can help them meet their goals.

- Advising people on the best approaches to meeting their financial goals.

- Answering questions about various investment choices.

- Offering seminars or workshops to educate people about financial matters.

- Researching investment opportunities.

- Identifying potential investment risks.

- Recommending specific investments.

- Selecting investments on behalf of their clients.

- Managing investment portfolios on behalf of their clients.

- Monitoring client accounts to identify opportunities for investment performance improvement.

---

**Consider This**

An investment adviser, is a "fiduciary" to the advisory clients. This means that they have a fundamental obligation to act in the best interests of their clients and to provide investment advice in their clients' best interests. They owe their clients a duty of undivided loyalty and utmost good faith. They should not engage in any activity in conflict with the interest of any client, and they should take steps reasonably necessary to fulfill their obligations. They must employ reasonable care to avoid misleading clients and must provide full and fair disclosure of all material facts to their clients and prospective clients. Generally, facts are "material" if a reasonable investor would consider them to be important. They must eliminate, or at least disclose, all conflicts of interest that might incline the client—consciously or unconsciously—to render advice that is not disinterested. If they do not avoid a conflict of interest that could impact the impartiality of their advice, they must make full and frank disclosure of the conflict. They cannot use their clients' assets for their own benefit or the benefit of other clients, at least without client consent. Departure from this fiduciary standard may constitute "fraud" upon the clients.

---

# Financial Planners

Financial planners are financial advisors who specialize in certain areas of money management. Some financial planners focus on one or two areas of finance, and others offer a wider range of services depending on the needs of their clients. Because financial planning services cover so many different aspects of money management, it is important to identify the kind of financial planning services you need before hiring a financial planner.

Examples of common financial planning services include:

- Comprehensive planning that covers all aspects of finance and money management, such as saving and investments for both short-term and long-term goals like retirement, tax planning, estate management, insurance needs, and so on.

- Planning specific aspects of financial planning, such as saving for retirement or a large future expense like paying for college tuition or buying a home.

- Preparation of detailed financial plans and strategies for meeting lifetime financial goals.

- Recommending specific investment products such as stocks, bonds, mutual funds, or securities.

- Management of existing investment portfolios.

Before hiring a financial planner, make sure you understand exactly which services they can provide, how much these services will cost, and how the financial planner is paid. Financial planners sometimes charge a flat rate fee for certain services and an hourly rate for other services. Some are paid a commission on each financial transaction they perform for you, or collect a percentage of the total money you have invested through their services. Depending on the financial planning services you need, these fees can add up quickly.

Once you have an idea of the financial planning services you need, it is equally important to learn about the professional background of any financial planner you are thinking of hiring. Find out where they went to school, what kind of professional experience they have, how long they have been working in financial planning, and if they have any professional credentials such as Certified Financial Professional or Chartered Financial Analyst. These credentials can be verified by the organization that issued the certification, usually via the organization's website or by phoning the organization's main office. You can learn more about professional credentials for financial planners on the Financial Industry Regulatory Authority's website (www.finra.org/investors/professional-designations). Depending on the size of their business, professional financial planners who provide advice on investments must be registered with the U.S. Securities and Exchange Commission (SEC) and/or the securities regulation authority in their state. Information about verifying state registrations is provided by the North American Securities Administrations Association at www.nasaa.org/about-us/contact-us/contact-your-regulator. The SEC provides assistance with verifying registrations online at www.sec.gov/investor/brokers.htm.

# How To Pick A Financial Professional

Because financial advisors and financial planners offer such a wide variety of services and collect their fees in different ways, it is important to evaluate more than one potential financial service providers before choosing one. Depending on your individual financial goals and money management needs, you may be able to get financial advice from a banker or a Certified Public Accountant (CPA). Or you may benefit more from working with an investment advisor, broker, or a financial planner who provides comprehensive money management services.

In any case, it is critical to evaluate the professional reputation of any potential financial advisor that you are considering. Before you hire any financial professional, ask for a copy of their registration Form ADV. Carefully read both parts of this form. The first part of Form

ADV provides information about the advisor's business and whether they have had any complaints or other problems with clients or regulatory authorities. The second part of the form explains the advisor's services, fees, and commonly used money management strategies. You can also get a copy of an advisor's Form ADV from the SEC's Investment Advisor Public Disclosure website (https://adviserinfo.sec.gov).

Money management strategies are one of the most important life decisions that most people will ever make. When choosing a financial professional, remember that you are looking for someone trustworthy to provide advice and services related to your hard-earned dollars. Make sure that you ask questions and that you completely understand the answers. Some questions to consider asking during your initial meeting with a potential advisor include:

- What is the advisor's educational background, including school, training, and other experience?

- Does the advisor hold any professional certifications or credentials? If so, which ones?

- How long has the advisor been in business?

- How many clients does the advisor have?

- Can the advisor provide any client references?

- What is the advisor's investment philosophy? Do they prefer risky short-term gains or long-term growth investments?

- What is the advisor's fee structure and how do they collect their fees? For example, by commission, flat rate, hourly rate, percentage, etc.

- What is the total cost of doing business with the advisor? Are there up-front costs, ongoing costs, or both?

> **Quick Tip**
>
> If a financial advisor collects fees or charges based on a percentage of the money they will manage for you, be sure to ask for the equivalent of that percentage in dollars. This will help you better understand the amount of money you will be charged for their services.

## References

1. "Fast Answers: Financial Planners," U.S. Securities and Exchange Commission (SEC), August 20, 2008.

2. "Personal Financial Advisors," Bureau of Labor Statistics (BLS), U.S. Department of Labor (DOL), Occupational Outlook Handbook, 2016-17 Ed.

3. "Investment Advisors: What You Need to Know Before Choosing One," U.S. Securities and Exchange Commission (SEC), August 7, 2012.

4. "How to Pick a Financial Professional," U.S. Securities and Exchange Commission (SEC), February 1, 2007.

# Chapter 17

# Understanding Securities Analyst Recommendations

A security is ownership of a financial asset that can be bought or sold. There are many types, but some of the most common ones are shares of stock, bonds, and options (the right to buy an asset). Companies and government agencies issue securities as a means of raising money for a variety of purposes, including operating expenses, expansion, and specific projects. The public buys securities as an investment, hoping that they will generate income and/or increase in value so they can be sold at a profit.

Securities analysts study the performance of different types of securities and, based on their research, training and experience, make recommendations for investors. In the simplest terms, these recommendations generally consist of "buy," "sell," or "hold," meaning the analyst thinks it's a good idea to purchase a particular asset or, if you already own it, to get rid of it or keep it. Analysts' recommendations, as well as their extensive reports, can not only influence the behavior of investors but may actually cause a company's stock to rise or fall in value due to increased buying or selling. And some extremely well-known and influential analysts can affect a stock or bond's value just by expressing an opinion about it.

Because securities analysts play a key role in the world of investing, it's important for investors to understand who analysts are, what they do, and what their recommendations mean. This is especially true in light of the abundance of information and opinion that's available today via radio and television reports, social media, and investing websites. New investors, in particular, can easily be overwhelmed by the flood of data and need to know how to decide whom to trust when it comes to financial advice.

---

In addition to rating securities so investors can decide whether to buy, sell, or hold, analysts also forecast the future performance of those securities. Although the accuracy of these predictions certainly varies a lot, they do provide one more piece of information for you to consider.

# Types Of Securities Analysts

Securities analysists generally fall into three major categories, and it's important to be aware of what they do and whom they work for:

- **Sell-side analysts**: These analysts research a particular market segment or business sector, then issue reports and make recommendations on the securities area they know well. They often work for large, full-service brokerage houses and investment banks, many of which also serve corporate clients, which could include those whose securities the analyst might cover.

- **Buy-side analysts**: Like sell-side analysts, those on the buy side also research securities, write reports, and make recommendations, but buy-side analysts combine their own research with that of many sell-side experts and use all the data to formulate recommendations. Buy-side analysts often work for mutual funds, investment advisers, and insurance companies, many of whom purchase securities for their own accounts, as well as those of clients.

- **Independent analysts**: As the name implies, independent analysts are not generally associated with any of the firms involved with the securities they cover. Rather than writing reports for an employer, they may be paid by the companies they research or sell the reports on a direct purchase or a subscription basis to anyone who wants to buy them.

All analysts are not the same. There are so many people with widely varying qualifications and experience giving investment advice that it's possible to get steered down a very bad road by listening to the wrong person. The first step in getting good recommendations is to be sure you're hearing the advice of a qualified securities analyst. Check the person's background before making an investment decision. Also, there are many investment magazines, websites, and newsletters where you can research an analyst's track record to ensure that their recommendations have been solid.

# The Language Of Securities Analyst

"Buy," "sell," and "hold" seem like fairly clear recommendations. But the fact is, these terms—and others—can mean different things from different analysts and different firms. Their definitions can usually be found on the firm's website or in its disclosure documents. And when you're comparing recommendations, it's critical to know the meaning of the various terms used by the ones you're researching. For example:

- **Buy**: A "buy" recommendation from one analyst can equate to "strong buy" or "on the recommended list" from a different analyst. And some firms use "moderate buy," "out-perform," or "over-weight" to indicate that it feels a stock will do better than the market return, which also means "buy."

- **Sell**: A "sell" from one analyst could be a "strong sell" or "liquidate" from another. And a "moderate sell" could equate to "weak hold," "underperform," or "under-weight," mean-ing that the stock is expected to do a bit worse than market return, so those are also "sell" indicators.

- **Hold**: Generally, "hold" is a common term that doesn't result in much confusion, but there are some analysts or firms that will use "neutral" or "market outperform" to mean the same thing.

Important research point from the U.S. Securities and Exchnage Commission (SEC): "Analysts are generally required to disclose possible conflicts of interest when they recommend the pur-chase or sale of a specific security. For example, analysts must divulge if they or the broker-age firm they work for has a financial position in a recommended security. Analysts also must disclose in a research report if their firms make a market in the security or have an investment banking relationship with the company."

*(Source: "Securities Analyst Recommendations," U.S. Securities and Exchange Commission (SEC).)*

# Possible Conflicts Of Interest

Although investment professionals, including securities analysts, have a code of ethics that is intended to ensure their unbiased recommendations and conduct, a variety of factors create pressure to influence even an independent analyst's objectivity. Examples include:

- **Investment bank conflicts.** If the analyst's firm provides investment banking services, such as underwriting or advising a company on a stock offering, the analyst could be under pressure to help make the offering a success by writing a positive report. However, because of his or her familiarity with the company, that analyst might also be in a good position to provide an accurate assessment.

- **Ownership in companies.** The analyst or his or her firm might have ownership interest in the companies or segments being covered. Sometimes the analyst and other employees of the firm are offered discounted shares in new companies. These arrangements mean the firm and its employees could profit, directly or indirectly, from positive reports.

- **Analyst pay.** Analysts are compensated in a variety of ways. For instance, their salaries and bonuses could be dependent on the number of investment banking contracts the analysts bring in or to the profitability of the firm's investment banking division.

- **Brokerage commissions.** A positive report from an analyst can bring money into the firm by prompting more stock purchases or sales of other securities, which generate brokerage commissions, fees brokers charge for advising on and executing transactions.

# Making Investment Decisions

Reports written by securities analysts are an invaluable source of information for investors, and analyst recommendations can serve as useful pointers toward good opportunities. But smart investors don't make decisions based only the recommendation of one—or even several—analysts. Rather, you should:

- **Talk to your broker.** If you have a broker or financial adviser, speak with him or her about the company and the prospects for its stock. You're paying brokerage or adviser fees, so it makes sense to make use of the service.

- **Research the company's reports.** New companies will have a prospectus for their stock offerings, and public companies will have quarterly and annual reports available at the SEC website. These will contain a lot of information about past performance (if applicable) and business plans for the future, which will help you decide if that company's stock fits your particular investment needs.

- **Research independent sources.** There's a lot of information available online and in print about companies, stock offerings, and possible legal issues associated with them. Make use of reliable news reports, websites, and other resources to get the information you need.

- **Look for conflicts of interest.** While you're conducting research, find out if the analyst or his or her firm is involved in underwriting or advising on a stock offering you're considering. Also learn whether the analyst or firm have any ownership interest in the company offering the stock.

When it comes to investing, the final decision is always yours. No matter what the experts say, whatever recommendations you receive or advice you get, you need to decide whether or not a particular stock, bond, or other investment fits your particular financial needs and goals.

## References

1. "Analyzing Analyst Recommendations," U.S. Securities and Exchange Commission, August 30, 2010.

2. Brantley, Chris. "How Do Stockbrokers and Financial Analysts Determine What Stocks to Buy?" Zacks.com, n.d.

3. Brownlee, Adam. "Understanding Analyst Ratings," Investopedia.com, n.d.

4. Simpson, Stephen D., CFA. "Buy Side Vs. Sell Side Analysts," Investopedia.com, December 28, 2015.

5. "Understanding Securities Analyst Recommendations," MItradingschool.com, n.d.

# Chapter 18

# How To Avoid The Most Common Investment Scams

A basic understanding of how scam artists work can help you avoid fraud and protect your money. Learning how to invest wisely can help you reach your financial goals. Here are some ways to help avoid being scammed:

## Question About Your Investments

- Is this investment product registered with the SEC and my state securities agency?

- Does this investment match my investment goals? Why is this investment suitable for me?

- How will this investment make money? (Dividends? Interest? Capital gains?) Specifically, what must happen for this investment to increase in value? (For example, increase in interest rates, real estate values, or market share?)

- What are the total fees to purchase, maintain, and sell this investment? Are there ways that I can reduce or avoid some of the fees that I'll pay, such as purchasing the investment directly? After all the fees are paid, how much does this investment have to increase in value before I break even?

- How liquid is this investment? How easy would it be to sell if I needed my money right away?

- What are the specific risks associated with this investment? What is the maximum I could lose? (For example, what will be the effect of changing interest rates, economic recession, high competition, or stock market ups and downs?)

About This Chapter: This chapter includes text excerpted from "How To Avoid Fraud," Investor.gov, U.S. Securities and Exchange Commission (SEC), December 3, 2016.

- How long has the company been in business? Is its management experienced? Has management been successful in the past? Have they ever made money for investors before?
- Is the company making money? How are they doing compared to their competitors?
- Where can I get more information about this investment? Can I get the latest reports filed by the company with the SEC: a prospectus or offering circular, or the latest annual report and financial statements?

*(Source: "Questions You Should Ask About Your Investments And What To Do If You Run Into Problems", U.S Securities and Exchange (SEC).)*

# What You Can Do To Avoid Investment Fraud

**Ask questions.** Fraudsters are counting on you not to investigate before you invest. Fend them off by doing your own digging. It's not enough to ask for more information or for references—fraudsters have no incentive to set you straight. Take the time to do your own independent research.

**Research before you invest.** Unsolicited emails, message board postings, and company news releases should never be used as the sole basis for your investment decisions. Understand a company's business and its products or services before investing. Look for the company's financial statements on the U.S. Securities and Exchange Commission's (SEC) Electronic Data Gathering, Analysis, and Retrieval (EDGAR) filing system. You can also check out many investments by searching EDGAR.

**Know the salesperson.** Spend some time checking out the person touting the investment before you invest—even if you already know the person socially. Always find out whether the securities salespeople who contact you are licensed to sell securities in your state and whether they or their firms have had run-ins with regulators or other investors. You can check out the disciplinary history of brokers and advisers for free using the SEC's and Financial Industry Regulatory Authority's (FINRA) online databases. Your state securities regulator may have additional information.

**Be wary of unsolicited offers.** Be especially careful if you receive an unsolicited pitch to invest in a company, or see it praised online, but can't find current financial information about it from independent sources. It could be a "pump and dump" scheme. Be wary if someone recommends foreign or "off-shore" investments. If something goes wrong, it's harder to find out what happened and to locate money sent abroad.

**Protect yourself online.** Online and social marketing sites offer a wealth of opportunity for fraudsters.

**Know what to look for.** Make yourself knowledgeable about different types of fraud and red flags that may signal investment fraud.

## Red Flags For Fraud And Common Persuasion Tactics

How do successful, financially intelligent people fall prey to investment fraud? Researchers have found that investment fraudsters hit their targets with an array of persuasion techniques that are tailored to the victim's psychological profile. Here are red flags to look for:

**If it sounds too good to be true, it is.** Watch for "phantom riches." Compare promised yields with current returns on well-known stock indexes. Any investment opportunity that claims you'll receive substantially more could be highly risky—and that means you might lose money. Be careful of claims that an investment will make "incredible gains," is a "breakout stock pick" or has "huge upside and almost no risk!" Claims like these are hallmarks of extreme risk or outright fraud.

**"Guaranteed returns" aren't.** Every investment carries some degree of risk, which is reflected in the rate of return you can expect to receive. If your money is perfectly safe, you'll most likely get a low return. High returns entail high risks, possibly including a total loss on the investments. Most fraudsters spend a lot of time trying to convince investors that extremely high returns are "guaranteed" or "can't miss." They try to plant an image in your head of what your life will be like when you are rich. Don't believe it.

**Beware the "halo" effect.** Investors can be blinded by a "halo" effect when a con artist comes across as likeable or trustworthy. Credibility can be faked. Check out actual qualifications.

**"Everyone is buying it."** Watch out for pitches that stress how "everyone is investing in this, so you should, too." Think about whether you are interested in the product. If a sales presentation focuses on how many others have bought the product, this could be a red flag.

**Pressure to send money right now.** Scam artists often tell their victims that this is a once-in-a-lifetime offer and it will be gone tomorrow. But resist the pressure to invest quickly and take the time you need to investigate before sending money.

**Reciprocity.** Fraudsters often try to lure investors through free investment seminars, figuring if they do a small favor for you, such as supplying a free lunch, you will do a big favor for them and invest in their product. There is never a reason to make a quick decision on an investment. If you attend a free lunch, take the material home and research both the investment and the individual selling it before you invest. Always make sure the product is right for you and that you understand what you are buying and all the associated fees.

# Protect Your Social Media Accounts

The Internet has made our lives easier in so many ways. However, you need to know how you can protect your privacy and avoid fraud. Remember, not only can people be defrauded when using the Internet for investing; the fraudsters use information online to send bogus materials, solicit or phish.

Phishing is the attempt to obtain financial or confidential information from Internet users. This phishing expedition usually begins with an email that looks as if it is from a legitimate source, often a financial institution. The email contains a link to a fake website that looks like the real site. Fraudsters want you to provide account and password information, and then they have access to your account.

## Here's What You Can Do To Protect Yourself When Using Social Media

**Privacy Settings:** Always check the default privacy settings when opening an account on a social media website. The default privacy settings on many social media websites are typically broad and may permit sharing of information to a vast online community. Modify the setting, if appropriate, before posting any information on a social media website.

**Biographical Information:** Many social media websites require biographical information to open an account. You can limit the information made available to other social media users. Consider customizing your privacy settings to minimize the amount of biographical information others can view on the website.

**Account Information:** Never give account information, Social Security numbers, bank information or other sensitive financial information on a social media website. If you need to speak to a financial professional, use a firm-sponsored method of communication, such as telephone, letter, firm e-mail or firm-sponsored website.

**Friends/Contacts:** When choosing friends or contacts on a social media site, think about why you use the website. Decide whether it is appropriate to accept a "friend" or other membership request from a financial service provider, such as a financial adviser or broker-dealer. There is no obligation to accept a "friend" request of a service provider or anyone you do not know or do not know well.

**Site Features:** Familiarize yourself with the functionality of the social media website before broadcasting messages on the site. Who will be able to see your messages—only specified recipients, or all users?

## Online Security Tips

As with all computer and web-based accounts, take precautions to keep your social media account information secure. Here are some security tips:

- Pick a "strong" password, keep it secure, and change it frequently.

- Use different passwords for different accounts.

- Use caution with public computers or wireless connections. Try to avoid accessing your social media accounts on public or other shared computers. But if you must do so, remember to log out completely by clicking the "logout" button on the social media website to terminate the online session.

- Be mindful of accessing your social media accounts on public wireless connections, such as at a coffee shop or airport. It is very easy to eavesdrop on Internet traffic, including passwords and other sensitive data, on a public wireless network.

- Be extra careful before clicking on links sent to you, even if by a friend.

- Secure your mobile devices. If your mobile devices are linked to your social media accounts, make sure that these devices are password protected in case they are lost or stolen.

# Types Of Fraud

Investment fraud comes in many forms. Whether you are a first-time investor or have been investing for many years, here are some basic facts you should know about different types of fraud.

- Affinity Fraud

- Advance Fee Fraud

- Binary Options Fraud

- High Yield Investment Programs

- Internet and Social Media Fraud

- Microcap Fraud

- Ponzi Scheme

- Pre-IPO Investment Scams

- Pyramid Schemes

- "Prime Bank" Investments

- Promissory Notes

- Pump and Dump Schemes

## Affinity Fraud

Affinity frauds target members of identifiable groups, such as the elderly, or religious or ethnic communities. The fraudsters involved in affinity scams often are – or pretend to be—members of the group. They may enlist respected leaders from the group to spread the word about the scheme, convincing them it is legitimate and worthwhile. Many times, those leaders become unwitting victims of the fraud they helped to promote.

These scams exploit the trust and friendship that exists in groups of people. Because of the tight-knit structure of many groups, outsiders may not know about the affinity scam. Victims may try to work things out within the group rather than notify authorities or pursue legal remedies.

Affinity scams often involve "Ponzi" or pyramid schemes where new investor money is used to pay earlier investors, making it appear as if the investment is successful and legitimate.

## Advance Fee Fraud

Advance fee frauds ask for payment up front before the deal can go through. The advance payment may be described as a fee, tax, commission, or incidental expense that will be repaid later. Some advance fee schemes target investors who already purchased underperforming securities and offer to sell those securities if an "advance fee" is paid.

One example is the so-called Nigerian advance fee fraud, where someone pretending to be a Nigerian official or businessperson promises high profits for help moving money out of Nigeria. This scam is so prevalent that the U.S. Secret Service has a task force devoted to it.

Other advance fee frauds try to fool investors with official-sounding websites and e-mail addresses. These addresses may contain ".gov" and end in ".us" or ".org." U.S. government agency websites or e-mail addresses end in ".gov," ".mil," or "fed.us." Be wary of a website or correspondence claiming to be from a U.S. government agency whose e-mail address does not end in ".gov," ".mil," or "fed.us."

## Binary Options Fraud

Much of the binary options market operates through Internet-based trading platforms that are not necessarily complying with applicable U.S. regulatory requirements and may be engaging in illegal activity. *Investors should be aware of fraudulent promotion schemes involving binary options and binary options trading platforms.*

### What Is A Binary Option?

A binary option is a type of options contract in which the payout depends entirely on the outcome of a yes/no proposition and typically relates to whether the price of a particular asset will rise above or fall below a specified amount. Once the option is acquired, there is no further decision for the holder to make regarding the exercise of the binary option because binary options exercise automatically. Unlike other types of options, a binary option does not give the holder the right to buy or sell the specified asset. When the binary option expires, the option holder receives either a pre-determined amount of cash or nothing at all.

The SEC has received numerous complaints of fraud associated with websites that offer an opportunity to buy or trade binary options through Internet-based trading platforms. The complaints fall into at least three categories:

- **Refusal to credit customer accounts or reimburse funds to customers**

  These complaints typically involve customers who have deposited money into their binary options trading account and who are then encouraged by "brokers" over the telephone to deposit additional funds into the customer account. When customers later attempt to withdraw their original deposit or the return they have been promised, the trading platforms allegedly cancel customers' withdrawal requests, refuse to credit their accounts, or ignore their telephone calls and emails.

- **Identity theft**

  These complaints allege that certain Internet-based binary options trading platforms may be collecting customer information (including copies of customers' credit cards, passports, and driver's licenses) for unspecified uses. Do not provide personal data.

- **Manipulation of software to generate losing trades**

  These complaints allege that the Internet-based binary options trading platforms manipulate the trading software to distort binary options prices and payouts. For example,

131

when a customer's trade is "winning," the countdown to expiration is extended arbitrarily until the trade becomes a loss.

## Beware Of Overstated Investment Returns For Binary Options

Additionally, some binary options Internet-based trading platforms may overstate the average return on investment by advertising a higher average return on investment than a customer should expect, given the payout structure.

For example, a customer may be asked to pay $50 for a binary option contract that promises a 50% return if the stock price of XYZ company is above $5 per share when the option expires. Assuming a 50/50 chance of winning, the payout structure has been designed in such a way that the expected return on investment is actually **negative**, resulting in a **net loss** to the customer. This is because the consequence if the option expires out of the money (approximately a 100% loss) significantly outweighs the payout if the option expires in the money (approximately a 50% gain). In this example, an investor could expect—on average—to lose money.

## Always Check The Background Of A Firm Or Financial Professional

Before investing, check out the background, including registration or license status, of any firm or financial professional you are considering dealing with through the SEC's Investment Adviser Public Disclosure (IAPD) database, available on Investor.gov, and the National Futures Association Background Affiliation Status Information Center's BASIC Search. If you cannot verify that they are registered, don't trade with them, don't give them any money, and don't share your personal information with them.

## High Yield Investment Programs

The Internet is awash in so-called "high-yield investment programs" or "HYIPs." These are unregistered investments typically run by unlicensed individuals—and they are often frauds. The hallmark of an HYIP scam is the promise of incredible returns at little or no risk to the investor. A HYIP website might promise annual (or even monthly, weekly, or daily!) returns of 30 or 40 percent—or more. Some of these scams may use the term "prime bank" program. *If you are approached online to invest in one of these, you should exercise extreme caution—it is likely a fraud.*

## Internet And Social Media Fraud

Many investors use the Internet and social media to help them with investment decisions. While these online tools can provide many benefits for investors, these same tools can make attractive targets for criminals. Criminals are quick to adapt to new technologies—and the Internet is no exception.

The Internet is a useful way to reach a mass audience without spending a lot of time or money. A website, online message, or social media site can reach large numbers with minimum effort. It's easy for fraudsters to make their messages look real and credible and sometimes hard for investors to tell the difference between fact and fiction. That's why you should think twice before you invest your money in any opportunity you find online. The key to avoiding investment fraud on social media sites or elsewhere on the Internet is to be an educated investor.

## Social Media

Social media, such as Facebook, YouTube, Twitter, and LinkedIn, have become key tools for U.S. investors. Whether they are seeking research on particular stocks, background information on a broker-dealer or investment adviser, guidance on an overall investment strategy, up to date news or to simply want to discuss the markets with others, investors turn to social media. Social media also offers a number of features that criminals may find attractive. Fraudsters can use social media in their efforts to appear legitimate, to hide behind anonymity, and to reach many people at low cost.

Always be wary of unsolicited offers to invest. Unsolicited sales pitches may be part of a fraudulent investment scheme. If you receive an unsolicited message from someone you don't know containing a "can't miss" investment, your best move maybe to pass up the "opportunity" and report it to the SEC Complaint Center.

## Online Investment Newsletters

While legitimate online newsletters contain valuable information, others are tools for fraud. Some companies pay online newsletters to "tout" or recommend their stocks. Touting isn't illegal as long as the newsletters disclose who paid them, how much they're getting paid, and the form of the payment, usually cash or stock. But fraudsters often lie about the payments they receive and their track records.

Fraudulent promoters may claim to offer independent, unbiased recommendations in newsletters when they stand to profit from convincing others to buy or sell certain stocks. They may spread false information to promote worthless stocks.

The fact that these so-called "newsletters" may be advertised on legitimate websites, including on the online financial pages of news organizations, does not mean that they are not fraudulent.

### Online Bulletin Boards And Chat Rooms

Online bulletin boards, chat rooms and social media sites are a way for investors to share information. While some messages may be true, many turn out to be bogus—or even scams. Fraudsters may use online discussions to pump up a company or pretend to reveal "inside" information about upcoming announcements, new products, or lucrative contracts.

You never know for certain who you're dealing with, or whether they're credible, because many sites allow users to hide their identity behind multiple aliases. People claiming to be unbiased observers may actually be insiders, large shareholders, or paid promoters. One person can easily create the illusion of widespread interest in a small, thinly traded stock by posting numerous messages under various aliases.

Other online offerings may not be fraudulent per se, but may nonetheless fail to comply with the applicable registration provisions of the federal securities laws. While the federal securities laws require the registration of solicitations or "offerings," some offerings are exempt. Always determine if a securities offering is registered with the SEC or a state, or is otherwise exempt from registration, before investing.

### Spam

"Spam"—junk e-mail—often is used to promote bogus investment schemes or to spread false information about a company. With a bulk e-mail program, spammers can send personalized messages to millions of people at once for much less than the cost of cold calling or traditional mail. Many scams, including advance fee frauds, use spam to reach potential victims.

Many of the frauds that show up on social media are not unique to the Internet. These frauds range from "pump and dump" schemes to promises of "guaranteed returns," from "High Yield Investment Programs" to affinity fraud.

## Microcap Fraud

If you are considering investing in a company based on an unsolicited stock promotion, be cautious. The promotion may be from a paid promoter or company insider who stands to profit at your expense from selling shares after creating a buying frenzy and pumping up the stock price as part of a pump and dump scheme.

**What are microcap stocks and why are they more susceptible to stock price manipulation?**

Publicly-available information about microcap stocks (low-priced stocks issued by the smallest of companies), including penny stocks (the very lowest priced stocks), often is scarce. This makes it easier for fraudsters to spread false information. In addition, it is often easier for fraudsters to manipulate the price of microcap stocks because microcap stocks historically have been less liquid than the stock of larger companies.

**What are some warning signs of microcap fraud?**

- **Unsolicited stock recommendation or heavy stock promotion**
  - Be wary if the company's stock seems to be more heavily promoted than its products or services.

- **No real business operations**
  - Penny stocks that are aggressively promoted may be stocks of dormant shell companies.

- **Unexplained increase in stock price or trading volume**
  - Some microcap stocks are quoted on "over-the-counter" (OTC) systems (e.g., OTC Bulletin Board and OTC Markets).

- **Frequent changes in company name or type of business**
  - Frequent changes in company name or business plan may suggest no real business operations.

**Where can I get information about a microcap company?**

Read recent reports that the company has filed with the SEC. Note that fraudsters often attempt to take advantage of the news as a hook for investment schemes touting "the latest growth industry." For example, they may promote companies that claim to be developing products or services relating to marijuana, Ebola, or Zika.

**What If I received the stock promotion through a legitimate source?**

Fraudsters may promote a stock in seemingly independent and unbiased sources including social media, investment newsletters, online advertisements, email, Internet chat rooms, direct mail, newspapers, magazines, and radio.

**What if the promoter discloses receiving compensation to promote the stock?**

Even if a promoter makes specific disclosures about being compensated for promoting a stock, be aware that fraudsters may make such disclosures to create the false appearance that the promotion is legitimate. Additionally, the disclosures may not reveal that the underlying source of the compensation is a company insider or affiliate.

## Ponzi Scheme

A Ponzi scheme is an investment fraud that pays existing investors with funds collected from new investors. Ponzi scheme organizers often promise to invest your money and generate high returns with little or no risk. But in many Ponzi schemes, the fraudsters do not invest the money. Instead, they use it to pay those who invested earlier and may keep some for themselves.

With little or no legitimate earnings, Ponzi schemes require a constant flow of new money to survive. When it becomes hard to recruit new investors, or when large numbers of existing investors cash out, these schemes tend to collapse.

Ponzi schemes are named after Charles Ponzi, who duped investors in the 1920s with a postage stamp speculation scheme.

## Ponzi Scheme "Red Flags"

Many Ponzi schemes share common characteristics. Look for these warning signs:

- **High returns with little or no risk.** Every investment carries some degree of risk, and investments yielding higher returns typically involve more risk. Be highly suspicious of any "guaranteed" investment opportunity.

- **Overly consistent returns.** Investments tend to go up and down over time. Be skeptical about an investment that regularly generates positive returns regardless of overall market conditions.

- **Unregistered investments.** Ponzi schemes typically involve investments that are not registered with the SEC or with state regulators. Registration is important because it provides investors with access to information about the company's management, products, services, and finances.

- **Unlicensed sellers.** Federal and state securities laws require investment professionals and firms to be licensed or registered. Most Ponzi schemes involve unlicensed individuals or unregistered firms.

- **Secretive, complex strategies.** Avoid investments if you don't understand them or can't get complete information about them.

- **Issues with paperwork.** Account statement errors may be a sign that funds are not being invested as promised.

- **Difficulty receiving payments.** Be suspicious if you don't receive a payment or have difficulty cashing out. Ponzi scheme promoters sometimes try to prevent participants from cashing out by offering even higher returns for staying put.

## Pre-IPO Investment Scams

The SEC's Office of Investor Education and Advocacy (OIEA) has issued an updated Investor Alert to warn investors about investment scams that purport to offer investors the opportunity to buy pre-IPO shares of companies, including social media and technology companies such as Facebook and Twitter. SEC staff is aware of a number of complaints and inquiries about these types of frauds, which may be promoted on social media and internet sites, by telephone, email, in person, or by other means.

## Pyramid Schemes

In the classic "pyramid" scheme, participants attempt to make money solely by recruiting new participants, usually where:

- The promoter promises a high return in a short period of time;

- No genuine product or service is actually sold; and

- The primary emphasis is on recruiting new participants.

All pyramid schemes eventually collapse, and most investors lose their money.

Fraudsters frequently promote pyramid schemes through social media, Internet advertising, company websites, group presentations, conference calls, YouTube videos, and other means. Pyramid scheme promoters may go to great lengths to make the program look like a business, such as a legitimate multi-level marketing (MLM) program. But the fraudsters use money paid by new recruits to pay off earlier stage investors (usually recruits as well). At some point, the schemes get too big, the promoter cannot raise enough money from new investors to pay earlier investors, and people lose their money.

**These are some of the hallmarks of a pyramid scheme:**

- **Emphasis on recruiting.** If a program focuses solely on recruiting others to join the program for a fee, it is likely a pyramid scheme. Be skeptical if you will receive more compensation for recruiting others than for product sales.

- **No genuine product or service is sold.** Exercise caution if what is being sold as part of the business is hard to value, like so-called "tech" services or products such as mass-licensed e-books or online advertising on little-used websites. Some fraudsters choose fancy-sounding "products" to make it harder to prove the company is a bogus pyramid scheme.

- **Promises of high returns in a short time period.** Be skeptical of promises of fast cash—it could mean that commissions are being paid out of money from new recruits rather than revenue generated by product sales.

- Easy money or passive income. There is no such thing as a free lunch. If you are offered compensation in exchange for doing little work such as making payments, recruiting others, or placing online advertisements on obscure websites, you may be part of an illegal pyramid scheme.

- **No demonstrated revenue from retail sales.** Ask to see documents, such as financial statements audited by a certified public accountant (CPA), showing that the company generates revenue from selling its products or services to people outside the program. As a general rule, legitimate MLM companies derive revenue primarily from selling products, not from recruiting members.

- **Complex commission structure.** Be concerned unless commissions are based on products or services that you or your recruits sell to people outside the program. If you do not understand how you will be compensated, be cautious.

## All Pyramid Schemes Collapse

When fraudsters attempt to make money solely by recruiting new participants into a program, that is a pyramid scheme, and there is only one possible mathematical result – collapse. Imagine if one participant must find six other participants, who, in turn, must find six new recruits each. In only 11 layers of the "downline," you would need more participants than the entire population of the United States to maintain the scheme. This infographic shows how all pyramid schemes are destined to collapse.

## "Prime Bank" Investments

If someone approaches you about investing in a so-called "Prime Bank" program, "Prime World Bank" financial instrument, or similar high-yield security, you should know that these investments do not exist. They are all scams.

Prime Bank programs often claim investors' funds will be used to buy and trade "Prime Bank" instruments. Promoters make the schemes seem legitimate, using complex, sophisticated and official-sounding terms. The investment may be described as debentures, standby letters of credit, bank guarantees, an offshore trading program, a high-yield investment program, or some variation.

To reassure investors, promoters may claim that the instrument is issued, traded, or guaranteed by a well-known organization such as the World Bank, the International Monetary

Fund (IMF), a central bank, such as the U.S. Federal Reserve, or the International Chamber of Commerce (ICC).

Secrecy is another tip-off. Prime Bank scheme promoters frequently claim that investment opportunities of this type are by invitation only and limited to select, wealthy customers. They cite secrecy if potential investors ask for references, and sometimes ask investors to sign non-disclosure agreements.

Some promoters are audacious enough to advertise in national newspapers. They may avoid using the term "Prime Bank note," and tell prospective investors that their programs do not involve Prime Bank instruments. Regardless of what they're called, the basic pitch remains the same, and investors should remain vigilant against offers to invest in high-yield, risk-free international finance programs.

## Promissory Notes

Promissory notes are a form of debt that companies sometimes use to raise money. They typically involve investors loaning money to a company in exchange for a fixed amount of periodic income. Although promissory notes can be appropriate investments for many individuals, some fraudsters use promissory notes to defraud investors, especially the elderly.

## Pump And Dump Schemes

"Pump and dump" schemes have two parts. In the first, promoters try to boost the price of a stock with false or misleading statements about the company. Once the stock price has been pumped up, fraudsters move on to the second part, where they seek to profit by selling their own holdings of the stock, dumping shares into the market. These schemes often occur on the Internet where it is common to see messages urging readers to buy a stock quickly. Often, the promoters will claim to have "inside" information about a development that will be positive for the stock. After these fraudsters dump their shares and stop hyping the stock, the price typically falls, and investors lose their money.

# Where Can I Go For Help?

If you have a question or concern about an investment, or you think you have encountered one of these frauds, please contact the U.S. Securities and Exchange Commission (SEC), Financial Industry Regulatory Authority (FINRA), or your state securities regulator to report the fraud and to get assistance.

# Chapter 19

# Beware Of Online Perils And Internet Fraud

The Internet has proven to be major boon for consumers making financial decisions. Information that at one time would've taken days or weeks to ferret out can now be found relatively easily in minutes. Annual reports and other corporate filings are available on SEC.gov, the website of the U.S. Securities and Exchange Commission (SEC), and most companies provide those documents and other valuable investor information on their own sites. In addition, thousands of other sites contain a wealth of data about investments, banks, online stores, and email offers, allowing consumers to perform in-depth research before making financial decisions.

Unfortunately the Web has also been a boon for scammers and has fostered a host of possible ways for people to lose money. It's an easy way for criminals to reach large numbers of people cheaply and without much effort and then lure them into traps using tools like social media, spam emails, pop-up ads, newsletters, discussion forums, and fake websites. So it's very important to learn to spot online scammers and fraudulent Internet practices in order to avoid becoming the next victim.

## Common Online Investment Scams

There are many thousands of ways unscrupulous individuals can take advantage of investors, and they're inventing more every day. But some have proven so successful that criminals keep using them over and over. A few of the most common ones include:

- **Online investment newsletters.** Online newsletters can provide valuable information for investors, but some are fraudulent. In these cases, companies often pay newsletter writers to recommend their stock. This isn't actually illegal if the newsletters follow SEC regulations and disclose who's paying them and how much they're getting. But many fail to do this and pose as unbiased sources of information while they convince the public to make poor investment choices.

- **Online bulletin boards or discussion forums.** These sites allow people to exchange information about investments, ask questions, and share their experiences. The problem is, you don't really know who's doing the posting. It could be a company, or someone it's hired, promoting a certain investment while posing as small investors or perhaps as someone with inside information. This is another cheap and easy way to disseminate false information and get people to buy stock.

- **Spam.** Spam is a fact of life for virtually anyone with an email address. Most people receive multiple messages each day trying to get them to buy products or use a service. Investment spam is one more way for scammers to reach a large audience and spread false information about a company or investment opportunity, usually making it sound much better than it really is.

- **"Pump and dump" schemes.** This term refers to a scheme in which a scammer acquires a large amount of cheap stock and then pumps up the price through the use of false information in emails, online discussion groups, and social media, urging people to buy the stock quickly. The sudden burst of promotion increases demand for the stock and drives up the price, at which point the fraudster sells all of his or her shares. Then the stock drops in value, and other investors lose money.

- **High-yield investment scheme.** Also known as "prime bank scams," these are unregistered investments, usually managed by unlicensed brokers, that are almost always fraudulent. They promise to deliver extremely high returns with little or no risk to the investor. Typically a high-yield promoter will use a website or other online means to convince people that their investment will net an annual return of 30 to 40 percent—or even 100 percent. In reality, it's likely that the scammer will simply take the money and disappear.

- **Advance fee scam.** Here a scammer typically uses spam emails to solicit up-front fees for investments. Often these are positioned as a commission, tax, deposit, or underwriting fee, and sometimes victims are told they'll get this money back at a future date. They are almost always accompanied by very official-looking email addresses or website, and often investors are instructed to send the fee to an attorney or other agent. Needless to say, the fraudster will vanish with no further word about the "investment."

- **Fraudulent online offerings.** These scams are instances in which investments in stocks, bonds, or other securities are offered to the public with false information intended to make the investment look better than it is. Usually this involves the promise of a higher return than is actually possible.

> Use common sense. If an online offer sounds too good to be true, it probably is. Scam artists are experts as using greed as leverage against their victims. If someone is promising you free stuff or large sums of money in exchange for a small investment on your part, your instinct should tell you that something doesn't add up.

# Other Online Scams

In addition to investment fraud, there are thousands of other ways criminals use the Internet to take people's money. Here are some common scams:

- **Phishing.** One of the most prevalent fraudulent online practices, phishing emails try to steal your personal information, such as birth date, passwords, and credit-card numbers. Typically they trick you into visiting a fake website made to look like a legitimate online store or banking site, often one with which you've done business in the past. There they may ask you to "verify" your personal info or enter financial details, which they can then use to hack into your accounts or steal your identity.

- **Greeting card scams.** Here you receive an e-card in your email box, but when you click on the link to see the card you're taken to a website that's rigged to download a malicious bot to your computer. Once there it can wreak all sorts of havoc, including stealing personal details and financial information.

- **Lottery frauds.** Lots of people dream of winning the lottery, and these scams prey on those hopes and dreams. The scammers send you an email saying you've won a lottery, and to collect the huge prize all you need to do is send them a "processing fee." Of course, there is no lottery, and they keep your fee.

- **Nigerian scam.** This one has been around for almost as long as the Internet, yet it continues to rob people every year. There are many variations of this scheme, which is similar to lottery fraud. An email from Nigerian royalty, or another very wealthy person, asks for your help in getting a large sum of money out of the country. You need to advance a small amount of money, and in return you're promised a big payoff once the transaction is completed. As with a lottery scam, there is no transaction, except the money you advanced.

- **Guaranteed acceptance fraud.** Here an email tells you that you've been pre-approved for a credit card or loan for a large sum of money, and to get it all you need to do is send an up-front "processing fee." These scams are particularly believable because banks and credit-card companies often do send consumers pre-approval offers. But in this case, of course, there's no card or loan.

- **Pyramid scheme.** This scam predates the Internet by many years, but where it once was perpetrated by mail, scammers now use email to reach a lot more victims. Pyramid schemes purport to be businesses that sell goods or services with growth accomplished by "associates" (sales people) recruiting more people into the scheme. Each new associate pays a fee to join. Often no goods or services ever exist, and the people at the top of the pyramid make all the money.

> Sign up to receive regular scam alerts at the Federal Trade Commission website, ftc.gov. There you'll also find valuable information on some of the latest scams and how to avoid them.

# How To Avoid Becoming A Victim

Fraudsters are clever, and they're always thinking up new ways to separate people from their money. With the Internet at their disposal they're able to reach more victims and can make their schemes look especially tempting with legitimate-appearing websites and emails. Young people are particularly susceptible to some of their scams, in part because they may not have been exposed to similar types of fraud in the past. But there are steps you can take to protect yourself from the scammers, such as:

- **Use the Internet to your advantage.** There's a wealth of information available online that can help you investigate investments or email offers before parting with your money. Often a simple Google search will uncover other people who've been victims. When it comes to investments, the SEC website or your state's securities regulation site can also be a valuable source of information about companies and their stocks or bonds.

- **Work with professionals.** When investing, use the services of a reputable broker or financial adviser. They can not only guide you to some of the most stable investments but can also provide assurance that you're putting your money into legitimate sources. If you're investing with an online broker, check out the site thoroughly to be sure it's not a scam.

- **Choose regular investments.** Get-rich-quick email schemes sound tempting, which is why so many people fall for them. But avoid any offers that sound too good to be true, and invest your money in more common securities, like stocks and bonds that are recommended by reputable analysts and advisers. These investments may not seem as exciting, but they're less likely to be scams.

- **Beware of imposters.** Scammers very often pose as a trusted source, such as a bank, a company you do business with, a government agency, or even a friend or family member. Don't send money to anyone until you check them out thoroughly. Typing their name, or the company's name, into a search engine followed by "scam" or "complaint" will often reveal the truth.

- **Don't pay up front.** Never make an advance payment or pay an up-front fee for any unsolicited offers. Scammers send emails for everything from prizes to job offers to pre-approved credit in order to get you to send money. Be wary of anyone asking for "processing" or "handling" fees.

- **Make a phone call.** If your research into an online offer turns up what appears to be a legitimate business, get the company's phone number and call for more information. If the offer is legitimate, they'll be glad to verify it and give you additional details.

- **Choose a safe online payment method.** The safest way to shop or make payments online is with credit cards, because they have the most built-in fraud protection. Debit cards are less secure; with those you will probably get your money back in case of fraud, but it will be more difficult and take more time. It's especially risky to wire money or use reloadable debit cards; if an online source insists that you use one of these payment methods, that should raise a red flag.

> If you suspect online fraud, you should report it to the FBI Internet Crime Complaint Center (ic3.gov), the U.S. Government's Online Safety page (usa.gov/online-safety), or the Better Business Bureau's Scam Tracker page (bbb.org/scamtracker/us/reportscam).

## References

1. "Avoiding Internet Investment Scams: Tips for Investors," U.S. Securities and Exchange Commission (SEC), August 15, 2007.

2. "Internet Fraud: How to Avoid Internet Investment Scams," Findlaw.com, n.d.

3. "Online Scams and Fraud: How Internet Users Can Minimize Exposure," Whoishostingthis.com, n.d.

4. Schock, Lori J. "Don't Get Scammed by Investment Fraud on the Internet," Militarysaves.org, February 3, 2015.

5. Smith, Lisa. "Avoiding Online Investment Scams," Investopedia.com, n.d.

# Part Three
## Banks And Bonds

# Chapter 20
# Basic Facts About Banks And Banking

The monetary system of the modern world is built around banks. They account for trillions of dollars in assets, making them a crucial driver of the global economy. And, closer to home, they provide a number of services that can help you manage your money wisely. But not everyone understands what banks are, what they do, and how they operate. Increasing your knowledge about banks can guide you to make better financial decisions and save you money in the long run.

## The Origin Of Banks

Although money-lending and the exchange of money for goods dates back to ancient times, the first institution most of us would recognize as a bank arose in fourteenth-century Italy. In the cities of Florence, Genoa, and Venice, prominent families established banks to loan money to merchants, finance military operations, and facilitate trade between city-states and regions.

Banks gradually sprang up throughout Europe from the fifteen to the seventeenth centuries. Most of them dealt in bullion (gold and silver bars or ingots) or coins made from gold, silver, copper, or other metals. But late in the seventeenth century, in Sweden, banks started issuing paper money, notes of credit that promised the holder could exchange the paper for a specified amount of precious metal. Banking continued to expand worldwide, and during the Industrial Revolution in the nineteenth century banks became the key component in international trade that they remain today.

# Types Of Banks

You're probably familiar with one kind of bank, the one near you with the drive-through ATM and where you may have a savings account. But there are actually a number of different types of banks, including:

- **Retail banks**: These are the ones you know. Also called consumer banks, they're usually local branches of larger banking systems that provide a variety of services to individual customers, including savings and checking accounts, loans, and credit and debit cards.

- **Savings and loans**: Less common than they once were, these institutions function similarly to a retail bank, but usually offer more limited services. Their main purpose is to take in savings deposits and make loans, primarily home mortgages.

- **Commercial banks**: These banks cater to business customers with basic services like savings and checking accounts. But they can also accept payments for customers, extend lines of credit to help businesses manage cash flow, and facilitate cash transfers from overseas customers.

- **Investment banks**: Investment banks are set up to facilitate large transactions. Their services can include handling investors' funds, guaranteeing payments, helping institutional clients with mergers or corporate reorganizations, and acting as a broker or financial adviser.

- **Online banks**: These are retail banks that have no physical location, operating instead completely via the Internet. They provide most of the same services as a traditional bank but frequently offer better savings interest rates and more favorable terms on loans.

- **Central banks**: Central banks are national banks that provide services for their country's government. They also implement the government's monetary policy and issue the country's currency. In the United States, this function is served by the Federal Reserve Bank, which was founded in 1913.

---

## Things To Consider When Choosing A Bank

- **Minimum deposit requirements**: Do you have to keep a minimum dollar amount in your account to earn interest or avoid account maintenance fees?
- **Limits on withdrawals**: Can you take money out whenever you want? Are there any penalties for doing so?

- **Interest**: Can you earn interest on your accounts? How much is it, and how frequently is it paid?
- **Online bill pay**: Can you pay your bills directly from your bank's website?
- **Deposit insurance**: Make sure that the bank is a member of the Federal Deposit Insurance Corporation (FDIC).
- **Mobile banking**: Can you access your accounts and make deposits from your mobile phone or tablet? Does the bank charge fees for this access?
- **Convenience**: Are there branches or ATMs close to where you to school, work, and live?

# Retail Bank Services

Since it's unlikely that you'll need the services of other types of banks at the moment, it might be useful to concentrate on your interaction with retail banks, which can include online banks. Some of the services these banks provide include:

- **Savings accounts**: There pay a relatively small amount of interest on your deposits but allow you to withdraw your money at any time. Then there are other types of accounts that earn a higher rate of interest in exchange for leaving your money in the bank for longer periods, such as certificates of deposit (CDs).

- **Checking accounts**: When you open a checking account you deposit funds and receive a book of checks, slips of paper that are a promise to pay a specified amount of money from your account. Checking accounts also let you make deposits and withdrawals from an ATM using a debit card, pay bills online, and transfer money between accounts.

- **Loans**: One of the primary ways banks make money is by taking funds it receives from depositors and lending it to people who need it. The bank makes money by charging a higher fee for these loans than it pays out in interest.

- **Credit cards**: These are actually a kind of loan. The bank advances funds to a merchant or other payee with the understanding that the customer will pay the money back to the bank at the end of the month, usually with no fee, or over time with a finance charge added.

- **Online and mobile banking**: Even physical banks now provide customers with access to their secure websites. This allows you to check your balances, transfer funds between accounts, and pay bills from any computer with an Internet connection. Most banks now also have mobile apps that allow you to perform these same functions from a phone or tablet.

> Most banks have savings and checking accounts designed specifically for students. You can find the details of these accounts, as well as tips and other useful information, on their websites.

# Bank Regulation

Through the many centuries of banking, there have been numerous abuses that have sometimes led to personal bankruptcies, bank failures, and even the collapse of the monetary systems of entire countries. As a result, governments place restrictions on banks that regulate the way they handle money and interact with customers. In the United States, banking is regulated by the federal government, as well as by individual states. Many regulations were enacted after the bank failures of the Great Depression that began in 1929, and more were passed following the financial crisis that started in 2007. A few of the federal agencies responsible for overseeing the huge number of bank regulations include:

- **Federal Deposit Insurance Corporation (FDIC)**: Created in 1933, the FDIC insures the money in your savings and checking accounts. This agency guarantees that your funds will be there when you need them.

- **Federal Reserve Board**: Often called "The Fed," this is the governing body of the Federal Reserve System, which provides central control of the country's monetary system. This includes regulating banks, ensuring a stable economy, and providing services to individual banks.

- **Office of the Comptroller of the Currency (OCC)**: Established in 1863, the purpose of the OCC is to charter, supervise, and regulate banks to help ensure the stability and proper functioning of the entire banking system.

- **Office of Thrift Supervision (OTS)**: This agency was created in 1989 by the Financial Institutions Reform, Recovery and Enforcement Act of that year. It primarily regulates savings and loans in the same way the OCC regulates other banks.

# Credit Unions

These financial institutions perform many of the functions of banks, providing customers with services like savings and checking accounts and loans. There are some differences, however, including:

- **Structure**: Most banks are corporations owned by shareholders who elect their governing boards. Credit unions are owned by their customers, called members. All members, regardless of the size of their deposits, get a vote when electing board members, and while banks pay their board members, credit unions are run by volunteers.

- **Profits**: Banks are in business to make money for their shareholders. Credit unions, on the other hand, are nonprofit organizations. When they make a profit from loans or other investments, they use it to increase interest rates on savings accounts or reduce the finance charges on loans to members.

- **Size**: Through the years, changes in regulations have resulted in the elimination of some restrictions on the way credit unions do business, bringing them more in line with banks. However, the fact remains that today even the biggest credit unions are tiny compared to most banks.

- **Regulations**: As we've seen, the many regulations on banks are overseen by a number of federal and state agencies. But national regulation of credit unions is handled by the National Credit Union Administration, as well as individual state authorities. One of the responsibilities of the NCUA is to manage the National Credit Union Share Insurance Fund, which is similar to the FDIC in that it insures depositor funds.

What's better, a bank or a credit union? Like a lot of questions, the answer depends on your individual circumstances. Credit unions have the reputation of providing better, more personal, customer service, which is an important factor for many people. They also generally pay higher interest rates on savings and charge lower fees for loans. But unlike banks, credit unions may offer limited access to ATMs. And you can't open an account at just any credit union; most of them have been created to serve specific organizations, employee groups, or geographic regions. But if you qualify for membership, a credit union may meet your needs. As with any financial decision, do your homework carefully before choosing an option.

> The **Reserve Requirement** is the amount of funds, set by the Federal Reserve Board of Governors, that a bank must have on hand every night, either as cash in its vault or as a deposit at the local Federal Reserve bank. Large banks with more than $79.5 million on deposit must maintain a reserve of 10 percent of deposits.

## References

1. Maxfield, John. "Credit Union vs. Bank: 4 Major Differences," Fool.com, June 7, 2015.

2. Roche, Cullen. "The Basics of Banking," Pragcap.com, n.d.

3. "The Role of Banks," ING.com, n.d.

4. Sylla, Richard. "The U.S. Banking System: Origin, Development, and Regulation," Gilderlehrman.org, n.d.

5. "Types of Banks & Federal Deposit Insurance Corporation (FDIC)," Teensguidetomoney.com, n.d.

# Chapter 21

# Internet And Tech-Based Banking Options

## Electronic Fund Transfers (EFT)

Electronic banking, also known as electronic fund transfer (EFT), uses computer and electronic technology in place of checks and other paper transactions. EFTs are initiated through devices like cards or codes that let you, or those you authorize, access your account. Many financial institutions use ATM or debit cards and Personal Identification Numbers (PINs) for this purpose. Some use other types of debit cards that require your signature or a scan. For example, some use radio frequency identification (RFID) or other forms of "contactless" technology that scan your information without direct contact with you. The federal Electronic Fund Transfer Act (EFT Act) covers some electronic consumer transactions.

---

### What Does It Mean?

"Internet banking" refers to systems that enable bank customers to access accounts and general information on bank products and services through a personal computer (PC) or other intelligent device.

Internet banking products and services can include wholesale products for corporate customers as well as retail and fiduciary products for consumers. Ultimately, the products and services obtained through Internet banking may mirror products and services offered through other bank delivery channels. Some examples of wholesale products and services include:

- Cash management.
- Wire transfer.

---

About This Chapter: Text under the heading "Electronic Fund Transfers (EFT)" is excerpted "Electronic Banking," Federal Trade Commission (FTC), August 2012; Text beginning with the heading "Using Technology To Remain Financially Fit" is excerpted from "Banking In A High-Tech World," Federal Deposit Insurance Corporation (FDIC), 2013.

> - Automated clearinghouse (ACH) transactions.
> - Bill presentment and payment.
>
> *(Source: "Internet Banking," Office of the Comptroller of the Currency (OCC), U.S. Department of the Treasury.)*

## Common EFT Services

**ATMs** are electronic terminals that let you bank almost virtually any time. To withdraw cash, make deposits, or transfer funds between accounts, you generally insert an ATM card and enter your PIN. Some financial institutions and ATM owners charge a fee, particularly if you don't have accounts with them or if your transactions take place at remote locations. Generally, ATMs must tell you they charge a fee and the amount on or at the terminal screen before you complete the transaction. Check with your institution and at ATMs you use for more information about these fees.

**Direct Deposit** lets you authorize specific deposits—like paychecks, Social Security checks, and other benefits—to your account on a regular basis. You also may pre-authorize direct withdrawals so that recurring bills—like insurance premiums, mortgages, utility bills, and gym memberships—are paid automatically. Be cautious before you pre-authorize recurring withdrawals to pay companies you aren't familiar with; funds from your bank account could be withdrawn improperly. Monitor your bank account to make sure direct recurring payments take place and are for the right amount.

**Pay-by-Phone Systems** let you call your financial institution with instructions to pay certain bills or to transfer funds between accounts. You must have an agreement with your institution to make these transfers.

**Personal Computer Banking** lets you handle many banking transactions using your personal computer. For example, you may use your computer to request transfers between accounts and pay bills electronically.

**Debit Card Purchase or Payment Transactions** let you make purchases or payments with a debit card, which also may be your ATM card. Transactions can take place in-person, online, or by phone. The process is similar to using a credit card, with some important exceptions: a debit card purchase or payment transfers money quickly from your bank account to the company's account, so you have to have sufficient funds in your account to cover your purchase. This means you need to keep accurate records of the dates and amounts of your debit card purchases, payments, and ATM withdrawals. Be sure you know the store or business before you provide your debit card information to avoid the possible loss of funds through fraud. Your liability for unauthorized use, and your rights for dealing with errors, may be different for a debit card than a credit card.

**Electronic Check Conversion** converts a paper check into an electronic payment in a store or when a company gets your check in the mail.

When you give your check to a cashier in a store, the check is run through an electronic system that captures your banking information and the amount of the check. You sign a receipt and you get a copy for your records. When your check is given back to you, it should be voided or marked by the merchant so that it can't be used again. The merchant electronically sends information from the check (but not the check itself) to your bank or other financial institution, and the funds are transferred into the merchant's account.

When you mail a check for payment to a merchant or other company, they may electronically send information from your check (but not the check itself) through the system; the funds are transferred from your account into their account. For a mailed check, you still should get notice from a company that expects to send your check information through the system electronically. For example, the company might include the notice on your monthly statement. The notice also should state if the company will electronically collect a fee from your account—like a "bounced check" fee—if you don't have enough money to cover the transaction.

Be careful with online and telephone transactions that may involve the use of your bank account information, rather than a check. A legitimate merchant that lets you use your bank account information to make a purchase or pay on an account should post information about the process on its website or explain the process on the phone. The merchant also should ask for your permission to electronically debit your bank account for the item you're buying or paying on. However, because online and telephone electronic debits don't occur face-to-face, be cautious about sharing your bank account information. Don't give out this information when you have no experience with the business, when you didn't initiate the call, or when the business seems reluctant to discuss the process with you. Check your bank account regularly to be sure that the right amounts were transferred.

Not all electronic fund transfers are covered by the EFT Act. For example, some financial institutions and merchants issue cards with cash value stored electronically on the card itself. Examples include prepaid phone cards, mass transit passes, general purpose reloadable cards, and some gift cards. These "stored-value" cards, as well as transactions using them, may not be covered by the EFT Act, or they may be subject to different rules under the EFT Act. This means you may not be covered for the loss or misuse of the card. Ask your financial institution or merchant about any protections offered for these cards.

# Using Technology To Remain Financially Fit

If you're interested in trying new bank technology but you're not sure what's available, FDIC Consumer News offers this overview of some current services, many of them free.

**Personal financial management and budgeting:** Financial planning tools, often referred to as personal financial management software, can include electronic check registers on your home computer (which many consumers will find much easier to use and balance than an old-fashioned paper check register) and "companion applications" for your smartphone that allow you to access your electronic check register wherever you are.

Mobile banking services go one step further by allowing you to access your account from anywhere using a smartphone, "tablet" computer or other device. An estimated 30 million Americans currently manage their finances using mobile devices.

"Mobile banking services can be very helpful if you are in a store contemplating a major purchase and need to know whether you have enough money in your account to cover the cost," said Jeff Kopchik, a Senior Policy Analyst with the FDIC's Technology Supervision Branch. "If your balance is low, you can use your mobile device to transfer funds from your savings account into your checking account to cover the purchase." But remember that the available balance shown in online banking may be less than you have to spend if any checks or other transactions have not yet been posted to your account.

Your bank also may offer free online budgeting tools that can help you track your spending by category, monitor investments and meet your savings goals. Some of them offer retirement planning advice and calculators to help you figure out such things as whether you should refinance your mortgage or how much you need to be saving for retirement every month. While not directly related to banking and not a new service, many consumers may wish to consider using tax-preparation software that can make preparing federal and state income tax returns easy and much less expensive than using a paid preparer.

**Depositing checks using your smartphone or other mobile device:** Many banks have rolled out a "remote deposit capture" (RDC) feature that allows customers to take a picture of a check with their mobile phone and deposit that check electronically, without visiting a branch or using an ATM. This service is becoming popular, especially among customers who don't live or work close to a bank branch. "Mobile RDC can provide convenience to a variety of consumers, from young people to senior citizens," noted Elizabeth Khalil, a Senior Policy

Analyst in the FDIC's Division of Depositor and Consumer Protection. If you use mobile RDC, carefully keep track of the checks you deposit. For instance, you can write the date you deposited the item on the front of the paper check and hold onto it until the check has cleared and the money is in your account. Then you can destroy the check, preferably using a high-quality paper shredder. Contact your bank with any questions.

**Account alerts:** Most mobile banking systems will allow you to sign up to get text messages on your mobile phone or e-mails if your account balance drops below a set dollar amount, which can help ensure that you don't overdraw your account. You may be able to receive text alerts if your bank observes "suspicious"— potentially fraudulent—transactions involving your account. Another possibility may be to get a notice of a certificate of deposit about to mature. "Mobile account alerts are probably the easiest and most effective way to monitor what is going on with your checking account in real time," suggested Kopchik.

**Mobile bill paying:** Most mobile banking services allow consumers to pay companies that already have been added to their "approved list" on their bank's online banking Website. However, if you want to make bill payment even easier, some banks allow customers to use their mobile phone to take a picture of a paper bill from any merchant (provided the bill shows the company's name and certain other information) and then click the "pay" button. "This new service eliminates the need for you to enter merchant payment information into your bank's bill-payment service. Your bank will take care of that automatically," said Khalil. As with any mobile banking service, always check with your bank before signing up to make sure you know about any fees or other key terms.

**"Loyalty" discount programs with retailers:** These are new and not in widespread use, but here's one example. You may be able to give your bank permission to analyze your debit and credit card transaction records and automatically arrange for some of your favorite retailers to send electronic coupons or other special offers to your home computer or mobile banking device. Some mobile payment programs that utilize a "mobile wallet" (an application that can be loaded onto your mobile phone) will enable specific merchants to send discount offers directly to your phone as you are walking by their store. Keep in mind that if you sign up for these programs you will have to share information about your buying habits with merchants or other third parties.

Finally, when using any mobile financial service, keep privacy and security issues in mind. "For one thing, mobile phones are much easier to lose or misplace than a desktop computer, so make sure that you keep track of your mobile phone and password-protect it," Kopchik advised.

# Protecting Your Plastic From High-Tech Criminals

While many consumers still like to use paper money and coins, more and more people are pulling out credit or debit cards to make purchases. And, as the popularity of payment cards has grown, so has the number of criminals trying to steal very valuable details, including the cardholder's name and the card's account number and expiration date, which are printed on the card itself as well as encoded (for machine readability) in the magnetic stripe or a computer chip.

"No matter how your card information is stored, it is in high demand by criminals who would like to retrieve that data to create a counterfeit version of your card or use the information to make purchases online or over the phone," said Michael Benardo, manager of the Federal Deposit Insurance Corporation's (FDIC) Cyber Fraud and Financial Crimes Section. If you're ever the victim or target of credit or debit card theft or fraud, catching it fast and reporting it to your card issuer are key to resolving the situation. And while federal laws and industry practices protect consumers in these situations, there are important differences depending on the type of card. In general, under the Truth in Lending Act, your cap for liability for unauthorized charges on a credit card is $50. But under the Electronic Fund Transfer Act, if your debit card or ATM card is lost or stolen or you notice an unauthorized purchase or other transfer using your checking or savings account, your maximum liability is limited to $50 only if you notify your bank within two business days. If you wait more than two business days, your debit/ATM card losses under the law could go up to $500, or perhaps much more. With either card, though, industry practices may further limit your losses, so check with your card issuer. What else can you do to keep thieves away from your cards and your money?

**Never give out your payment card numbers in response to an unsolicited e-mail, text message or phone call, no matter who the source supposedly is.** An "urgent" email or phone call appearing to be from a well-known organization is likely a scam attempting to trick you into divulging your card information. It's called "phishing," a high-tech variation of the concept of "fishing" for account information. If they get confidential details, the criminals can use the information to make counterfeit cards and run up charges on your accounts.

**Take precautions at the checkout counter, ATM and gas pump.** "Be on the lookout for credit and debit card reading devices that look suspicious, such as a plastic sleeve inside a card slot," Benardo said. "Crooks are getting very good at attaching their own devices over legitimate card readers and gathering account information from the cards that consumers swipe through those readers."

Also be alert when you hand your payment card to an employee at a restaurant or retail establishment. For example, if he or she swipes your card through two devices instead of one, that second device could be recording your account information to make a fraudulent card. Report that situation to a manager and your card issuer.

To help combat payment card fraud, many card issuers have turned to the technology known as radio frequency identification (RFID). This uses wireless radio signals to identify people or objects from a distance. It is also being used with items such as highway toll passes, subway fare cards and pay-at-the-pump cards to add convenience and speed up many routine transactions. While some news reports indicate that payment cards with RFID chips may be more vulnerable to fraud than traditional cards with magnetic stripes on the back, Benardo said that's not the case. "Today an RFID card is nearly impossible to breach because the chip in it creates an encrypted signal that is extremely difficult to hack or compromise," he said. "If

## What To Know If Criminals Disrupt A Bank's Internet Services

You may have seen recent news reports about financial institutions' Websites and online banking services being temporarily disrupted due to cyberattacks from a variety of sources. These assaults, generally referred to as denial-of-service attacks, occur when criminals deliberately inundate computers that handle Internet traffic (also called Web servers) with so many requests at the same time that they cause a financial institution's site to "crash" for anywhere from a few minutes to several days.

"The motive behind most denial-of-service attacks to date has been to damage the targeted institution's reputation by keeping customers from accessing its Website or online banking system and causing people to believe something is seriously wrong with the bank," said Michael Benardo, manager of the FDIC's Cyber Fraud and Financial Crimes Section. "In reality, denial-of-service attacks to date have done little more than temporarily inconvenience Internet banking customers. The financial industry has responded well to these attacks, and customer information and accounts have remained secure." Benardo also noted that federal banking regulators review how individual institutions carry out security measures and manage denial-of-service incidents. Part of that is making sure every bank has contingency plans for how to handle a prolonged service interruption.

Also, the regulators require that banks issue notices if there has been unauthorized access to sensitive data, including Social Security numbers (SSN), account numbers, passwords and other information that could result in "substantial harm or inconvenience to any customer." Benardo added that "if you receive one of these notices, your financial institution will explain what you should do to protect yourself." If you have questions or concerns about cyberattacks, speak with a bank representative.

you have questions or concerns about a payment card that is RFID-enabled, ask your bank about the precautions it takes to safeguard your card information."

**Closely monitor your bank statements and credit card bills.** "Look at your account statements as soon as they arrive in your mailbox or electronic inbox and report a discrepancy or anything suspicious, such as an unauthorized withdrawal," advised FDIC attorney Richard M. Schwartz. "While federal and state laws limit your losses if you're a victim of fraud or theft, your protections may be stronger the quicker you report the problem." These days, it's also easy to monitor your accounts using online banking or even your mobile phone.

Also, don't assume that a small unauthorized transaction isn't worth reporting to your bank. Some thieves are making low-dollar withdrawals or charges in hopes those will go unnoticed by the account holders. In one recent example, a federal court temporarily halted an operation that allegedly debited hundreds of thousands of consumers' bank accounts and billed their credit cards for more than $25 million—in small charges—without their consent.

And, contact your institution if your bank statement or credit card bill doesn't arrive when you normally expect it because that could be a sign that an identity thief has stolen your mail and/or account information to commit fraud in your name. Periodically review your credit reports for warning signs of fraudulent activity. Credit reports, which are prepared by companies called credit bureaus (or consumer reporting agencies), summarize a consumer's history of paying debts and other bills. But if a credit report shows a credit card, loan or lease you never signed up for, this could indicate you are a victim of ID theft. You are entitled to at least one free credit report every 12 months from each of the nation's three major credit bureaus. To maximize your protection against fraud, some experts suggest spreading out your requests throughout the year, such as by getting one free report every four months instead of all three at the same time. To request your free report, go to www.AnnualCreditReport.com or call toll-free 1-877-322-8228.

For additional information on how to protect your credit or debit card from fraud, start with consumer information about identity theft on the Federal Trade Commission Website. Resources from other federal agencies can also be found at www.mymoney.gov.

# Chapter 22
# Pros And Cons Of Different Savings Options

Once you eliminate piggy banks, mattresses, and coffee cans buried in the backyard, any place you choose to save your money is really an investment. And smart investors know it's important to do your homework, consider all your options, and make an informed decision before turning your money over to anyone to manage for you. The options for saving money are almost limitless, but learning a little about some of the more common ones will pay off in the long run.

> One of the biggest factors affecting your decision about where to save or invest is your degree of risk-tolerance. If you're not comfortable risking your initial deposit or investment, there are plenty of safe or very safe places to save your money. And if you think you can tolerate a lot of risk, it's especially important for you to work with a qualified adviser before make a decision.

## Savings Accounts

The basic savings account at the local bank is the type of account you're already familiar with. Your parents might have started one for you when you were young, or maybe you opened your own account with gift money or the salary earned from part-time jobs.

### Pros

- **They're easy to open.** It usually takes just a few minutes, and you can open an account in person at a bank, over the phone, or even online.

---

"Pros And Cons Of Different Savings Options," © 2017 Omnigraphics.

- **Interest.** While money stashed in a drawer just sits there, a bank will pay you to deposit funds in a savings account. And the interest accrued gets added to your total, and then it earns more interest, which is called compounding.

- **Security.** Funds deposited in a bank affiliated with the Federal Deposit Insurance Corporation (FDIC), which is almost all of them, are insured up to $250,000. That makes banks the safest places to keep your money.

- **Availability.** With automated teller machines (ATMs), you have access to at least some of your money 24 hours per day, 365 days per year. There are limits on ATM withdrawals, but if you go into the bank you can take out all your funds at any time.

## Cons

- **Low interest rates.** Savings accounts generally pay the lowest rate of interest you can get. The amounts vary, though, so it pays to shop around before deciding on a bank. Don't forget to check credit unions and online banks, which tend to pay higher rates.

- **There may be fees.** Many banks charge a monthly fee to manage your account if you don't keep a minimum balance in it. But there are a lot of no-fee accounts available, so be sure to do your research.

- **There are no tax advantages.** There are places you can put your money that offer a variety of tax benefits, but bank savings accounts are not among them. If you earn enough interest on your savings you'll be required to pay tax on the profit.

- **Availability.** Yes, this can be a disadvantage, too. With money in a savings account, you might be tempted to make withdrawals too easily, thus defeating your long-term saving goals.

# Checking Accounts

At one time checking accounts were just for writing paper checks to pay bills and buy stuff. But now they've become much more.

## Pros

- **Convenience.** When you open a checking account, you have access to online and mobile-phone banking and bill-paying. You also get a debit card that allows you to withdraw money from the account at an ATM or make purchases at stores, restaurants, or online shops.

- **No need to carry cash.** Many places will take paper checks, and almost everyone will let you use a debit card to make purchases. This is both a convenience and a safety feature.

- **Help managing your finances.** With a checking account, you quickly learn that you need to keep track of your spending. That way you can deduct purchases from your available balance and always know how much is in your account.

- **Security.** As with savings accounts, checking accounts at member banks are insured by the FDIC, so you're protected against loss.

- **Direct deposit.** Many employers will deposit your paycheck directly into your bank account, saving you the trouble of cashing a paper check. If you have money deposited directly into your checking account, you can then pay expenses from the same account.

## Cons

- **Most don't pay interest.** Some checking accounts pay interest if you maintain a fairly high balance, but in most cases the bank is getting free use of your money in exchange for convenience.

- **There may be fees.** Not only do most banks not pay interest on checking accounts, but some charge you a monthly fee if you don't maintain a minimum balance. There could also be hefty overdraft fees if you spend more from the account than you actually have in the bank. And there are almost always fees when you use an ATM that's not affiliated with your own bank.

- **Security.** Checks, and especially debit cards, make checking accounts less secure than savings accounts. If someone gets hold of your checks or debit-card information, they may be able to drain the money from your account. If this happens, you'll likely get your money back, but it may take a while, and you won't have access to it in the meantime.

# High-Yield Reward Checking Accounts

High-yield reward checking accounts pay higher rates than traditional interest-paying checking accounts, and they offer other perks as well, but they have more requirements, too.

## Pros

- **Higher interest rates.** High-yield means these accounts offer rates of interest beyond the typical checking or savings account, even online accounts. The rates vary, of course, so it's important to shop for the best terms you can get.

165

- **Wide selection.** High-yield reward checking accounts have become very popular, with hundreds of banks making them available to customers. So it's relatively easy to find several near you and make comparisons between terms.

- **No fees.** Most banks don't charge a monthly maintenance fee for these types of accounts. Some do, however, so be careful.

- **Rewards.** There are a variety of perks that can come with these accounts, including reward points for debit-card use, refunds of fees charged for using ATMs at other banks, and better interest rates on savings accounts at the same bank.

## Cons

- **Minimum balance requirements.** With most high-yield reward checking accounts you're required to keep a certain amount of money in the account each month. This amount can vary a lot, so do your research before making a commitment.

- **Monthly debit card use requirements.** Most reward checking accounts require you to make at least 10 debit card purchases every month. If you don't, your interest rate drops for the month, and you may not receive other benefits.

- **Small purchases may be flagged.** Most banks don't have a minimum dollar amount per purchase to count toward the debit card use requirement, but some do. In those cases, if you make too many small purchases, the bank might eliminate some benefits or eventually even close the account.

- **The interest rate may top out.** Most high-yield checking accounts have a maximum amount on which the bank will pay the high rate of interest (usually $25,000). Any amount above that will earn at the bank's normal interest rate.

# Certificates Of Deposit

A certificate of deposit (CD) is similar to a savings account in some ways. For example, most people typically get them from a bank where they're already doing business. But there are some important distinctions.

## Pros

- **Higher interest.** Banks adjust savings account interest rates periodically to reflect the state of the economy, so the interest you're paid on your savings account can vary from time to time. With a CD, interest is fixed at a predictable rate for the term of the certificate. In addition, the interest rate on a CD is usually higher than that on a savings account, depending on how long you agree to let the bank keep your money.

- **Security.** As with savings and checking accounts, funds put into a CD at a member bank are insured by the FDIC.

- **Good way to start investing.** CDs provide a great first step into the world of investing. Since they have a fixed interest rate and they're insured, they carry virtually no risk, unlike stocks or bonds.

- **Easy to get.** Because CDs can be purchased in just a few minutes from virtually any bank, you don't need a financial adviser or other expert to guide you through the process. But, of course, you should comparison shop to be sure you're getting the best terms.

## Cons

- **Poor access to funds.** The essence of a CD is that you agree to let the bank keep your money for a set period of time, ranging from a few months to several years. You can withdraw funds during that period, but you'll pay a cash penalty to do so.

- **Varying terms.** In order to get the best interest rate on a CD, you need to leave your money in the bank for a greater length of time, or invest a larger amount of money, or both. CDs terms vary widely so, again, make sure to do your research.

- **Inflation risk.** One advantage of CDs is their predictable, fixed interest rate. But if there's an increase in inflation during the life of your CD, you could find yourself with less buying power than you started with.

- **Low interest rates.** While CDs generally pay better interest rates than a savings account, those rates probably won't equal what you could make with other investments, such as stocks. That's the price you pay for a guaranteed return and FDIC insurance.

---

Before turning over your money to an investment professional, the U.S. Securities and Exchange Commission suggests you ask these questions:

What training and experience do you have? How long have you been in business?

What is your investment philosophy? Do you take a lot of risks or are you more concerned about the safety of my money?

---

Describe your typical client. Can you provide me with references, the names of people who have invested with you for a long time?

How do you get paid? By commission? Based on a percentage of assets you manage? Another method?

Do you get paid more for selling your own firm's products?

How much will it cost me in total to do business with you?

*(Source: "Saving And Investing For Students," U.S. Securities and Exchange Commission (SEC).)*

# U.S. Treasury Bonds And Notes

When you buy government notes and bonds, you're loaning money to the federal government. In return, you receive regular interest payments, and when the bond matures you get your initial investment back. Next to CDs, these financial instruments are considered some of the easiest and safest ways to begin investing your money.

## Pros

- **Security.** U.S. Treasury bonds and notes are backed by the U.S. government, which makes them one of the safest and most popular investments worldwide. There are no guarantees, but the full authority of government agencies helps ensure the security of your funds.

- **Favorable terms.** When it comes to extremely low-risk investments, these instruments offer some of the best terms available. Time commitments range from two to 30 years, profit increase as the length goes up, and U.S. Treasury investments pay higher and more frequent dividends than most other safe investments.

- **Liquidity.** There's almost always a strong market for Treasury instruments, making it easy to buy and sell them if you need the money before the bond matures.

- **Tax benefits.** Interest earned on U.S. Treasury bonds and notes is often exempt from state and local taxes. Before investing, find out if this is the case where you live.

## Cons

- **Relatively low interest rates.** Because of their low risk, U.S. Treasury bonds and notes don't generally pay as much as some higher-risk investments, such as corporate bonds.

- **Time commitments.** The investments that offer the best interest rates are generally the ones that require you to part with your money for the longest period of time. For example, notes usually mature in two to seven years, and bonds in ten years and up. You need to make sure the investment you choose matches your preferred timeframe.

- **Interest rate risk.** Government bonds and notes lose value when interest rates and inflation rise. They're not good investments for short-term investors during periods when interest rates are low, and they're not good for those hoping for a high rate of return in a short time.

- **Default risk.** One reason government investments are low risk is that the U.S. Treasury can print more currency to repay debt. But there's always the slight chance that Congress won't approve the expenditure, which could result in default.

# Municipal Bonds

An investment in municipal bonds is a loan to state or local governments, usually for projects like the construction of a hospital, road, bridge, or school. In practice, they work similarly to federal government bonds.

## Pros

- **Security.** Although they're not as safe as U.S. Treasury bonds, municipal bonds are still considered a low-risk investment, since they're backed by government agencies.

- **Favorable terms.** Municipal bonds tend to pay a bit less interest than federal government bonds, but, depending on the time to maturity, they still usually beat bank rates. There are many, many kinds of municipal bonds, so compare terms carefully to get the best deal.

- **Liquidity.** Municipal bonds are traded vigorously. That means that if you need cash for emergency, you can usually get it quickly without incurring a penalty for selling before maturity.

- **Tax benefits.** Municipal bonds are exempt from federal taxes. But some states and municipalities exempt these bonds from their taxes, as well, if you live in that jurisdiction and invest in local projects.

## Cons

- **Relatively low interest rates.** Just as with federal bonds, you pay for the low risk of municipal bonds with a lower rate of return than many other investments. In some cases, the interest on the bond may not even keep up with inflation.

- **Interest rate risk.** When interest rates go up, your current municipal bond holdings lose value. This isn't much of an issue if you plan to hold the bonds to maturity, but if you need to cash out early, you could lose money.

- **Call risk.** A call occurs when the bond issuer chooses to repay the principal on outstanding bonds early. Although not all municipal bonds have a call provision, if that does happen, you'll get back the money you invested, but you won't get the interest you expected if the bond had reached maturity.

- **Default risk.** Unlike the federal government, states and municipalities can't release more money to pay their debts, so the risk of default with a municipal bond is greater than with a federal bond. So even though municipal bonds have an extremely low default rate, it's not impossible.

# Corporate Bonds

Companies usually issue corporate bonds to raise money for various business activities, such as expansion, new facilities, and other kinds of growth or improvement. Just like with other types of bonds, investors receive regular interest payments and get back their principal when the bond matures.

## Pros

- **Security.** Although corporate bonds are not generally as secure as those issued by a government, they are considered a safer, less volatile way to invest in a company than buying shares of that firm's stock. In addition, bond-holders usually rank higher as creditors than stockholders, which means if the company should default, you have a better chance of getting your money back.

- **Stability.** Corporate bonds are generally less susceptible to inflation and interest rate increases than government bonds, primarily due to their shorter timeframes.

- **Favorable terms.** Corporate bonds almost always pay interest at a higher rate than U.S. government or municipal bonds. Interest rates and other terms vary even more widely than other kinds of bonds, so shop wisely.

- **Liquidity.** Many corporate bonds are traded actively, so investors can usually buy and sell them easily, especially if the company is a known quantity. By doing so, it's possible for you to "buy low and sell high," making a nice profit.

## Cons

- **Default risk.** This is the primary reason corporate bonds pay higher interest rates than government bonds. There's a greater chance that a business will fail completely or default on a bond than a government entity. Large, well-known companies don't default on bonds as much as small companies or startups, but it's not unheard of.

- **Event risk.** The ability of a company to pay investors is dependent on the firm generating cash. If the company is unable to earn money, this may have an impact on its ability to both pay interest and repay the principal to bondholders.

- **Interest rate risk.** Although corporate bonds are less vulnerable to interest rate fluctuations than government bonds, they're not impervious. Rising interest rates can affect the company's ability to generate cash flow, which is one kind of event that might reduce its ability to repay investors. High interest rates can also make it difficult to sell a corporate bond, and result in a loss, if you need cash in an emergency.

- **Risk of economic downturn.** If the economy takes a general downturn, corporate bonds are much more vulnerable than government bonds. A poor economy can have disastrous results for individual corporations and entire industries, and without the government guarantees, bond-holders could lose their investments.

# Money Market Funds

A money market fund is a type of mutual fund—a group of investors whose money is pooled together and managed by an expert—that is designed to invest in short-term government bonds, and other relatively safe, fixed-income cash-oriented properties.

## Pros

- **Security.** Although they're not guaranteed, money market funds are considered low-risk investments. Their goal is to pay investors a modest rate of interest while retaining the value of the initial investment.

- **Stability.** When the stock market is volatile, money market funds can be a great place to invest. Because they pool money into low-risk vehicles like CDs and government bonds, they tend to be less susceptible to stock and interest fluctuations.

- **Liquidity.** Because money market funds invest in reliable known quantities, they are generally in very high demand on the open market, making it easy for investors to sell if they need some ready cash.

- **Return on investment.** Money market funds, while being relatively secure and stable, pay a better return than interest on a savings account. And this can make them a good choice for new investors.

## Cons

- **Investment risk.** While money market funds are considered low-risk, they're not no-risk. When you invest in such a fund, there are no guarantees and most of them are not insured by the FDIC.

- **Low rate of return.** True, money market funds can usually beat bank interest rates, but they still lag behind some other types of investments. For example, common stocks might return 8 to10 percent over time, while a money market fund will typically yield about 2 or 3 percent.

- **Returns can be at risk.** Although money market funds tend to pool money into safe investments, they do occasionally take some risks in order to maximize returns for investors. This can lead to losses. In the long run, these are usually offset by gains, but there could be short-term consequences for investors.

## References

1. "The Basics of Municipal Bonds," Investopedia.com, January 12, 2017.

2. Bovaird, Charles. "Corporate Bonds: Advantages and Disadvantages," Investopedia.com, August 22, 2016.

3. Brown, Jeff. "The Pros and Cons of Municipal Bonds," USnews.com, August 15, 2016.

4. Coleman, Hank. "Benefits and Drawbacks of Money Market Funds," Moneyqanda.com, n.d.

5. Curtis, Glenn. "The Pros And Cons of Money Market Funds," Investopedia.com, n.d.

6. Duff, Victoria. "Advantages and Disadvantages of U.S. Treasury Notes and Bonds," Thefinancebase.com, n.d.

7. Gaille, Brandon. "10 Pros and Cons of Corporate Bonds," Brandongaille.com, June 7, 2016.

8. Guina, Ryan. "Pros and Cons of Rewards Checking Accounts," Cashmoneylife.com, n.d.

9. Morley, Miranda. "Advantages and Disadvantages of Savings and Checking Accounts," Synonym.com, n.d.

10. "Pros and Cons of Certificates of Deposit," Ally.com, September 2016.

11. "Savings Account Pros and Cons," Ally.com, June 2014.

12. Tumin, Ken. "10 Pros and Cons of High-Yield Reward Checking Accounts," Depositaccounts.com, n.d.

13. VanBaren, Jennifer. "Checking Account Pros & Cons," Sapling.com, May 18, 2010.

14. "What Are the Advantages and Disadvantages of U.S. Treasury Bonds and Notes?" Fool.com, n.d.

# Chapter 23

# Account Choices To Consider For Saving Money

A bank account provides a safe place to put your money; can be less costly, over the long term, than using a check casher or other non-bank service; and can help you save money. When it comes to choosing an account, there are many options, such as:

- **Savings:** This is a deposit account that earns interest known as an annual percentage rate or APR.

- **Checking:** These accounts allow you to deposit money, withdraw money, and write checks to pay for purchases and bills. Most banks will also provide a debit or ATM card and a checkbook to allow you to withdraw cash, transfer funds between accounts, and make deposits at your bank's ATM machines.

- **Certificate of deposit (CD):** This is a deposit-only account that offers a guaranteed interest rate for a specified term usually ranging from 6 months to 5 years—if you promise not to touch the money for the agreed upon term. Most banks charge a penalty for early withdrawal.

- **Money market:** These are deposit accounts that pay interest. Money market accounts provide a higher interest rate than traditional savings accounts and usually come with high minimum balance requirements.

---

About This Chapter: Text in this chapter begins with the excerpts from "Choose A Bank Account," USA.gov, U.S. General Service Administration (GSA), September 28, 2012; Text under the heading "Choosing And Using The Right Bank Account" is excerpted from "Choosing And Using The Right Bank Account," Federal Deposit Insurance Corporation (FDIC), November 8, 2016; Text under the heading "Selecting A Lower-Risk Account" is excerpted from "Consumer Guide To Selecting A Lower-Risk Account," Consumer Financial Protection Bureau (CFPB), February 3, 2016.

Each has different rules and benefits that fit different needs. The bank or credit union must provide you with the account terms and conditions when you open your account.

# Important Things To Consider

When choosing an account that is right for you, think about these factors:

- **Minimum deposit requirements:** Do you have to keep a minimum dollar amount in your account to earn interest or avoid account maintenance fees?

- **Limits on withdrawals:** Can you take money out whenever you want? Are there any penalties for doing so?

- **Interest:** Can you earn interest on your accounts? How frequently is it paid (monthly, quarterly)? Check with banks or credit unions to compare their current published rates.

- **Online bill pay:** Can you pay your bills directly from your bank or credit union's website?

- **Deposit insurance:** Make sure that the bank is a member of the Federal Deposit Insurance Corporation (FDIC) or that a credit union is insured by the National Credit Union Share Insurance Fund (NCUSIF).

- **Mobile banking:** Can you access your accounts and make deposits from your mobile phone or tablet? Does the bank charge fees for this access?

- **Convenience:** Are there branches or ATMs close to where you work and live? Can you bank by phone or Internet?

If you are considering a checking account or another type of account with check-writing privileges, add these items to your list of things to think about:

- **Number of checks:** Is there a maximum number of checks you can write per month without incurring a charge?

- **Check fees:** Is there a monthly fee for the account or a charge for each check you write?

- **Holds on checks:** Is there a waiting period for checks to clear before you can withdraw money from your account?

- **Overdraft protection:** Many banks and credit unions offer overdraft protection, but you must opt-in to get the service. This prevents you from cashing a check, withdrawing money, or using your debit card for an amount greater than the amount of money in your checking account. Banks can't impose overdraft fees if you haven't opted in.

- **Debit card fees:** Are there fees for using your debit card?

- **Account fees:** Does the bank charge fees on your checking or savings accounts to cover things like maintenance, withdrawals, or minimum balance rules?

# Choosing And Using The Right Bank Account

When managing your money, the right tools can make all the difference. That's why it helps to start by opening a bank account that best fits your lifestyle and your financial goals. Federal Deposit Insurance Corporation (FDIC) provides some simple pointers to help you choose wisely and streamline how you manage your checking and savings accounts.

## Before You Open An Account

Consider what you need or want from a bank account. Think about your day-to-day life and how you like to handle your money. For example: Do you receive a fixed paycheck or pension on a regular basis or does the amount and frequency of your income vary? Do you prefer to pay for purchases using cash, credit cards, debit cards, paper checks or online bill-paying services? Is one of your personal financial goals to set aside money regularly for savings? Are you concerned about possible overdrafts and the fees you might incur as a result? The answers to questions like these will help you make an informed decision about opening a bank account that works for you.

Comparison shop. There are many types of bank products and services, and the fees, interest rates and special promotional offers will vary from institution to institution. Some banks will charge fees for using another bank's automated teller machines (ATMs), while others won't charge fees and they may even reimburse customers for fees (up to a certain dollar amount) charged by the ATM owner. So if you often withdraw cash from ATMs, you may want to look closely at how ATM fees are handled before signing up.

Also, some bank accounts may have minimum balance requirements or monthly maintenance fees. Many banks will reduce or even eliminate these requirements if you have your paycheck directly deposited or you have a minimum number of electronic transactions.

Read the agreement from the bank that describes the account's terms and conditions before making a final decision. Federal rules require certain information to be disclosed to consumers before opening an account. You can review a bank's account agreements online or by stopping by a branch. Looking at a legal document may appear intimidating or time-consuming, but many banks offer simplified disclosures and knowing how the account works is worth it to ensure that you understand all aspects of the account, including the potential fees and when they may be assessed. That's the best way to avoid surprises.

Never give out or confirm financial or other sensitive information, including your bank account, credit card, or Social Security number, unless you know who you're dealing with. Scam artists, like fake debt collectors, can use your information to commit identity theft—charging your existing credit cards, opening new credit card, checking, or savings accounts, writing fraudulent checks, or taking out loans in your name. If you get a call about a debt that may be legitimate—but you think the collector may not be—contact the company you owe money to about the calls.

*(Source: "Government Imposter Scams," Federal Trade Commission (FTC).)*

## Managing An Account

Follow your transactions and balance your accounts. Some consumers use pen and paper, a check register, a computer spreadsheet, a website or an app to ensure that they stay on top of what is happening in their accounts. Whichever method you choose, track every transaction—be it a deposit, check, ATM transaction, debit card transaction or online bill payment—to handle your money effectively and avoid spending more than you're comfortable with. You also can monitor your transactions using online services provided by your bank. In addition, many banks offer alerts via email or text to notify customers when their account balance drops below a specified level or when a check has cleared.

Understand how to avoid overdraft fees for withdrawing more than what is in your account. Opening a checking account has long been the way customers establish a relationship with a financial institution. However, a traditional checking account may not be for everyone and can quickly become harmful to your finances if you're not careful about incurring fees, including overdraft fees.

Today, many financial institutions offer a "checkless" checking account. These types of accounts generally do not come with the ability to write paper checks, but enable customers to pay bills, make purchases and otherwise withdraw money electronically by banking online or using debit cards or mobile apps.

Checkless accounts may be a great option for consumers who prefer to use their computer, smartphone or other mobile device for banking. Generally, these accounts do not come with the ability to be overdrawn, so users will not be subject to the high overdraft or insufficient funds fees that come with many traditional checking accounts.

For those who prefer typical checking accounts, a careful decision should be made regarding whether or not to "opt in" (agree) to overdraft coverage. Most banks offer overdraft programs that allow customers to make ATM withdrawals or perform certain debit card transactions that exceed the customer's available balance. These overdraft transactions trigger fees that may reach $35 or more per overdrafted item, but banks are only allowed to assess fees for paying an ATM or one-time debit card transaction if the customer has opted in to overdraft coverage.

If you choose not to opt in, be aware that ATM and one-time debit card transactions that go over the amount of funds in your account will be declined.

"Think carefully before deciding to opt into this kind of fee-based overdraft program," said Heather St. Germain, a senior consumer affairs specialist at the FDIC. "You could be charged several overdraft fees in a single day because most banks will assess a separate fee for each transaction that exceeds your account balance, so the costs can add up quickly."

Another option is to ask your bank if you can link your savings account to your checking account to automatically transfer funds to cover transactions when you don't have enough money in your checking account. A bank may charge a fee for this automatic transfer service, but the fee is typically smaller than an overdraft fee. Find out how the fees compare by reviewing the bank's account agreement or fee schedule. These documents are usually available online or can be picked up at a local bank branch.

The easiest way to avoid overdraft charges is to keep a close eye on your account balance and on how much you plan to spend. Also, make sure you have enough in the account to cover any automatic (typically monthly) payments you have set up.

Direct deposit your pay and benefit checks. Direct deposit allows your money to be safely and securely electronically deposited into your bank account. With this feature you don't have to worry about finding time to make deposits yourself. Using the service may also help you with savings, as you can set up your direct deposit to have a certain amount from each check automatically sent to your savings account.

In addition, some banks offer incentives if you sign up for direct deposit, such as increasing the account's interest rate or waiving certain minimum balance requirements and fees.

Earn more interest, but be mindful of any conditions. If you have money in your checking account that you do not expect to use right away, moving it to a savings account or a certificate of deposit (for a set period of time) can be a good personal-finance strategy for building short-term savings and earning more interest. But before switching accounts, find out if there may be restrictions or requirements.

"Be aware of limitations on how soon you can withdraw funds from a certificate of deposit without paying a penalty, and restrictions on the number of withdrawals during a month from a savings account," said Luke W. Reynolds, chief of the FDIC's Outreach and Program Development Section. "Your institution may also offer a different checking account product that pays a higher rate of interest, but you might need to meet certain requirements, such as having a set number of debit card withdrawals post to your statement during the month. Be sure you are likely to meet any requirements based on how you normally handle your finances."

Help guard your accounts from theft and fraud. Check your accounts regularly for suspicious transactions. Protect your passwords and PINs. Also avoid clicking on links or responding to emails requesting personal information such as Social Security and bank account numbers, no matter how legitimate they may look. That's because criminals create fictitious websites and emails claiming to be from government agencies or trusted companies. In general, legitimate companies will never contact you unprompted requesting sensitive information. Contact your bank to learn more about the security features it offers or tips it suggests for customers.

The bottom line: Having a bank account brings important benefits, including access to safe and affordable financial services in good times and bad. If you choose well and manage wisely, your banking relationship can evolve and grow as you do—affording you access to more options for credit, savings and investment when you are ready and when you need them.

## Selecting A Lower-Risk Account

Finding and choosing a checking or prepaid account that puts you in control. It's important to shop around to find financial products and services that meet your needs. If you are new to banking, need to stay within a fixed budget, or simply want to limit costly or unexpected fees, it may be especially important to find an account that gives you the control you need and helps prevent you from overspending or racking up fees. Banks and credit unions provide safe places to keep your money. Transaction account products, such as checking accounts and prepaid accounts, allow you to store money, make payments and purchases, and send money to others. Prepaid accounts are also available through a number of non-bank providers as well. However, many of these products come with fees or features that can make them expensive. This can be risky if you don't monitor your payments and account balance regularly or anticipate delays in the time it takes to make the funds available from your deposits. Also, it can be difficult to successfully manage your account and keep costs under control if you are unable to keep enough money in your account. Before you select a checking or prepaid account, you should understand the features you need to conduct your day-to-day financial transactions, and how much you will pay for those features.

It's important to understand overdraft and the risks you may be taking on. Overdrafts occur when the total of your payments and withdrawals exceed your account balance. Your bank or credit union will usually charge you a fee, often as high as $35 or more, each time you overdraw your account. The financial institution will automatically take out of your account both the fee and the amount that you overdrafted when your next deposit arrives. Sometimes your bank or credit union will charge an additional fee if your account balance stays negative for a certain number of days.

If you can't pay the overdraft, there could be negative repercussions. You could lose your account. You could also be reported to a checking account reporting company, and the negative information could remain on your report for up to seven years under the federal Fair Credit Reporting Act. This means that you may have a difficult time opening a new bank account for several years after such an event. This is because many banks and credit unions use information from these reporting companies—and specifically, incidents of unpaid balances and account closures—to evaluate new account applicants.

Here are some steps you can take to identify and select a checking account that works for you:

## Know Your Options

Know what products are offered. A number of banks and credit unions today offer products, such as some checking accounts or prepaid accounts, that do not authorize you to spend money beyond what you have in your account. Such products are designed to help consumers manage their spending and avoid overdrafts. (Prepaid accounts are available through a number of non-bank providers as well.) These lower-risk products can help you manage your spending and avoid overdrafts and overdraft fees. This will reduce the likelihood that you will lose your account privileges because of unpaid overdrafts.

Some banks may not offer these lower-risk products, or may not market them prominently. Therefore, it's important to shop around. Ask whether the bank or credit union offers an account designed to help you spend only the money that you have and to minimize fees.

Don't be discouraged if a bank or credit union denies you for an account. If you've have trouble managing an account in the past, look for an account that is designed to help you manage spending and avoid overdrafting. Some banks may be more likely to offer you a product that is considered less risky for both the consumer and the bank, such as a checkless checking account or a prepaid account. These products may be good options for you to consider if you have had trouble with a prior checking account, have negative information on your credit or checking account report, or if you want to avoid the risk of spending more than you have in your account check around at multiple banks and credit unions.

Know what product features you need and any tradeoffs. Some products that are designed to help you manage spending and avoid overdrawing your account may also have limited features, such as no check-writing and no online bill payment capabilities. Decide which features are most important to you. You may pay a monthly fee for these products, although you can anticipate and budget for those fees.

Product design and pricing for both checking accounts and prepaid accounts can vary greatly between providers, so it's important to shop around and to ask questions about both features and price.

## Ask Questions

There are a number of important considerations when selecting an account, which will depend on your particular needs and financial situation. Below is a list of suggested questions to ask when considering a lower-risk account. These are intended to help you better understand your account choices and to help you decide between products or product features:

1. Consider how important it is that you have an account that won't allow you to spend more than what you have. You might consider the following questions:

   - Have I overdrawn an account in the past?

   - Have I had an account closed in the past?

   - Is my income sometimes inconsistent and unpredictable?

   - Can I maintain a sufficient balance in my account?

   - Do I want to avoid unplanned overdrafts or fees?

2. Ask questions about whether the product offered exposes you to the risk of overdrawing your account:

   - How does the account help me avoid overdrawing my account?

   - Can I transfer funds (for example, by linking an account to savings) to avoid or reduce the costs of overdrafts?

3. Consider the costs associated with maintaining the account, including:

   - What are the fees? How much would it cost for:

   - monthly account maintenance,

   - going below the minimum balance,

   - making purchases,

   - account inactivity,

   - making a deposit,

- overdrafting, or

- having a check or bill payment returned for insufficient funds?

A fee that you pay every month may still be cheaper in the long run than piling up overdraft fees.

- Can I waive the monthly fee with direct deposit or another way?

- What types of ATM fees can I expect and are there ways to reduce these? Where can I use an ATM without a fee?

4. Consider the types of features you need and whether the product you are considering meets these needs.

- Do I need to pay anyone, such as a contractor or landlord, via check?

- Do I need to pay any bills online?

- When will the funds I deposit become available?

---

**What is overdraft protection?**

Overdraft protection is an agreement with the bank or financial institution to cover overdrafts on a checking account. This service will typically involve a fee and be limited to a preset maximum amount.

**Can the bank pay a check if my account is overdrawn?**

National banks can either return the check unpaid or they can pay the check. If paying the check results in an overdraft, the bank can assess an insufficient funds fee against your account if disclosed in the account agreement.

**Can the bank charge a fee if my check overdraws my account?**

The bank can assess a fee if a check overdraws your account provided that the fee has been disclosed to you. Read your account agreement for information about the fees that may be assessed.

*(Source: "Answers About Overdraft Fees And Protection," Office Of The Comptroller Of The Currency (OCC), U.S. Department of the Treasury.)*

---

There are other questions to consider when selecting an account, including those pertaining to other product's features and requirements, protections for your money, and convenience and accessibility.

The Consumer Financial Protection Bureau (CFPB) has additional resources to help you decide what types of financial products and services are right for you.

# Chapter 24

# A Guide To Deposit Insurance Coverage

## What Is The Federal Deposit Insurance Corporation (FDIC)?

The FDIC—short for the Federal Deposit Insurance Corporation—is an independent agency of the United States government. The FDIC protects depositors of insured banks located in the United States against the loss of their deposits if an insured bank fails. Any person or entity can have FDIC insurance coverage in an insured bank. A person does not have to be a U.S. citizen or resident to have his or her deposits insured by the FDIC. FDIC insurance is backed by the full faith and credit of the United States government. Since the FDIC began operations in 1934, no depositor has ever lost a penny of FDIC-insured deposits.

## FDIC Coverage Basics

FDIC insurance covers depositors' accounts at each insured bank, dollar-for-dollar, including principal and any accrued interest through the date of the insured bank's closing, up to the insurance limit. FDIC insurance covers all types of deposits received at an insured bank but does not cover investments, even if they were purchased at an insured bank.

## What The FDIC Covers

- Checking accounts
- Negotiable Order of Withdrawal (NOW) accounts

---

About This Chapter: This chapter includes text excerpted from "Your Insured Deposits," Federal Deposit Insurance Corporation (FDIC), August 13, 2014.

- Savings accounts
- Money market deposit accounts (MMDA)
- Time deposits such as certificates of deposit (CDs)
- Cashier's checks, money orders, and other official items issued by a bank

## What The FDIC Does Not Cover

- Stock investments
- Bond investments
- Mutual funds
- Life insurance policies
- Annuities
- Municipal securities
- Safe deposit boxes or their contents
- U.S. Treasury bills, bonds or notes*

*These investments are backed by the full faith and credit of the U.S. government.

The standard deposit insurance amount is $250,000 per depositor, per insured bank, for each account ownership category.

The FDIC insures deposits that a person holds in one insured bank separately from any deposits that the person owns in another separately chartered insured bank. For example, if a person has a certificate of deposit at Bank A and has a certificate of deposit at Bank B, the amounts would each be insured separately up to $250,000. Funds deposited in separate branches of the same insured bank are not separately insured.

The FDIC provides separate insurance coverage for funds depositors may have in different categories of legal ownership. The FDIC refers to these different categories as "ownership categories." This means that a bank customer who has multiple accounts may qualify for more than $250,000 in insurance coverage if the customer's funds are deposited in different ownership categories and the requirements for each ownership category are met.

## Ownership Categories

This section describes the following FDIC ownership categories and the requirements a depositor must meet to qualify for insurance coverage above $250,000 at one insured bank.

- Single Accounts

- Certain Retirement Accounts

- Joint Accounts

- Revocable Trust Accounts

- Irrevocable Trust Accounts

- Employee Benefit Plan Accounts

- Corporation/Partnership/Unincorporated Association Accounts

- Government Accounts

## Single Accounts

- A single account is a deposit owned by one person. This ownership category includes:

- An account held in one person's name only, provided the owner has not designated any beneficiary(ies) who are entitled to receive the funds when the account owner dies

- An account established for one person by an agent, nominee, guardian, custodian, or conservator, including Uniform Transfers to Minors Act accounts, escrow accounts and brokered deposit accounts

- An account held in the name of a business that is a sole proprietorship (for example, a "Doing Business As" or DBA account)

- An account established for or representing a deceased person's funds—commonly known as a decedent's estate account

- An account that fails to qualify for separate coverage under another ownership category

If an account title identifies only one owner, but another person has the right to withdraw funds from the account (e.g., as Power of Attorney or custodian), the FDIC will insure the account as a single ownership account.

The FDIC adds together all single accounts owned by the same person at the same bank and insures the total up to $250,000.

## Certain Retirement Accounts

A retirement account is insured under the Certain Retirement Accounts ownership category only if the account qualifies as one of the following:

- Individual Retirement Account (IRA):
  - Traditional IRA
  - Roth IRA
  - Simplified Employee Pension (SEP) IRA
  - Savings Incentive Match Plans for Employees (SIMPLE) IRA
- Self-directed defined contribution plan account includes
  - Self-directed 401(k) plan
  - Self-directed SIMPLE IRA held in the form of a 401(k) plan
  - Self-directed defined contribution profit-sharing plan
- Self-directed Keogh plan account (or H.R.10 plan account) designed for self-employed individuals
- Section 457 deferred compensation plan account, such as an eligible deferred compensation plan provided by state and local governments regardless of whether the plan is self-directed

The FDIC adds together all retirement accounts listed above owned by the same person at the same insured bank and insures the total amount up to $250,000.

The FDIC defines the term "self-directed" to mean that plan participants have the right to direct how the money is invested, including the ability to direct that deposits be placed at an FDIC-insured bank. The FDIC will consider an account to be self-directed if the participant of the retirement plan has the right to choose a particular bank's deposit accounts as an investment option. For example:

- If a plan has deposit accounts at a particular insured bank as its default investment option, then the FDIC would deem the plan to be self-directed for insurance coverage purposes because, by inaction, the participant has directed the placement of such deposits
- If a plan consists only of a single employer/employee, and the employer establishes the plan with a single investment option of deposit accounts at a particular insured bank, then the plan would be considered self directed for insurance coverage purposes

The following types of deposits do not qualify as **Certain Retirement Accounts:**

- A plan for which the only investment vehicle is the deposit accounts of a particular bank, so that participants have no choice of investments

- Deposit accounts established under section 403(b) of the Internal Revenue Code (annuity contracts for certain employees of public schools, tax-exempt organizations and ministers), which are insured as Employee Benefit Plan accounts

- Defined-benefit plan deposits (plans for which the benefits are determined by an employee's compensation, years of service and age), which are insured as Employee Benefit Plan accounts

- Defined contribution plans that are not self-directed, which are insured as Employee Benefit Plan Accounts

- Coverdell Education Savings Accounts (formerly known as Education IRAs), Health Savings Accounts or Medical Savings Accounts

## Joint Accounts

A joint account is a deposit owned by two or more people. FDIC insurance covers joint accounts owned in any manner conforming to applicable state law, such as joint tenants with right of survivorship, tenants by the entirety and tenants in common. To qualify for insurance coverage under this ownership category, all of the following requirements must be met:

1. All co-owners must be living people. Legal entities such as corporations, trusts, estates or partnerships are not eligible for joint account coverage.

2. All co-owners must have equal rights to withdraw deposits from the account. For example, if one co-owner can withdraw deposits on his or her signature alone but the other co-owner can withdraw deposits only with the signature of both co-owners, the co-owners would not have equal withdrawal rights.

3. All co-owners must sign the deposit account signature card unless the account is a CD or is established by an agent, nominee, guardian, custodian, executor or conservator.

If all of these requirements are met, each co-owner's shares of every joint account that he or she owns at the same insured bank are added together and the total is insured up to $250,000.

The FDIC assumes that all co-owners' shares are equal unless the deposit account records state otherwise. The balance of a joint account can exceed $250,000 and still be fully insured. For example, if the same two co-owners jointly own both a $350,000 CD and a $150,000 savings account at the same insured bank, the two accounts would be added together and insured up to $500,000, providing up to $250,000 in insurance coverage for each co-owner. This example assumes that the two co-owners have no other joint accounts at the bank. There is no kinship requirement for joint account coverage. Any two or more people that co-own funds can qualify for insurance coverage in the joint account ownership category provided the requirements listed above are met. Insurance coverage of joint accounts is not increased by rearranging the owners' names or Social Security numbers or changing the styling of their names. Alternating the use of "or," "and" or "and/or" to separate the names of co-owners in a joint account title also does not affect the amount of insurance coverage provided.

## Revocable Trust Accounts

This section explains FDIC insurance coverage for revocable trust accounts, and is not intended as estate planning advice or guidance. Depositors should contact a legal or financial advisor for assistance with estate planning.

A revocable trust account is a deposit account owned by one or more people that identifies one or more beneficiaries who will receive the deposits upon the death of the owner(s). A revocable trust can be revoked, terminated or changed at any time, at the discretion of the owner(s). In this section, the term "owner" means the grantor, settlor, or trustor of the revocable trust. When calculating deposit insurance coverage, the designation of trustees, co-trustees and successor trustees is not relevant. They are administrators and are not considered in calculating deposit insurance coverage. This ownership category includes both informal and formal revocable trusts:

- **Informal revocable trusts**—often called payable on death, Totten trust, in trust for, or as trustee for accounts—are created when the account owner signs an agreement, usually part of the bank's signature card, directing the bank to transfer the funds in the account to one or more named beneficiaries upon the owner's death.

- **Formal revocable trusts**—known as living or family trusts— are written trusts created for estate planning purposes. The owner controls the deposits and other assets in the trust during his or her lifetime. The agreement establishes that the deposits are to be paid to one or more identified beneficiaries upon the owner's death. The trust generally becomes irrevocable upon the owner's death.

An owner who identifies a beneficiary as having a life estate interest in a formal revocable trust is entitled to insurance coverage up to $250,000 for that beneficiary. A life estate beneficiary is a beneficiary who has the right to receive income from the trust or to use trust deposits during the beneficiary's lifetime, where other beneficiaries receive the remaining trust deposits after the life estate beneficiary dies. For example: A husband is the sole owner of a living trust that gives his wife a life estate interest in the trust deposits, with the remainder going to their two children upon his wife's death. Maximum insurance coverage for this account is calculated as follows: $250,000 times three different beneficiaries equals $750,000.

## Irrevocable Trust Accounts

Irrevocable trust accounts are deposit accounts held in connection with a trust established by statute or a written trust agreement in which the owner (also referred to as a grantor, settlor or trustor) contributes deposits or other property to the trust and gives up all power to cancel or change the trust. An irrevocable trust also may come into existence upon the death of an owner of a revocable trust. A revocable trust account that becomes an irrevocable trust account due to the death of the trust owner may continue to be insured under the rules for revocable trusts. Therefore, in such cases, the rules in the revocable trust section may be used to determine coverage.

The interests of a beneficiary in all deposit accounts under an irrevocable trust established by the same settlor and held at the same insured bank are added together and insured up to $250,000, only if all of the following requirements are met:

- The trust must be valid under state law

- The insured bank's deposit account records must disclose the existence of the trust relationship

- The beneficiaries and their interests in the trust must be identifiable from the bank's deposit account records or from the trustee's records

- The amount of each beneficiary's interest must not be contingent as defined by FDIC regulations

If the owner retains an interest in the trust, then the amount of the owner's retained interest would be added to the owner's other single accounts, if any, at the same insured bank and the total insured up to $250,000.

For example, if the grantor of an irrevocable trust is still living, and the trust provides that trust assets can either be used by the grantor or by a trustee on behalf of the grantor, the grantor would be deemed to have a retained interest. Thus, this irrevocable trust account would not be insured under the irrevocable trust ownership category, but as a single ownership deposit of the grantor. The balance of the account would be added together with any other single ownership accounts the grantor has at the same bank, and the total would be insured up to $250,000.

## Employee Benefit Plan Accounts

An employee benefit plan account is a deposit of a pension plan, defined benefit plan or other employee benefit plan that is not self-directed. An account insured under this category must meet the definition of an employee benefit plan in section 3(3) of the Employee Retirement Income Security Act (ERISA) of 1974, with the exception of plans that qualify under the Certain Retirement Account ownership category. The FDIC does not insure the plan itself, but insures the deposit accounts owned by the plan.

Additional requirements for coverage:

- The investment and management decisions relating to the account must be controlled by a plan administrator (not self-directed by the participant).

- The plan administrator must maintain documentation supporting the plan and the beneficial interest of the participants

- The account must be properly titled as an employee benefit account with the bank

When all of these requirements are met, the FDIC will insure each participant's interest in the plan up to $250,000, separately from any accounts the employer or employee may have in the same FDIC insured institution. The FDIC often refers to this coverage as "pass-through coverage" because the insurance coverage passes through the employer (agent) that established the account to the employee who is considered the owner of the funds.

Even when plans qualify for pass-through coverage, insurance coverage cannot be determined simply by multiplying the number of participants by $250,000 because plan participants frequently have different interests in the plan.

To determine the maximum amount a plan can have on deposit in a single bank and remain fully insured, the plan administrator must first identify the participant who has the largest share of the plan assets, and calculate the participant's share as a percentage of overall plan assets. Then, the plan administrator must divide $250,000 by that percentage to arrive at the maximum fully insured amount that a plan can have on deposit at one bank.

## Corporations/Partnerships/Unincorporated Associations Accounts

Deposits owned by corporations, partnerships, and unincorporated associations, including for-profit and not-for-profit organizations, are insured under the same ownership category. Such deposits are insured separately from the personal deposits of the organization's owners, stockholders, partners or members. Unincorporated associations typically insured under this category include churches and other religious organizations, community and civic organizations and social clubs. To qualify for insurance coverage under this ownership category, a corporation, partnership or unincorporated association must be engaged in an "independent activity," meaning that the entity is operated primarily for some purpose other than to increase deposit insurance coverage.

All deposits owned by a corporation, partnership, or unincorporated association at the same bank are combined and insured up to $250,000.

## Fiduciary Accounts

### What are fiduciary accounts?

Fiduciary accounts are deposit accounts owned by one party but held in a fiduciary capacity by another party. Fiduciary relationships may include, but are not limited to, an agent, nominee, guardian, executor or custodian. Common fiduciary accounts include Uniform Transfers to Minors Act accounts, escrow accounts, Interest On Lawyer Trust Accounts and deposit accounts obtained through a broker.

### What are the FDIC requirements for fiduciary accounts?

The fiduciary nature of the account must be disclosed in the bank's deposit account records (e.g., "Jane Doe as Custodian for Susie Doe" or "First Real Estate Title Company, Client Escrow Account"). The name and ownership interest of each owner must be ascertainable from the deposit account records of the insured bank or from records maintained by the agent (or by some person or entity that has agreed to maintain records for the agent). Special disclosure rules apply to multi-tiered fiduciary relationships. If an agent pools the deposits of several owners into one account and the disclosure rules are satisfied, the deposits of each owner will be insured as that owner's deposits.

### How does the FDIC insure funds deposited by a fiduciary?

Funds deposited by a fiduciary on behalf of a person or entity (the owner) are insured as the deposits of the owner if the disclosure requirements for fiduciary accounts are met.

### Are funds deposited by a fiduciary insured separately from an owner's other deposit accounts at the same bank?

Funds deposited by a fiduciary on behalf of a person or entity (the owner) are added to any other deposits the owner holds in the same ownership category at the same bank, and insured up to the applicable limit.

**For Example:** A broker purchases a CD for $250,000 on a customer's behalf at ABC Bank. The customer already has a checking account in his or her name at ABC Bank for $15,000. The two accounts are added together and insured up to $250,000 in the single ownership account category. Since the customer's single ownership deposits total $265,000, $15,000 is uninsured.

Accounts owned by the same corporation, partnership, or unincorporated association but designated for different purposes are not separately insured. For example: If a corporation has both an operating account and a reserve account at the same bank, the FDIC would add both accounts together and insure the deposits up to $250,000. Similarly, if a corporation has divisions or units that are not separately incorporated, the FDIC would combine the deposit accounts of those divisions or units with any other deposit accounts of the corporation at the bank and the total would be insured up to $250,000. The number of partners, members, stockholders or account signatories established by a corporation, partnership or unincorporated association does not affect insurance coverage. For example: The FDIC insures deposits owned by a homeowners' association at one insured bank up to $250,000 in total, not $250,000 for each member of the association.

## Government Accounts

The category known as government accounts (also called Public Unit accounts) includes deposit accounts owned by:

- The United States, including federal agencies

- Any state, county, municipality (or a political subdivision of any state, county or municipality), the District of Columbia, Puerto Rico and other government possessions and territories

- An Indian tribe

Insurance coverage of a government account is unique in that the insurance coverage extends to the official custodian of the deposits belonging to the government or public unit, rather than to the government unit itself. Accounts held by an official custodian of a government unit will be insured as follows:

**In-state accounts:**

- Up to $250,000 for the combined amount of all time and savings accounts (including NOW accounts)

- Up to $250,000 for the combined amount of all interest bearing and noninterest-bearing demand deposit accounts (since July 21, 2011, banks have been allowed to pay interest on demand deposit accounts)

**Out-of-state accounts:**

- up to $250,000 for the combined amount of all deposit accounts

## Health Savings Accounts

**What is a Health Savings Account?**

A Health Savings Account (HSA) is an IRS qualified tax exempt trust or custodial deposit that is established with a qualified HSA trustee, such as an FDIC-insured bank, to pay or reimburse a depositor for certain medical expenses.

**How does the FDIC insure an HSA?**

An HSA, like any other deposit, is insured based on who owns the funds and whether beneficiaries have been named. If a depositor opens an HSA and names beneficiaries either in the HSA agreement or in the bank's records, the FDIC would insure the deposit under the Revocable Trust Account ownership category. If a depositor opens an HSA and does not name any beneficiaries, the FDIC would insure the deposit under the single account ownership category.

**How should an HSA be titled?**

The identification of a deposit as an HSA, such as "John Smith's HSA," is sufficient for titling the deposit to be eligible for single account or revocable trust account coverage, depending on whether eligible beneficiaries are named.

# Frequently Asked Questions

## What Happens To My Deposits If My Bank Fails?

In the unlikely event of a bank failure, the FDIC acts quickly to protect insured deposits by arranging a sale to a healthy bank, or by paying depositors directly for their deposit accounts to the insured limit.

- **Purchase and Assumption Transaction:** This is the preferred and most common method, under which a healthy bank assumes the insured deposits of the failed bank. Insured depositors of the failed bank immediately become depositors of the assuming bank and have access to their insured funds. The assuming bank may also purchase loans and other assets of the failed bank.

- It is important for account owners to note that their deposit contract was with the failed bank and is considered void upon the failure of the bank. The assuming institution has no obligation to maintain either the failed bank rates or terms of the account agreement. Depositors of a failed bank, however, do have the option of either setting up a new account with the acquiring institution or withdrawing some or all of their funds without penalty.

195

- **Deposit Payoff:** When there is no open bank acquirer for the deposits, the FDIC will pay the depositor directly by check up to the insured balance in each account. Such payments usually begin within a few days after the bank closing.

## What Happens To My Insurance Coverage If I Have Deposits At Two Insured Banks That Merge?

When two or more insured banks merge, deposits from the assumed bank are separately insured from deposits at the assuming bank for at least six months after the merger. This grace period gives a depositor the opportunity to restructure his or her accounts, if necessary. CDs from the assumed bank are separately insured until the earliest maturity date after the end of the six-month grace period. CDs that mature during the six-month period and are renewed for the same term and in the same dollar amount (either with or without accrued interest) continue to be separately insured until the first maturity date after the six-month period. If a CD matures during the six-month grace period and is renewed on any other basis, it would be separately insured only until the end of the six-month grace period.

Note that in situations of a bank failure where a depositor already has deposits at the acquiring bank, the six-month grace period described would also apply to their deposits.

## What Happens To Insurance Coverage After An Account Owner Dies?

The FDIC insures a deceased person's accounts as if the person were still alive for six months after the death of the account holder. During this grace period, the insurance coverage of the owner's accounts will not change unless the accounts are restructured by those authorized to do so. Also, the FDIC will not apply this grace period if it would result in less coverage.

## How Does The Death Of A Beneficiary Of An Informal Revocable Trust Affect Insurance Coverage?

There is no grace period if the beneficiary of an informal revocable trust (e.g., POD account) dies. In most cases, insurance coverage for the deposits would be reduced immediately. For example: A mother deposits $500,000 in a POD account at an insured bank with her two children named as the beneficiaries in the account records of the bank. While the owner and both beneficiaries are alive, the account is insured up to $500,000 ($250,000 times two beneficiaries = $500,000). If one beneficiary dies, insurance coverage for the mother's POD account is immediately reduced to $250,000 ($250,000 times one beneficiary = $250,000).

## How Does The Death Of A Beneficiary Of A Formal Revocable Trust Affect The Insurance Coverage?

Like informal revocable trusts, the six-month grace period does not apply to the death of a beneficiary named in a formal revocable trust account. However, the terms of the formal revocable trust may provide for a successor beneficiary or some other redistribution of the trust deposits. Depending on these terms, the insurance coverage may or may not change.

# Chapter 25

# What You Should Know About Certificates Of Deposit (CD)

## What Are Certificates Of Deposit (CD)?

A certificate of deposit (CD) is a savings account that holds a fixed amount of money for a fixed period of time, such as six months, one year, or five years, and in exchange, the issuing bank pays interest. When you cash in or redeem your CD, you receive the money you originally invested plus any interest. Certificates of deposit are considered to be one of the safest savings options. A CD bought through a federally insured bank is insured up to $250,000. The $250,000 insurance covers all accounts in your name at the same bank, not each CD or account you have at the bank.

As with all investments, there are benefits and risks associated with CDs. The disclosure statement should outline the interest rate on the CD and say if the rate is fixed or variable. It also should state when the bank pays interest on the CD, for example, monthly or semi-annually, and whether the interest payment will be made by check or by an electronic transfer of funds. The maturity date should be clearly stated, as should any penalties for the "early withdrawal" of the money in the CD. The risk with CDs is the risk that inflation will grow faster than your money, and lower your real returns over time.

## Broker Certificates Of Deposit

Although most CDs are purchased directly from banks, many brokerage firms and independent salespeople also offer CDs. These individuals and entities, known as "deposit brokers,"

---

About This Chapter: Text beginning with the heading "What Are Certificates Of Deposit?" is excerpted from "Certificates of Deposit (CDs)," Investor.gov, U.S. Securities and Exchange Commission (SEC), November 23, 2016; Text beginning with the heading "The ABCs Of Certificate Of Deposits" is excerpted from "High-Yield CDs: Protect Your Money By Checking The Fine Print," U.S. Securities and Exchange Commission (SEC), November 9, 2015.

can sometimes negotiate a higher rate of interest for a CD by promising to bring a certain amount of deposits to the institution. The deposit broker can then offer these "brokered CDs" to their customers.

Thoroughly check out the background of the issuer or deposit broker to ensure that the CD is from a reputable institution. Deposit brokers are not licensed or certified, and no state or federal agency approves them. Since anyone can claim to be a deposit broker, always check whether the deposit broker or the company he or she works for has a history of complaints or fraud. Many deposit brokers are affiliated with investment professionals. You can check out their disciplinary history using the SEC's and FINRA's online databases. Your state securities regulator may have additional information. To research the background of deposit brokers who are not affiliated with an investment firm, start by contacting your state's consumer protection office.

When looking for a low-risk investment for their hard-earned cash, many Americans turn to certificates of deposit (CDs). In combination with recent market volatility, advertisements for CDs with attractive yields have generated considerable interest in CDs.

The U.S. Securities and Exchange Commission's (SEC) Office of Investor Education and Advocacy (OIEA) is issuing this Alert to inform investors about the potential risks of some high-yield CDs. While most CDs feature federal deposit insurance, some CDs are more complex and may carry more risk, especially with respect to getting money back early or locking in an attractive interest rate.

# The ABCs Of Certificate Of Deposits

When you purchase a CD, you invest a fixed sum of money for a fixed period of time—six months, one year, five years, or more—and, in exchange, the issuing bank pays you interest, typically at regular intervals. When you cash in or redeem your CD, you receive the money you originally invested plus any accrued interest. If you redeem your CD before it matures, you may have to pay an "early withdrawal" penalty or forfeit a portion of the interest you earned.

Although most individuals purchase CDs directly from banks, many brokerage firms and independent salespeople also offer CDs. These individuals and entities—known as "deposit brokers"—can sometimes negotiate a higher rate of interest for a CD by promising to bring a certain amount of deposits to the institution. The deposit broker can then offer these "brokered CDs" to their customers.

At one time, most CDs paid a fixed interest rate until they reached maturity. But, like many other products in today's markets, CDs have become more complicated. Investors may now choose among variable rate CDs, long-term CDs, and CDs with other special features.

Some long-term, high-yield CDs have "call" features, meaning that the issuing bank may choose to terminate—or call—the CD after only one year or some other fixed period of time. Only the issuing bank may call a CD, not the investor. For example, a bank might decide to call its high-yield CDs if interest rates fall. But if you've invested in a long-term CD and interest rates subsequently rise, you'll be locked in at the lower rate.

## Few Questions And Answers About Certificate Of Deposit (CD)

**My CD matured today, but the bank will not release the funds to me.**

Generally, the financial institution may not process the CD at the branch. It will be forwarded for processing, and you will receive a check in the mail.

**My CD matured, but I didn't redeem it. What happened to my funds?**

Review your time deposit agreement to determine the bank's policy.

**What are the penalties for withdrawing money early from a Time Certificate of Deposit (CD)?**

Federal law stipulates that all time certificates of deposit (CD) that are cashed out early are subject to a minimum penalty. If you withdraw an amount within the first six days after deposit, the penalty consists of at least seven days' simple interest. Other than that, national banks can set their own penalties; there is no maximum.

Additionally, you may want to review the Account Agreement that the bank provided when you opened the account, as it explains the early withdrawal penalties.

**Does the bank have to continue to pay interest on my Time Certificate of Deposit (CD) after it matures?**

Not necessarily. If you choose to roll over/renew the time certificate of deposit (CD) for another term at the bank, the bank can continue to pay the interest.

Let's say you haven't decided in advance. Once the CD matures, you have 10 days to decide whether to renew or withdraw the funds. The bank can continue to pay interest until you decide, but it's entirely up to the bank. You may want to review your Account Agreement, which explains if interest is paid after maturity. You should have received this Agreement when you opened the account.

**I cashed my Time Certificate of Deposit (CD) before it matured, and the bank charged me an early withdrawal penalty. Can it do this?**

Yes. Time Certificates of Deposits (CD) are not liquid: When you buy one, you enter into a contract involving a fixed amount of money (principal) for a predetermined period of time (the term) and an agreed-upon interest rate and yield. Banks are permitted to assess an early withdrawal penalty whenever funds from a time deposit are withdrawn prior to the date of maturity. This penalty should be explained in the Account Agreement you received when you opened your account.

*(Source: "Answers About CDs And Certificates Of Deposit," Office of the Comptroller of the Currency (OCC), U.S. Department of the Treasury.)*

# Picking A Certificate Of Deposit

Don't be dazzled by high yields. The right CD for you might have a lower yield, and less risk, than other CDs you are considering. Before you purchase a CD, make sure you fully understand all of its terms and carefully read its disclosure statement. Remember to ask questions and check out the answers with an unbiased source. These basic tips can help you decide if you're picking a CD that's appropriate for you:

## Think About Your Financial Goals

Before you make any investing decision, sit down and take an honest look at your entire financial situation, especially if you've never made a financial plan before. The first step to successful investing is figuring out your goals and risk tolerance, either on your own or with the help of a financial professional. CDs and other cash equivalents, such as savings deposits, treasury bills, money market deposit accounts, and money market funds, can be important part of a diversified portfolio. The principal concern for individuals investing in cash equivalents is inflation risk, which is the risk that inflation will outpace and erode returns over time.

## Find Out When The CD Matures

As simple as this sounds, many individuals fail to confirm the maturity dates for their CDs and are later shocked to learn that they've tied up their money for five, ten, or even twenty years. Before you purchase a CD, ask to see the maturity date in writing.

## Investigate Any Call Features

Your ability to lock in a good interest rate for a long time is restricted with a callable CD. Callable CDs give the issuing bank the right to terminate—or "call"— the CD after a set period of time, but they do not give you that same right. If interest rates fall, the issuing bank might call the CD. In that case, you should receive the full amount of your original deposit plus any unpaid accrued interest. But you'll have to shop for a new one with a lower rate of return

---

### Potential Pitfall

Do you understand the difference between a CD's call period and maturity date? Don't assume that a "federally insured one-year non-callable" CD matures in one year. It doesn't. These words mean the bank cannot redeem the CD during the first year, but they have nothing to do with the CD's maturity date. A "one-year non-callable" CD may still have a maturity date 15 or 20 years in the future.

---

## Confirm The Interest Rate You'll Receive And How You'll Be Paid

You should receive a disclosure document that tells you the interest rate on your CD and whether the rate is fixed or variable. Be sure to ask how often the bank pays interest (for example, monthly or semi-annually) and confirm how you'll be paid (for example, by check or by an electronic transfer of funds).

## Ask Whether The Interest Rate Ever Changes

If you're considering investing in a variable-rate CD, make sure you understand when and how the rate can change. Some variable-rate CDs feature a "multi-step" or "bonus rate" structure in which interest rates increase or decrease over time according to a pre-set schedule. Other variable-rate CDs pay interest rates that track the performance of a specified market index, such as the S&P 500 or the Dow Jones Industrial Average.

Research Any Penalties for Early Withdrawal—Be sure to find out how much you'll have to pay if you cash in your CD before maturity.

## Special Considerations For Brokered CDs

Brokered CDs typically are more complex and may carry more risks than CDs offered directly by banks. For example, if you buy a brokered CD and need to get your money back early, you may lose some of your principal. Be sure to read the fine print about the features of any brokered CD you are considering. In addition, since brokered CDs are sold through an intermediary, you'll need to take extra steps to avoid fraud. These additional tips can help you evaluate a brokered CD:

## Thoroughly Check Out The Background Of The Deposit Broker

Deposit brokers do not have to go through any licensing or certification procedures, and no state or federal agency licenses, examines, or approves them. Since anyone can claim to be a deposit broker, you should always check whether your deposit broker or the company he or she works for has a history of complaints or fraud. Many deposit brokers are affiliated with investment professionals. You can check out the disciplinary history of investment professionals quickly using the SEC's and Financial Industry Regulatory Authority's (FINRA) online databases. Your state securities regulator may have additional information on investment professionals. To research the background of a deposit broker who is not affiliated with an investment firm, start by contacting your state government's consumer protection office. You should continue researching until you are comfortable that the deposit broker is reputable. If you have concerns about a deposit broker, you should consider purchasing a CD through another deposit broker or buying one directly from a bank.

## Identify The Issuer

Because federal deposit insurance is limited to a total aggregate amount of $250,000 for each depositor in each bank or thrift institution, it is very important that you know which bank or thrift issued your CD. In other words, find out where the deposit broker plans to deposit your money. Your deposit broker may plan to put your money in a bank or thrift where you already have CDs or other deposits. You risk not being fully insured if the brokered CD would push your total deposits over the $250,000 federal deposit insurance limit.

## Ask About Your Deposit Broker's Record-Keeping

Good account records by your deposit broker can ensure your CD will have federal deposit insurance and, in the event of a bank closing, you'll be paid quickly. For example, unlike traditional bank CDs, brokered CDs are sometimes held by a group of unrelated investors. Instead of owning the entire CD, each investor owns a piece. Confirm with your broker how your CD is held, and be sure to ask for a copy of the exact title of the CD. If several investors own the CD, the deposit broker will probably not list each person's name in the title. But you should make sure that the account records reflect that the broker is merely acting as an agent for you and the other owners (for example, "XYZ Brokerage as Custodian for Customers"). This will ensure that your portion of the CD qualifies for full federal deposit insurance coverage.

## Find Out What Would Happen If You Needed To Withdraw Your Money Early

If you are the sole owner of a brokered CD, you may be able to pay an early withdrawal penalty to the bank that issued the CD to get your money back. But if you share the CD with other customers, your broker will have to find a buyer for your portion. If interest rates have fallen since you purchased your CD and the bank hasn't called it, your deposit broker may be able to sell your portion for a profit. But if interest rates have risen, there may be less demand for your lower-yielding CD. That means you would have to sell the CD at a discount and lose some of your original deposit.

# Bottom Line

The bottom-line question you should always ask yourself is: Does the CD make sense for me? A brokered CD with some potential risks and the possibility of a higher yield might be a good fit for your portfolio. On the other hand, you may only be comfortable purchasing a CD directly from a bank. In any case, the safest choice is to educate yourself about your options because the CD with the highest yield may not be the right one for you.

If you have a problem with a certificate of deposit, send your complaint using the online complaint form at www.sec.gov/complaint.shtml. You can also reach them by regular mail at:

U.S. Securities and Exchange Commission (SEC)

Office of Investor Education and Advocacy (OIEA)

100 F Street, N.E.

Washington, D.C. 20549-0213

You should also contact the banking regulator that oversees the bank that issued the CD:

- The Board of Governors of the Federal Reserve System oversees state-chartered banks and trust companies that belong to the Federal Reserve System.

- The Federal Deposit Insurance Corporation (FDIC) regulates state-chartered banks that do not belong to the Federal Reserve System.

- The National Credit Union Administration (NCUA) regulates federally charted credit unions and insures state-chartered credit unions.

- The Office of the Comptroller of the Currency (OCC) regulates all national banks and federal savings associations as well as federal branches and agencies of foreign banks.

# Chapter 26
# What Are Bonds?

A bond is a debt security, similar to an IOU (I owe you) document. Borrowers issue bonds to raise money from investors willing to lend them money for a certain amount of time. When you buy a bond, you are lending to the issuer, which may be a government, municipality, or corporation. In return, the issuer promises to pay you a specified rate of interest during the life of the bond and to repay the principal, also known as face value or par value of the bond, when it "matures," or comes due after a set period of time.

## Why Do People Buy Bonds?

Investors buy bonds because:

- They provide a predictable income stream. Typically, bonds pay interest twice a year.

- If the bonds are held to maturity, bondholders get back the entire principal, so bonds are a way to preserve capital while investing.

- Bonds can help offset exposure to more volatile stock holdings.

Companies, governments and municipalities issue bonds to get money for various things, which may include:

- Providing operating cash flow

- Financing debt

About This Chapter: Text in this chapter begins with excerpts from "Bonds," Investor.gov, U.S. Securities and Exchange Commission (SEC), December 3, 2016; Text beginning with the heading "The Effect Of Market Interest Rates On Bond Prices And Yield" is excerpted from "Interest Rate Risk—When Interest Rates Go Up, Prices Of Fixed-Rate Bonds Fall," U.S. Securities and Exchange Commission (SEC), June 26, 2013.

- Funding capital investments in schools, highways, hospitals, and other projects

# What Types Of Bonds Are There?

There are three main types of bonds:

- **Corporate bonds** are debt securities issued by private and public corporations.

- **Investment-grade.** These bonds have a higher credit rating, implying less credit risk, than high-yield corporate bonds.

- **High-yield.** These bonds have a lower credit rating, implying higher credit risk, than investment-grade bonds and, therefore, offer higher interest rates in return for the increased risk.

- **Municipal bonds,** called "munis," are debt securities issued by states, cities, counties and other government entities. Types of "munis" include:

  - **General obligation bonds.** These bonds are not secured by any assets; instead, they are backed by the "full faith and credit" of the issuer, which has the power to tax residents to pay bondholders.

  - **Revenue bonds.** Instead of taxes, these bonds are backed by revenues from a specific project or source, such as highway tolls or lease fees. Some revenue bonds are "non-recourse," meaning that if the revenue stream dries up, the bondholders do not have a claim on the underlying revenue source.

  - **Conduit bonds.** Governments sometimes issue municipal bonds on behalf of private entities such as non-profit colleges or hospitals. These "conduit" borrowers typically agree to repay the issuer, who pays the interest and principal on the bonds. If the conduit borrower fails to make a payment, the issuer usually is not required to pay the bondholders.

- **U.S. Treasuries** are issued by the U.S. Department of the Treasury on behalf of the federal government. They carry the full faith and credit of the U.S. government, making them a safe and popular investment. Types of U.S. Treasury debt include:

  - **Treasury Bills.** Short-term securities maturing in a few days to 52 weeks

  - **Notes.** Longer-term securities maturing within ten years

  - **Bonds.** Long-term securities that typically mature in 30 years and pay interest every six months

- **TIPS.** Treasury Inflation-Protected Securities (TIPS) are notes and bonds whose principal is adjusted based on changes in the Consumer Price Index. TIPS pay interest every six months and are issued with maturities of five, ten, and 30 years.

# What Are The Benefits And Risks Of Bonds?

Bonds can provide a means of preserving capital and earning a predictable return. Bond investments provide steady streams of income from interest payments prior to maturity. The interest from municipal bonds generally is exempt from federal income tax and also may be exempt from state and local taxes for residents in the states where the bond is issued.

As with any investment, bonds have risks. These risks include:

- **Credit risk**: The issuer may fail to timely make interest or principal payments and thus default on its bonds.

- **Interest rate risk**: Interest rate changes can affect a bond's value. If bonds are held to maturity the investor will receive the face value, plus interest. If sold before maturity, the bond may be worth more or less than the face value. Rising interest rates will make newly issued bonds more appealing to investors because the newer bonds will have a higher rate of interest than older ones. To sell an older bond with a lower interest rate, you might have to sell it at a discount.

- **Inflation risk**: Inflation is a general upward movement in prices. Inflation reduces purchasing power, which is a risk for investors receiving a fixed rate of interest.

- **Liquidity risk**: This refers to the risk that investors won't find a market for the bond, potentially preventing them from buying or selling when they want.

---

## All Bonds Are Subject To Interest Rate Risk—Even If the Bonds Are Insured Or Government Guaranteed

The seesaw effect between interest rates and bond prices applies to all bonds, even to those that are insured or guaranteed by the U.S. government. When the U.S. government guarantees a bond, it guarantees that it will make interest payments on the bond on time and that it will pay the principal in full when the bond matures. There is a misconception that, if a bond is insured or is a U.S. government obligation, the bond will not lose value. In fact, the U.S. government does not guarantee the market price or value of the bond if you sell the bond before it matures. This is because the market price or value of the bond can change over time based on several factors, including market interest rates.

---

- **Call risk**: The possibility that a bond issuer retires a bond before its maturity date, something an issuer might do if interest rates decline, much like a homeowner might refinance a mortgage to benefit from lower interest rates.

## Avoiding Fraud

Corporate bonds are securities and, if publicly offered, must be registered with the U.S. Securities and Exchange Commission (SEC). The registration of these securities can be verified using the SEC's Electronic Data Gathering, Analysis, and Retrieval (EDGAR) system. Be wary of any person who attempts to sell non-registered bonds. Most municipal securities issued after July 3, 1995 are required to file annual financial information, operating data, and notices of certain events with the Municipal Securities Rulemaking Board (MSRB).

## The Effect Of Market Interest Rates On Bond Prices And Yield

A fundamental principle of bond investing is that market interest rates and bond prices generally move in opposite directions. When market interest rates rise, prices of fixed-rate bonds fall. This phenomenon is known as interest rate risk.

A seesaw, such as the one pictured below, can help you visualize the relationship between market interest rates and bond prices. Imagine that one end of the seesaw represents the market interest rate and the other end represents the price of a fixed-rate bond.

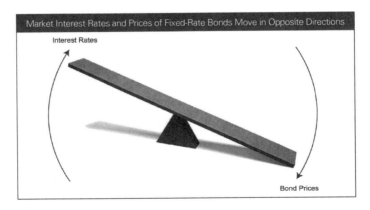

*Figure 26.1.* **Interest Rates On Bond Prices And Yield**

Higher market interest rates —> lower fixed-rate bond prices
Lower market interest rates —> higher fixed-rate bond prices

> **Remember:**
>
> Lower market interest rates —> higher fixed-rate bond prices —> lower fixed-rate bond yields —> higher interest rate risk to rising market interest rates
>
> Because of this relationship, it is particularly important for investors to consider interest rate risk when they purchase bonds in a low-interest rate environment.

A bond's yield to maturity shows how much an investor's money will earn if the bond is held until it matures. For example, as the table below illustrates, let's say a treasury bond offers a 3% coupon rate, and a year later market interest rates fall to 2%. The bond will still pay a 3% coupon rate, making it more valuable than new bonds paying just a 2% coupon rate. If you sell the 3% bond before it matures, you will probably find that its price is higher than it was a year ago. Along with the rise in price, however, the yield to maturity of the bond will go down for anyone who buys the bond at the new higher price.

**Table 26.1.** If Market Interest Rates Decrease By One Percent

| Financial Term | Today | One Year Later |
|---|---|---|
| Market Interest Rate | 3% | 2% |
| Coupon Rate (semi-annual payments) | 3% | 3% |
| Face Value | $1,000 | $1,000 |
| Maturity | 10 years | 9 years remaining |
| Price | $1,000 | $1,082 |
| Yield to Maturity | 3% | 2% |

*Lower market interest rates —> higher fixed-rate bond prices lower —> fixed-rate bond yields*

Now suppose market interest rates rise from 3% to 4%, as the table below illustrates. If you sell the 3% bond, it will be competing with new treasury bonds that offer a 4% coupon rate. The price of the 3% bond may be more likely to fall. The yield to maturity, however, will rise as the price falls.

**Table 26.2.** If Market Interest Rates Increase By One Percent

| Financial Term | Today | One Year Later |
|---|---|---|
| Market Interest Rate | 3% | 4% |
| Coupon Rate (semi-annual payments) | 3% | 3% |
| Face Value | $1,000 | $1,000 |

**Table 26.2.** Continued

| Financial Term | Today | One Year Later |
|---|---|---|
| Maturity | 10 years | 9 years remaining |
| Price | $1,000 | $925 |
| Yield to Maturity | 3% | 4% |

# The Effect Of Coupon Rates On Interest Rate Risk

Interest rate risk is common to all bonds, even U.S. Treasury bonds. A bond's maturity and coupon rate generally affect how much its price will change as a result of changes in market interest rates. If two bonds offer different coupon rates while all of their other characteristics (e.g., maturity and credit quality) are the same, the bond with the lower coupon rate generally will experience a greater decrease in value as market interest rates rise. Bonds offering lower coupon rates generally will have higher interest rate risk than similar bonds that offer higher coupon rates.

Lower fixed-rate bond coupon rates—>higher interest rate risk

Higher fixed-rate bond coupon rates—>lower interest rate risk

For example, imagine one bond that has a coupon rate of 2% while another bond has a coupon rate of 4%. All other features of the two bonds—when they mature, their level of credit risk, and so on—are the same. If market interest rates rise, then the price of the bond with the 2% coupon rate will fall more than that of the bond with the 4% coupon rate.

A bond's maturity is the specific date in the future at which the face value of the bond will be repaid to the investor. A bond may mature in a few months or in a few years. Maturity can also affect interest rate risk. The longer the bond's maturity, the greater the risk that the bond's value could be impacted by changing interest rates prior to maturity, which may have a negative effect on the price of the bond. Therefore, bonds with longer maturities generally have higher interest rate risk than similar bonds with shorter maturities.

Longer maturity —> higher interest rate risk

Shorter maturity —> lower interest rate risk

To compensate investors for this interest rate risk, long-term bonds generally offer higher coupon rates than short-term bonds of the same credit quality.

Longer maturity —> higher interest rate risk —> higher coupon rate

Shorter maturity —> lower interest rate risk —> lower coupon rate

If you intend to hold a bond to maturity, the day-to-day fluctuations in the bond's price may not be as important to you. The bond's price may change, but you will be paid the stated interest rate, as well as the face value of the bond, upon maturity. On the other hand, instead of holding the bond to maturity, you might be able to sell the bond and reinvest the proceeds into another bond that pays a higher coupon rate.

# Chapter 27
# Understanding Savings Bonds

Savings bonds are debt securities issued by the U.S. Department of the Treasury to help pay for the U.S. government's borrowing needs. U.S. savings bonds are considered one of the safest investments because they are backed by the full faith and credit of the U.S. Government.

Starting January 1, 2012, you can no longer buy paper savings bonds at financial institutions. But you can go online to purchase two types of electronic savings bonds. Under the rules, an individual can buy a maximum of $10,000 worth in each series in a single calendar year, or a total of $20,000.

**Series EE U.S. Savings Bonds** are an appreciation-type (or accrual-type) savings security. They are sold at face value, so you'll pay $50 for a $50 bond. The bond is worth its full value upon redemption. The interest is issued electronically to your designated account. You cannot buy more than $10,000 (face value) of Series EE bonds in any calendar year. If you redeem the bonds in the first five years of buying them, you'll forfeit interest payments for the three most recent months. After five years, you won't be penalized for redemptions.

**Series I U.S. Savings Bonds** are inflation-indexed. They are sold at face value and you can buy up to $10,000 (face value) of Series I bonds in any calendar year. Series I Bonds offer a fixed rate of interest, adjusted for inflation. As with Series EE Bonds, if you redeem Series I Bonds in the first five years, you'll forfeit the three most recent months' interest. After five years, you won't be penalized for redemptions.

About This Chapter: Text in this chapter begins with the excerpts from "Savings Bonds," Investor.gov, U.S. Securities and Exchange Commission (SEC), November 23, 2016; Text under the heading "Series EE U.S. Savings Bonds" is excerpted from "Series EE Savings Bonds," TreasuryDirect, U.S. Department of the Treasury, November 1, 2016; Text under the heading "Series I U.S. Savings Bonds" is excerpted from "I Savings Bonds," TreasuryDirect, U.S. Department of the Treasury, September 17, 2015.

Key advantages of savings bonds include:

- **Popularity as gifts:** Savings bonds are a popular birthday and graduation gift and also can be used toward financing education, supplemental retirement income, and other special events. Unlike other securities, minors may hold U.S. savings bonds in their own name.

- **Tax advantages:** You pay no state or local taxes on the interest on the bonds, and you can defer paying federal taxes on the interest until you cash in the bond or until it matures. In addition, tax benefits are available for eligible taxpayers when Series EE and Series I savings bonds are used for qualified education expenses.

You can buy these electronic savings bonds in penny increments, from $25 up to $5,000 each year. (In paper form, these bonds were only available in specific denominations.) You can use the Savings Bond Calculator and compare the different types of securities issued by the Treasury.

# Series EE U.S. Savings Bonds

Use EE bonds to

- save in a reliable, low-risk, government-backed product

- supplement your retirement income

- give as a gift

- pay for education

## What Is An EE Bond?

These EE bonds earn the same rate of interest (a fixed rate) for up to 30 years. When you buy the bond, you know what rate of interest it will earn. Treasury announces the rate each May 1 and November 1 for new EE bonds.

## Were Older EE Bonds Different?

Yes. EE bonds bought from May 1997 through April 2005 earn a rate of interest that changes every six months (a variable rate). EE bonds bought before May 1997 earn interest at different rates depending on when they were bought.

## If I Buy An EE Bond Now, What Interest Will It Earn?

The interest rate for bonds bought from November 1, 2016 through April 30, 2017, is an annual rate of 0.10%.

## Is It Taxable?

Federal income tax: Yes

State and local income tax: No

Using the money for higher education may keep you from paying federal income tax on your interest.

## Minimum And Maximum Purchase

**Minimum:** $25 for a $25 EE bond.

**Maximum:** $10,000 each calendar year for each Social Security Number.

**Available bonds:** Any amount from $25 to $10,000 to the penny. For example, you could buy an EE Bond for $50.23.

## How Long Must I Keep An EE Bond?

EE bonds earn interest for up to 30 years.

You can cash them after 1 year. But if you cash them before 5 years, you lose the last 3 months' interest. (For example, if you cash an EE bond after 18 months, you get the first 15 months of interest.)

# Series I U.S. Savings Bonds

Use I Bonds to

- save in a low-risk product that helps protect your savings from inflation

- supplement your retirement income

- give as a gift

- pay for education

## What Is An I Bond?

A security that earns interest based on combining a fixed rate and an inflation rate.

## What Interest Does An I Bond Earn?

A combination of a fixed rate and an inflation rate that can and usually does change twice-a-year.

## Is It Taxable?

Federal income tax: Yes

State and local income tax: No

Using the money for higher education may keep you from paying federal income tax on your savings bond interest.

## Minimum And Maximum Purchase

**Minimum:** Electronic: $25 for a $25 I Bond

**Maximum:** $10,000 each calendar year for each Social Security Number. You may buy up to $10,000 in electronic I Bonds, and up to $5,000 in paper I Bonds bought with your IRS tax refund.

**Available Bonds:**

**Electronic:** Any amount from $25 to $10,000 to the penny. For example, with electronic bonds, you could buy an I Bond for $50.23.

## How Long Must I Keep An I Bond?

I Bonds are meant to be long-term investments. They continue to earn interest for up to 30 years.

You can cash them in after one year. But if you cash them in before five years, you lose the last three months of interest. (If you cash in an I Bond after 18 months, you get the first 15 months of interest.)

## How Do I Bonds Earn Interest?

Interest on an I Bond rates is a combination of two rates:

1. A fixed rate of return which remains the same throughout the life of the I Bond and

2. A variable inflation rate which is calculated twice a year, based on changes in the non seasonally adjusted Consumer Price Index for all Urban Consumers (CPI-U) for all items, including food and energy (CPI-U for March compared with the CPI-U for September of the same year, and then CPI-U for September compared with the CPI-U for March of the following year).

Interest is earned on the bond every month. (However, values displayed by the Savings Bond Calculator for bonds that are less than five years old do not include the latest three months of interest. These values reflect the interest penalty.)

The interest is compounded semiannually: Every six months, on the 6th and 12th month anniversaries of the issue date, all interest the bond has earned in previous months is in the bond's new principal value on which interest is earned for the next 6 months.

# Chapter 28
# Treasury Bonds And Other Treasury Instruments

Treasury bonds are issued in terms of 30 years and pay interest every six months until they mature. When a Treasury bond matures, you are paid its face value. The price and yield of a Treasury bond are determined at auction. The price may be greater than, less than, or equal to the face value of the bond.

Treasury bonds are sold in TreasuryDirect (but not in Legacy Treasury Direct, which is being phased out) and by banks and brokers.

Two types of bids are accepted:

- With a **noncompetitive bid**, you agree to accept the interest rate determined at auction. With this bid, you are guaranteed to receive the bond you want, and in the full amount you want.

- With a **competitive bid**, you specify the yield you are willing to accept. Your bid may be:

  - accepted in the full amount you want if your bid is equal to or less than the yield determined at auction,

  - accepted in less than the full amount you want if your bid is equal to the high yield, or

  - rejected if the yield you specify is higher than the yield set at auction.

About This Chapter: Text in this chapter begins with the excerpts from "Treasury Bonds In Depth," TreasuryDirect, U.S. Department of the Treasury, July 13, 2015; Text beginning with the heading "Price And Interest" is excerpted from "Treasury Bonds: Rates & Terms," TreasuryDirect, U.S. Department of the Treasury, July 13, 2015; Text under the heading "TIPS In Depth" is excerpted from "TIPS In Depth," TreasuryDirect, U.S. Department of the Treasury, January 21, 2014; Text under the heading "Treasury Bonds: FAQs" is excerpted from "Treasury Bonds: FAQs," TreasuryDirect, U.S. Department of the Treasury, November 25, 2015; Text under the heading "Treasury Bills" is excerpted from "Treasury Bills In Depth," TreasuryDirect, U.S. Department of the Treasury, January 17, 2014; Text under the heading "Treasury Notes" is excerpted from "Treasury Notes In Depth," TreasuryDirect, U.S. Department of the Treasury, January 21, 2014.

To place a noncompetitive bid, you may use TreasuryDirect, a bank, or a broker.

To place a competitive bid, you must use a bank or broker.

Bonds exist in either of two formats: as paper certificates (these are older bonds) or as electronic entries in accounts. Today, the Treasury bonds are issued in electronic form, not paper. Paper Treasury bonds can be converted to electronic form.

## Key Facts

- The yield on a bond is determined at auction.

- Bonds are sold in increments of $100. The minimum purchase is $100.

- You can hold a Treasury bond until it matures or sell it before it matures.

- In a single auction, a bidder can buy up to $5 million in bonds by non-competitive bidding or up to 35 percent of the initial offering amount by competitive bidding.

# Price And Interest

The price and interest rate of a bond are determined at auction. The price may be greater than, less than, or equal to the bond's par amount (or face value).

The price of a fixed rate security depends on its yield to maturity and the interest rate. If the yield to maturity (YTM) is greater than the interest rate, the price will be less than par value; if the YTM is equal to the interest rate, the price will be equal to par; if the YTM is less than the interest rate, the price will be greater than par.

Here are some hypothetical examples of these conditions:

**Table 28.1.** Price And Interest

| Condition | Type Of Security | Yield At Auction | Interest Coupon Rate | Price | Explanation |
|---|---|---|---|---|---|
| Discount (price below par) | 30-year bond Issue Date: 8/15/2005 | 4.35% | 4.25% | 98.333317 | Below par price required to equate to 4.35% yield |
| Premium (price above par) | 30-year bond reopening Issue Date: 9/15/2005 | 3.99% | 4.25% | 104.511963 | Above par price required to equate to 3.99% yield |

Sometimes when you buy a bond, you are charged accrued interest, which is the interest the security earned in the current semiannual interest period before you took possession of the security. If you are charged accrued interest, it will be paid back to you as part of your next semiannual interest payment.

For example, you buy a 30-Year Treasury bond issued February 15, 2016 and maturing February 15, 2046. If February 15, 2016 fell on a Saturday, Treasury would issue the bond on the next business day, Monday February 17, 2016. Besides the purchase price, you would pay Treasury for the interest accrued from February 15 to February 17, 2016. When you get the first semiannual interest payment, it will include the accrued interest you paid.

If you are a TreasuryDirect customer, you should look at your Current Holdings, Pending Transactions Detail after 5 pm Eastern Time on auction day and check the price per $100 and accrued interest to determine the total price of the security. Next, make sure the source of funds you selected has sufficient funds to cover the total price. If you need to add funds to cover the purchase price, you have to do so before the issue date of the security.

If you buy from a bank or broker, please consult the bank or broker to learn payment arrangements.

Bonds pay interest every six months.

# Options At Maturity—And Before

You can hold a bond until it matures or sell it before it matures.

If you don't sell, your options at maturity depend on where you hold your bond:

- **TreasuryDirect:** Redeem the bond or use its proceeds to reinvest into another bond of the same term.

- **Legacy Treasury Direct:** Redeem the bond. (Bonds cannot be reinvested in Legacy Treasury Direct, which is being phased out.)

- **Bank or Broker:** For your options, consult your bank or broker.

## Treasury Bonds: How To Buy
**Buying Directly From the U.S. Treasury**

To buy Treasury bonds directly from U.S. Department of the Treasury, you must have an account in TreasuryDirect.

By bidding for a bond in TreasuryDirect, you:

- Agree to accept whatever yield is determined at auction
- Are guaranteed to receive the bond you want, in the amount you want

(This is called noncompetitive bidding.)

### Submit a Bid in TreasuryDirect

The bid submission process in TreasuryDirect is completely online. Login to your account and click the BuyDirect® tab. Follow the prompts to specify the security you want, the purchase amount, and other requested information.

You also can set up reinvestments into securities of the same type and term. For instance, you can use the proceeds from a maturing 30-year bond to buy another 30-year bond.

### Payments and Receipts in TreasuryDirect

The price that you pay for a bond can include either a premium or a discount, and accrued interest. For a full discussion of the price of a security.

When you buy a bond in TreasuryDirect, the purchase price from the source of funds that you specify is withdrawn, which could be one of your bank accounts or your Certificate of Indebtedness (C of I). When the bond matures, payments are deposited into your bank account or your C of I, whichever you specify.

### Buying Through a Bank, Broker, or Dealer

Banks, brokers, and dealers offer two types of bidding for bonds:

- Competitive
  - You specify the yield you will accept.
  - Depending on what yield is determined at the auction, you may or may not receive the bond you want, and if you receive it, you may receive it in less than the amount you want.
- Noncompetitive
  - You agree to accept whatever yield is determined at auction.
  - You are guaranteed to receive the bond you want, in the amount you want

*(Source: "Treasury Bonds: How To Buy," U.S. Department of the Treasury.)*

# Auction Pattern

30-Year Bond

- Original Issues—February, May, August, November

- *Reopenings—January, March, April, June, July, September, October, December

*In a reopening, an additional amount of a previously issued security is sold. The reopened security has the same maturity date and interest rate as the original security. However, as compared to the original security, the reopened security has a different issue date and usually a different purchase price.*

# Paper Bonds Or Electronic Bonds

Treasury bonds exist in either of two formats: as paper certificates or as electronic entries in accounts. Paper Treasury bonds can be converted to electronic form.

For information on this and other issues about paper Treasury bonds, contact by any of these methods:

- Send an e-mail

- Call 844-284-2676 (toll free)

- Write to:

  Bureau of the Fiscal Service

  P.O. Box 426

  Parkersburg, WV 26106-0426

# Treasury Inflation-Protected Securities (TIPS)

## How TIPS Are Tied To Inflation

Treasury Inflation-Protected Securities (TIPS) are marketable securities whose principal is adjusted by changes in the Consumer Price Index. With inflation (a rise in the index), the principal increases. With a deflation (a drop in the index), the principal decreases.

The relationship between TIPS and the Consumer Price Index affects both the sum you are paid when your TIPS matures and the amount of interest that a TIPS pays you every six months. TIPS pay interest at a fixed rate. Because the rate is applied to the adjusted principal, however, interest payments can vary in amount from one period to the next. If inflation occurs, the interest payment increases. In the event of deflation, the interest payment decreases.

At the maturity of a TIPS, you receive the adjusted principal or the original principal, whichever is greater. This provision protects you against deflation.

Treasury provides TIPS Inflation Index Ratios to allow you to easily calculate the change to principal resulting from changes in the Consumer Price Index.

## Methods Of Buying TIPS

TIPS are sold in TreasuryDirect, and through banks and brokers. TIPS no longer are sold in Legacy Treasury Direct, which is being phased out.

The price of a TIPS can be less than, equal to, or greater than the face value.

You can bid for TIPS in either of two ways:

With a noncompetitive bid, you agree to accept the yield determined at auction. With this bid, you are guaranteed to receive the TIPS you want, and in the full amount you want.

With a competitive bid, you specify the yield you are willing to accept. Your bid may be:

1.  accepted in the full amount you want if your bid is less than the yield determined at auction,

2.  accepted in less than the full amount you want if your bid is equal to the high yield, or

3.  rejected if the yield you specify is higher than the yield set at auction.

To place a noncompetitive bid, you may use TreasuryDirect, a bank, or a broker.

To place a competitive bid, you must use a bank or broker.

## Key Facts

*   TIPS are issued in terms of 5, 10, and 30 years.

*   The interest rate on a TIPS is determined at auction.

*   TIPS are sold in increments of $100. The minimum purchase is $100.

*   TIPS are issued in electronic form.

*   You can hold a TIPS until it matures or sell it in the secondary market before it matures.

*   In a single auction, a bidder can buy up to $5 million in TIPS by non-competitive bidding or up to 35% of the initial offering amount by competitive bidding.

# Treasury Bonds: FAQs

## What Are The Maturity Terms For Treasury Bonds?

Treasury bonds are sold in a term of 30 years.

## How Do I Know When Treasury Bonds Will Be Auctioned?

Treasury bonds are auctioned on a monthly basis. Bonds are auctioned at original issue in February, May, August, and November, and are auctioned them as reopenings in the other eight months.

## What Are Reopenings, Premiums, And Accrued Interest?

In a reopening, we auction additional amounts of a previously issued security. Reopened securities have the same maturity date and interest rate as the original securities, but a different issue date and usually a different price.

When you buy a reopened security, you have to pay a premium if the price of the security at reopening is greater than the face value of the security. The price of the reopened security will be determined at auction. Because the security is being auctioned at two separate times, market conditions probably won't be the same and, therefore, the prices likely won't be the same either.

Also, when you buy a reopened security, regardless of its price, you may have to pay accrued interest—interest the security earns from the original issue date of the security until the date the security is issued to you. However, the accrued interest will be paid back to you in your first semiannual interest payment.

These bonds are reopenings: the ones that are auctioned in January, March, April, June, July, September, October, and December.

## Do You Still Issue Treasury Bonds In Paper Form?

No. All Treasury bonds are now issued electronically.

## Do Some Treasury Bonds Still Exist In Paper Form?

Yes. These are Treasury bonds that were issued in paper form and haven't matured. If you own one of these, you can convert it to electronic form and hold it in an account with U.S. Department of the Treasury, or keep it in paper form. For information on paper Treasury bonds, contact:

- Send an e-mail
- Call 844-284-2676 (toll free)
- Write to:

  Bureau of the Fiscal Service

  P.O. Box 426

  Parkersburg, WV 26106-0426

### How Can I Place A Competitive Bid For A Treasury Bond?

By using a bank, broker, or dealer. (Our system, TreasuryDirect, accepts only noncompetitive bids.)

### How Do I Transfer A Treasury Bond From Legacy Treasury Direct* To TreasuryDirect?

Take these steps:

1. Open an account in TreasuryDirect. (If you already have an account, you may skip this step.)

2. Complete the form "Security Transfer Request" (FS Form 5179). In the form's section 3, check the box for "Transfer to an Established Online TreasuryDirect Account Number." Your signature on this form must be certified. Your bank may provide this service.

3. Mail the form to the address shown on the form.

*Legacy Treasury Direct is being phased out.*

# Treasury Bills

Treasury bills, or T-bills, are typically issued at a discount from the par amount (also called face value). For example, if you buy a $1,000 bill at a price per $100 of $99.986111, then you would pay $999.86 ($1,000 x .99986111 = $999.86111).* When the bill matures, you would be paid its face value, $1,000. Your interest is the face value minus the purchase price. It is possible for a bill auction to result in a price equal to par, which means that Treasury will issue and redeem the securities at par value. You can buy a bill in TreasuryDirect or through a bank or broker.

# Treasury Notes

Treasury notes, or T-notes, are issued in terms of 2, 3, 5, 7, and 10 years, and pay interest every six months until they mature. The price of a note may be greater than, less than, or equal to the face value of the note. When a note matures, you are paid its face value.

Notes are sold in TreasuryDirect, and by banks and brokers. (Notes are no longer sold in Legacy Treasury Direct, which is being phased out.)

You can bid for a note in either of two ways:

• To place a noncompetitive bid, you may use TreasuryDirect, a bank, or a broker.

• To place a competitive bid, you must use a bank or broker.

# Chapter 29
# Municipal And Corporate Bonds

## Municipal Bonds

### What Are Municipal Bonds?

Municipal bonds (or "munis" for short) are debt securities issued by states, cities, counties, and other governmental entities to fund day-to-day obligations and to finance capital projects such as building schools, highways or sewer systems. By purchasing municipal bonds, you are in effect lending money to the bond issuer in exchange for a promise of regular interest payments, usually semi-annually, and the return of the original investment, or "principal." A municipal bond's maturity date (the date when the issuer of the bond repays the principal) may be years in the future. Short-term bonds mature in one to three years, while long-term bonds won't mature for more than a decade.

Generally, the interest on municipal bonds is exempt from federal income tax. The interest may also be exempt from state and local taxes if you reside in the state where the bond is issued. Bond investors typically seek a steady stream of income payments and, compared to stock investors, may be more risk-averse and more focused on preserving, rather than increasing, wealth. Given the tax benefits, the interest rate for municipal bonds is usually lower than on taxable fixed-income securities such as corporate bonds.

---

About This Chapter: Text under the heading "Municipal Bonds" is excerpted from "What Are Municipal Bonds?" U.S. Securities and Exchange Commission (SEC), November 23, 2016; Text under the heading "Corporate Bonds" is excerpted from "What Are Corporate Bonds?" U.S. Securities and Exchange Commission (SEC), November 23, 2016.

The two most common types of municipal bonds are the following:

- **General obligation bonds** are issued by states, cities or counties and not secured by any assets. Instead, general obligation are backed by the "full faith and credit" of the issuer, which has the power to tax residents to pay bondholders.

- **Revenue bonds** are not backed by government's taxing power but by revenues from a specific project or source, such as highway tolls or lease fees. Some revenue bonds are "non-recourse," meaning that if the revenue stream dries up, the bondholders do not have a claim on the underlying revenue source.

In addition, municipal borrowers sometimes issue bonds on behalf of private entities such as non-profit colleges or hospitals. These "conduit" borrowers typically agree to repay the issuer, who pays the interest and principal on the bonds. In cases where the conduit borrower fails to make a payment, the issuer usually is not required to pay the bondholders.

## Where Can Investors Find Information About Municipal Bonds?

Investors wishing to research municipal bonds may access a range of information online free of charge at the Municipal Securities Rulemaking Board's Electronic Municipal Market Access (EMMA) website. Information available to you includes:

- Disclosure documents going back as early as 1990, including a bond's official statement, which is a disclosure document similar to a prospectus that includes important characteristics, such as type, yield, maturity, credit quality, call features and risk factors, as well as audited financial statements, material event notices and other continuing disclosures (including ratings changes, principal and interest payment delinquencies and non-payment related defaults).

- Historical and real-time transaction price data, including information relating to a type of municipal bond called a "variable rate demand obligation" that resets its interest rate periodically. Investors should be aware that recent price information may not be available for bonds that do not trade frequently.

## What Are Some Of The Risks Of Investing In Municipal Bonds?

As with any investment, investing in municipal bonds entails risk. Investors in municipal bonds face a number of risks, specifically including:

**Call risk:** Call risk refers to the potential for an issuer to repay a bond before its maturity date, something that an issuer may do if interest rates decline—much as a homeowner might refinance a mortgage loan to benefit from lower interest rates. Bond calls are less likely when interest rates are stable or moving higher. Many municipal bonds are "callable," so investors who want to hold a municipal bond to maturity should research the bond's call provisions before making a purchase.

**Credit risk:** This is the risk that the bond issuer may experience financial problems that make it difficult or impossible to pay interest and principal in full (the failure to pay interest or principal is referred to as "default"). Credit ratings are available for many bonds. Credit ratings seek to estimate the relative credit risk of a bond as compared with other bonds, although a high rating does not reflect a prediction that the bond has no chance of defaulting.

**Interest rate risk:** Bonds have a fixed face value, known as the "par" value. If bonds are held to maturity, the investor will receive the face value amount back, plus interest that may be set at a fixed or floating rate. The bond's market price will move up as interest rates move down and it will decline as interest rates rise, so that the market value of the bond may be more or less than the par value. U.S. interest rates have been low for some time. If they move higher, investors who hold a low fixed-rate municipal bond and try to sell it before it matures could lose money because of the lower market value of the bond.

**Inflation risk:** Inflation is a general upward movement in prices. Inflation reduces purchasing power, which is a risk for investors receiving a fixed rate of interest. It also can lead to higher interest rates and, in turn, lower market value for existing bonds.

**Liquidity risk:** This refers to the risk that investors won't find an active market for the municipal bond, potentially preventing them from buying or selling when they want and obtaining a certain price for the bond. Many investors buy municipal bonds to hold them rather than to trade them, so the market for a particular bond may not be especially liquid and quoted prices for the same bond may differ.

---

## In Addition To The Risks, What Other Factors Should You Consider When Investing In Municipal Bonds?

**Tax implications:** Consider consulting a tax professional to discuss the bond's tax implications, including the possibility that your bond may be subject to the federal alternative minimum tax or eligible for state income tax benefits.

**Broker compensation:** Most brokers are compensated through a markup over the cost of the bond to the firm. This markup is usually not disclosed on your confirmation statement.

If a commission is charged, it will be reported on your confirmation statement. You should ask your broker about markups and commissions.

**The background of the broker or adviser selling the bond:** A securities salesperson must be properly licensed, and, depending on the type of business the firm conducts, his or her firm must be registered with the Municipal Securities Rulemaking Board (MSRB) and with Financial Industry Regulatory Authority (FINRA), the U.S. Securities and Exchange Commission (SEC) or a state securities regulator.

# Corporate Bonds

## What Is A Corporate Bond?

A bond is a debt obligation, like an IOU document. Investors who buy corporate bonds are lending money to the company issuing the bond. In return, the company makes a legal commitment to pay interest on the principal and, in most cases, to return the principal when the bond comes due, or matures.

To understand bonds, it is helpful to compare them with stocks. When you buy a share of common stock, you own equity in the company and will receive any dividends declared and paid by the company. When you buy a corporate bond, you do not own equity in the company. You will receive only the interest and principal on the bond, no matter how profitable the company becomes or how high its stock price climbs. But if the company runs into financial difficulties, it still has a legal obligation to make timely payments of interest and principal. the company has no similar obligation to pay dividends to shareholders. In a bankruptcy, bond investors have priority over shareholders in claims on the company's assets. Like all investments, bonds carry risks. One key risk to a bondholder is that the company may fail to make timely payments of interest or principal. If that happens, the company will default on its bonds. This "default risk" makes the creditworthiness of the company— that is, its ability to pay its debt obligations on time—an important concern to bondholders.

## What Are The Basic Types Of Corporate Bonds?

Corporate bonds make up one of the largest components of the U.S. bond market, which is considered the largest securities market in the world. Other components include U.S. Treasury bonds, other U.S. government bonds, and municipal bonds.

Companies use the proceeds from bond sales for a wide variety of purposes, including buying new equipment, investing in research and development, buying back their own stock, paying shareholder dividends, refinancing debt, and financing mergers and acquisitions.

Bonds can be classified according to their maturity, which is the date when the company has to pay back the principal to investors. Maturities can be short term (less than three years), medium term (four to 10 years), or long term (more than 10 years). Longer-term bonds usually offer higher interest rates, but may entail additional risks.

Bonds and the companies that issue them are also classified according to their credit quality. Credit rating agencies assign credit ratings based on their evaluation of the risk that the company may default on its bonds. Credit rating agencies periodically review their bond ratings and may revise them if conditions or expectations change.

Based on their credit ratings, bonds can be either investment grade or non-investment grade. Investment grade bonds are considered more likely than non-investment grade bonds to be paid on time. Non-investment grade bonds, which are also called high-yield or speculative bonds, generally offer higher interest rates to compensate investors for greater risk. Bonds also differ according to the type of interest payments they offer. Many bonds pay a fixed rate of interest throughout their term. Interest payments are called coupon payments, and the interest rate is called the coupon rate. With a fixed coupon rate, the coupon payments stay the same regardless of changes in market interest rates.

Other bonds offer floating rates that are reset periodically, such as every six months. these bonds adjust their interest payments to changes in market interest rates. Floating rates are based on a bond index or other benchmark. For example, the floating rate may equal the interest rate on a certain type of treasury bond plus 1%.

One type of bond makes no interest payments until the bond matures. These are called zero-coupon bonds, because they make no coupon payments. Instead, the bond makes a single payment at maturity that is higher than the initial purchase price. For example, an investor may pay $800 to purchase a five-year, zero-coupon bond with a face value of $1,000. The company pays no interest on the bond for the next five years, and then, at maturity, pays $1,000— equal to the purchase price of $800 plus interest, or original issue discount, of $200. Investors in zero-coupon bonds generally must pay taxes each year on a prorated share of the interest before the interest is actually paid at maturity.

## What Happens If A Company Goes Into Bankruptcy?

If a company defaults on its bonds and goes bankrupt, bondholders will have a claim on the company's assets and cash flows. The bond's terms determine the bondholder's place in line, or the priority of the claim. Priority will be based on whether the bond is, for example, a secured bond, a senior unsecured bond or a junior unsecured (or subordinated) bond.

In the case of a secured bond, the company pledges specific collateral—such as property, equipment, or other assets that the company owns—as security for the bond. If the company defaults, holders of secured bonds will have a legal right to foreclose on the collateral to satisfy their claims.

Bonds that have no collateral pledged to them are unsecured and may be called debentures. Debentures have a general claim on the company's assets and cash flows. They may be classified as either senior or junior (subordinated) debentures. If the company defaults, holders of senior debentures will have a higher priority claim on the company's assets and cash flows than holders of junior debentures.

Bondholders, however, are usually not the company's only creditors. The company may also owe money to banks, suppliers, customers, pensioners, and others, some of whom may have equal or higher claims than certain bondholders. Sorting through the competing claims of creditors is a complex process that unfolds in bankruptcy court.

## What Are The Financial Terms Of A Bond?

The basic financial terms of a corporate bond include its price, face value (also called par value), maturity, coupon rate, and yield to maturity. Yield to maturity is a widely used measure to compare bonds. This is the annual return on the bond if held to maturity taking into account when you bought the bond and what you paid for it.

A bond often trades at a premium or discount to its face value. this can happen when market interest rates rise or fall relative to the bond's coupon rate. If the coupon rate is higher than market interest rates, for example, then the bond will likely trade at a premium.

**Table 29.1.** Financial Terms

| Financial Term | Bond A | Bond B | Bond C |
| --- | --- | --- | --- |
| Price (as a % of face value) | 100 | 90 | 110 |
| Maturity | 10 years | 10 years | 10 years |
| Face value | $1,000 | $1,000 | $1,000 |
| Coupon rate | 4.00% | 4.00% | 4.00% |
| Yield to maturity | 4.00% | 5.31% | 2.84% |

**Bond A.** Bond prices may be quoted in dollars or as a percentage of its face value. Bond A's price is 100% of the face value, or $1,000. the bond will pay 4% of the face value, or $40 per year.

Most bonds are paid semi-annually, so Bond A will pay $20 every six months. In addition, the bond will make a principal payment of $1,000 at the end of the 10 years. the bond pays a 4.00% yield to maturity because it is not trading at either a premium or a discount.

**Bond B.** Bond B's price is 90% of its face value, or $900. Notwithstanding this, investors in Bond B will still receive a total of $40 per year in coupon payments and when Bond B matures, bondholders will still receive the face value of $1,000. the discounted price results in Bond B having a yield to maturity of 5.31%.

**Bond C.** This bond sells for a premium at $1,100, or 110% of face value. Like Bonds A and B, investors in Bond C will receive a total of $40 per year in coupon payments and the bond's face value of $1,000 at maturity. Because of the premium price, the yield to maturity on Bond C at 2.84% is lower than the coupon rate.

## What Is The Relationship Among Bond Prices, Interest Rates, And Yield?

The price of a bond moves in the opposite direction than market interest rates—like opposing ends of a seesaw. When interest rates go up, the price of the bond goes down. And when interest rates go down, the bond's price goes up. As shown above, a bond's yield also moves inversely with the bond's price.

For example, let's say a bond offers 3% interest, and a year later market interest rates fall to 2%. the bond will still pay 3% interest, making it more valuable than newly issued bonds paying just 2% interest. If you sell the 3% bond, you will probably find that its price is higher than a year ago. Along with the rise in price, however, the yield to maturity for any new buyer of the bond will go down.

Now suppose market interest rates rise from 3% to 4%. If you sell the 3% bond, it will be competing with new bonds that offer 4% interest. The price of the 3% bond may be more likely to fall. the yield to maturity for any new buyer, however, will rise as the price falls.

It's important to keep in mind that despite swings in trading price with a bond investment, if you hold the bond until maturity, the bond will continue to pay the stated rate of interest as well as its face value upon maturity, subject to default risk.

## What Are Some Of The Risks Of Corporate Bonds?

### Credit Or Default Risk

Credit or default risk is the risk that a company will fail to timely make interest or principal payments and thus default on its bonds. Credit ratings try to estimate the relative credit risk of a bond based on the company's ability to pay. Credit rating agencies periodically review their bond ratings and may revise them if conditions or expectations change.

The corporate bond contract (called an indenture) often includes terms called covenants designed to limit credit risk. For instance, the terms may limit the amount of debt the company can take on, or may require it to maintain certain financial ratios. Violating the terms of a bond may constitute a default. The bond trustee monitors the company's compliance with the terms of its indenture. The trustee acts on behalf of the bondholders and pursues remedies if the bond covenants are violated.

## Interest Rate Risk

As discussed above, the price of a bond will fall if market interest rates rise. this presents investors with interest rate risk, which is common to all bonds, even U.S. Treasury bonds. A bond's maturity and coupon rate generally affect its sensitivity to changes in market interest rates. the longer the bond's maturity, the more time there is for rates to change and, as a result, affect the price of the bond. Therefore, bonds with longer maturities generally present greater interest rate risk than bonds of similar credit quality that have shorter maturities. To compensate investors for this interest rate risk, long-term bonds generally offer higher interest rates than short-term bonds of the same credit quality.

If two bonds offer different coupon rates while all of their other characteristics are the same, the bond with the lower coupon rate will generally be more sensitive to changes in market interest rates. For example, imagine one bond that has a coupon rate of 2% while another bond has a coupon rate of 4%. All other features of the two bonds—when they mature, their level of credit risk, and so on—are the same. If market interest rates rise, then the price of the bond with the 2% coupon rate will fall by a greater percentage than that of the bond with the 4% coupon rate. This makes it particularly important for investors to consider interest rate risk when they purchase bonds in a low-interest rate environment.

## Inflation Risk

Inflation is a general rise in the prices of goods and services, which causes a decline in purchasing power. With inflation over time, the amount of money received on the bond's interest and principal payments will purchase fewer goods and services than before.

## Liquidity Risk

Liquidity is the ability to sell an asset, such as a bond, for cash when the owner chooses. Bonds that are traded frequently and at high volumes may have stronger liquidity than bonds that trade less frequently. liquidity risk is the risk that investors seeking to sell their bonds may not receive a price that reflects the true value of the bonds (based on the bond's interest rate and creditworthiness of the company). If you own a bond that is not traded on an exchange, you may have to go to a broker when you want to sell it. In addition, the bond market does not have the same pricing transparency as the equity market, as the dissemination of pricing information is more limited for corporate bonds in comparison to equity securities such as common stock.

## Call Risk

The terms of some bonds give the company the right to buy back the bond before the maturity date. This is known as calling the bond, and it represents "call risk" to bondholders. For example, a bond with a maturity of 10 years may have terms allowing the company to call the bond any time after the first five years. If it calls the bond, the company will pay back the principal (and possibly an additional premium depending on when the call occurs). One reason the company may call the bond back is if market interest rates have fallen relative to the coupon rate on the bond. That same decline in market interest rates would likely make the bond more valuable to bondholders. Thus, what is financially advantageous to the company is likely to be financially disadvantageous to the bondholder. Bondholders may be unable to reinvest at a comparable interest rate for the same level of risk. Investors should check the terms of the bond for any call provisions or other terms allowing for prepayment.

## How Can Investors Reduce Their Risks?

Investors can reduce their risks by diversifying their assets. Bonds are one type of asset, along with shares of stock (or equity), cash, and other investments. Investors also can diversify the types of bonds they hold. For example, investors could buy bonds of different maturities—balancing short-term, intermediate, and long-term bonds—or diversify the mix of their bond holdings by combining corporate, treasury, or municipal bonds. Investors with a greater risk tolerance may decide to buy bonds of lower credit quality, accepting higher risks in pursuit of higher yields. More conservative investors, however, may prefer to limit their bond holdings solely to high-quality bonds, avoiding riskier or more speculative bonds. Instead of holding bonds directly, investors can invest in mutual funds or exchange-traded funds (ETFs) with a focus on bonds. Investors should base their decisions on their individual circumstances.

## How Do I Research My Bond Or Bond Fund Investment?

A prospectus is the offering document filed with the SEC by a company that issues bonds for sale to the public in a registered transaction. Among other things, the prospectus relating to a corporate bond issuance describes the terms of the bond, significant risks of investing in the offering, the financial condition of the company issuing the bond, and how the company plans to use the proceeds from the bond sale. similarly, if you are investing in a bond-focused mutual fund or ETF, these funds also prepare prospectuses detailing important information about the fund. Investors can ask their broker-dealer for the prospectus of any bond or bond fund in which they are interested. Prospectuses also are available to the public without charge on the SEC's EDGAR website. You can also find a bond fund's prospectus at the bond fund's website.

Regular periodic reports are filed by both companies that have sold bonds in a public offering and by bond-focused mutual funds and ETFs. Companies that have sold bonds in a public offering file quarterly reports on Form 10-Q and annual reports on Form 10-K, among other filings. You can use these reports to learn about and monitor a company's financial condition. Mutual funds and ETFs file annual and semiannual reports that detail the performance and holdings of the fund. these reports are available to the public without charge on the SEC's EDGAR website. You can also often find the reports of a bond fund at the bond fund's website.

# Part Four
Stocks And Mutual Funds

# Chapter 30
# Understanding Stocks

## What Are Stocks?

Stocks are a type of security that gives stockholders a share of ownership in a company. Stocks also are called "equities."

## Why Do People Buy Stocks?

Investors buy stocks for various reasons. Here are some of them:

- Capital appreciation, which occurs when a stock rises in price

- Dividend payments, which come when the company distributes some of its earnings to stockholders

- Ability to vote shares and influence the company

## Why Do Companies Issue Stock?

Companies issue stock to get money for various things, which may include:

- Paying off debt

- Launching new products

- Expanding into new markets or regions

- Enlarging facilities or building new ones

About This Chapter: This chapter includes text excerpted from "Stocks," Investor.gov, U.S. Securities and Exchange Commission (SEC), November 23, 2016.

---

## What Are The Differences Between Saving And Investing?

Your "savings" are usually put into the safest places or products that allow you access to your money at any time. Examples include savings accounts, checking accounts, and certificates of deposit. At some banks and savings and loan associations your deposits may be insured by the Federal Deposit Insurance Corporation (FDIC). But there's a trade-off for the security and ready availability of these savings methods: your money is paid a low wage as it works for you.

When you "invest," you have a greater chance of losing your money than when you "save." Unlike FDIC-insured deposits, the money you invest in securities, stocks, mutual funds, and other similar investments is not federally insured. You could lose your "principal," which is the amount you've invested. That's true even if you purchase your investments through a bank. But when you invest, you also have the opportunity to earn more money than when you save. There is a trade-off between the higher risk of investing and the potential for greater rewards.

*(Source: "Differences Between Saving And Investing," U.S. Securities and Exchange Commission (SEC).)*

---

# What Kinds Of Stocks Are There?

There are two main kinds of stocks, common stock and preferred stock.

1. **Common** stock entitles owners to vote at shareholder meetings and receive dividends.

2. **Preferred** stockholders usually don't have voting rights but they receive dividend payments before common stockholders do, and have priority over common stockholders if the company goes bankrupt and its assets are liquidated.

Common and preferred stocks may fall into one or more of the following categories:

- **Growth stocks** have earnings growing at a faster rate than the market average. They rarely pay dividends and investors buy them in the hope of capital appreciation. A start-up technology company is likely to be a growth stock.

- **Income stocks** pay dividends consistently. Investors buy them for the income they generate. An established utility company is likely to be an income stock.

- **Value stocks** have a low price-to-earnings (PE) ratio, meaning they are cheaper to buy than stocks with a higher PE. Value stocks may be growth or income stocks, and their low PE ratio may reflect the fact that they have fallen out of favor with investors for some reason. People buy value stocks in the hope that the market has overreacted and that the stock's price will rebound.

- **Blue-chip stocks** are shares in large, well-known companies with a solid history of growth. They generally pay dividends.

Another way to categorize stocks is by the size of the company, as shown in its market capitalization. There are large-cap, mid-cap, and small-cap stocks. Shares in very small companies are sometimes called "microcap" stocks. The very lowest priced stocks are known as "penny stocks." These companies may have little or no earnings. Penny stocks do not pay dividends and are highly speculative.

# What Are The Benefits And Risks Of Stocks?

Stocks offer investors the greatest potential for growth (capital appreciation) over the long haul. Investors willing to stick with stocks over long periods of time, say 15 years, generally have been rewarded with strong, positive returns.

But stock prices move down as well as up. There's no guarantee that the company whose stock you hold will grow and do well, so you can lose money you invest in stocks.

If a company goes bankrupt and its assets are liquidated, common stockholders are the last in line to share in the proceeds. The company's bondholders will be paid first, then holders of preferred stock. If you are a common stockholder, you get whatever is left, which may be nothing.

Even when companies aren't in danger of failing, their stock price may fluctuate up or down. Large company stocks as a group, for example, have lost money on average about one out of every three years. If you have to sell shares on a day when the stock price is below the price you paid for the shares, you will lose money on the sale.

Market fluctuations can be unnerving to some investors. A stock's price can be affected by factors inside the company, such as a faulty product, or by events the company has no control over, such as political or market events.

Stocks usually are one part of an investor's holdings. If you are young and saving for a long-term goal such as retirement, you may want to hold more stocks than bonds. Investors nearing or in retirement may want to hold more bonds than stocks.

The risks of stock holdings can be offset in part by investing in a number of different stocks. Investing in other kinds of assets that are not stocks, such as bonds, is another way to offset some of the risks of owning stocks.

> ## Difference Between Stocks And Bonds
>
> Stocks: If the company profits or is perceived as having strong potential, its stock may go up in value and pay dividends. You may make more money than from the bonds.
>
> Risk in Stock: The company may do poorly, and you'll lose a portion or all of your investment.
>
> Bonds: The company promises to return money plus interest
>
> Risk in Bond : If the company goes bankrupt, your money may be lost. But if there is any money left, you will be paid before stockholders.
>
> *(Source: "Savings And Investing For Students," U.S Securities and Exchange Commission (SEC).)*

# How To Buy And Sell Stocks

You can buy and sell stocks through:

- A direct stock plan

- A dividend reinvestment plan

- A discount or full-service broker

- A stock fund

**Direct stock plans:** Some companies allow you to buy or sell their stock directly through them without using a broker. This saves on commissions, but you may have to pay other fees to the plan, including if you transfer shares to a broker to sell them. Some companies limit direct stock plans to employees of the company or existing shareholders. Some require minimum amounts for purchases or account levels.

Direct stock plans usually will not allow you to buy or sell shares at a specific market price or at a specific time. Instead, the company will buy or sell shares for the plan at set times—such as daily, weekly, or monthly—and at an average market price. Depending on the plan, you may be able to automate your purchases and have the cost deducted automatically from your savings account.

**Dividend reinvestment plans:** These plans allow you to buy more shares of a stock you already own by reinvesting dividend payments into the company. You must sign an agreement with the company to have this done. Check with the company or your brokerage firm to see if you will be charged for this service.

**Discount or full-service broker:** Brokers buy and sell shares for customers for a fee, known as a commission.

**Stock funds:** These are a type of mutual fund that invests primarily in stocks. Depending on its investment objective and policies, a stock fund may concentrate on a particular type of stock, such as blue chips, large-cap value stocks, or mid-cap growth stocks. Stock funds are offered by investment companies and can be purchased directly from them or through a broker or adviser.

# Understanding Fees

Buying and selling stocks entails fees. A direct stock plan or a dividend reinvestment plan may charge you a fee for that service. Brokers who buy and sell stocks for you charge a commission. A discount brokerage charges lower commissions than what you would pay at a full-service brokerage. But generally you have to research and choose investments by yourself. A full-service brokerage costs more, but the higher commissions pay for investment advice based on that firm's research.

# Avoiding Fraud

Stocks in public companies are registered with the U.S. Securities and Exchange Commission (SEC) and in most cases, public companies are required to file reports to the SEC quarterly and annually. Annual reports include financial statements that have been audited by an independent audit firm. Information on public companies can be found on the SEC's Electronic Data Gathering, Analysis, and Retrieval (EDGAR) system.

# Chapter 31

# How The Stock Market Works

Do you trade baseball cards, videotapes or Pokemon cards? Anything becomes valuable if someone wants it badly enough. Have you heard about trading stocks and bonds on television or at home? Stocks are shares in a business that you get when you invest money in that company. Stocks are traded on the Stock Market and, on 1865, the New York Stock Exchange (NYSE) opened its first permanent headquarters near Wall Street in New York City. New York Stock Market Opened on Wall Street January 4, 1865.

## What Do You Think Makes The Price Of Stock Rise?

The more stocks you buy the bigger the piece of the company you own. If the company becomes popular, many people will invest their money, buy more stock, and the price of the stock will go up. If the company becomes unpopular, the stock price will drop. Bonds are different from stocks. Bonds are loans, usually made to your city, state, or the federal government, that are repaid with interest at a certain date in the future.

## How The Trading Of Stocks And Bonds Started

Although the official Stock Exchange opened in 1865, the trading of stocks and bonds began much earlier. The federal government started the U.S. investment market in 1790 to

About This Chapter: Text in this chapter begins with excerpts from "New York Stock Market Opened On Wall Street January 4, 1865," America's Library, Library of Congress (LOC), December 15, 2016; Text beginning with the heading "How Stock Markets Work" is excerpted from "How Stock Markets Work," Investor.gov, U.S. Securities and Exchange Commission (SEC), December 3, 2016; Text under the heading "Market Indices" is excerpted from "Market Indices," U.S. Securities and Exchange Commission (SEC), October 15, 2012; Text under the heading "After-Hours Trading" is excerpted from "Investor Bulletin: After-Hours Trading," U.S. Securities and Exchange Commission (SEC), May 2011.

issue bonds (loans) that would help pay off the debt from the American Revolution against Great Britain, which America won in 1783. Today the New York Stock Exchange is the biggest stock exchange in this country and it is located just a few doors away from this original stock exchange building.

---

All investments involve taking on risk. It's important that you go into any investment in stocks, bonds or mutual funds with a full understanding that you could lose some or all of your money in any one investment. While over the long term the stock market has historically provided around 10% annual returns (closer to 6% or 7% "real" returns when you subtract for the effects of inflation), the long term does sometimes take a rather long, long time to play out. Those who invested all of their money in the stock market at its peak in 1929 (before the stock market crash) would wait over 20 years to see the stock market return to the same level. However, those that kept adding money to the market throughout that time would have done very well for themselves, as the lower cost of stocks in the 1930s made for some hefty gains for those who bought and held over the course of the next twenty years or more.

*(Source: "Savings And Investing For Students," U.S Securities and Exchange Commission (SEC).)*

---

# How Stock Markets Work

Let's take a closer look at what you need to know about how stocks are traded.

## Public Companies

Public companies are a key part of the American economy. They play a major role in the savings, investment, and retirement plans of many Americans. If you have a pension plan or own a mutual fund, chances are that the plan or mutual fund owns stock in public companies. Like millions of Americans, you may also invest directly in public companies.

## What Is A Public Company?

The term "public company" can be defined in various ways. There are two commonly understood ways in which a company is considered public: first, the company's securities trade on public markets; and second, the company discloses certain business and financial information regularly to the public.

In general, the term refers to a company that has public reporting obligations. Companies are subject to public reporting requirements if they:

- Sell securities in a public offering (such as an initial public offering, or IPO;

- Allow their investor base to reach a certain size, which triggers public reporting obligations; OR

- Voluntarily register with SEC.

A private company also can become subject to public reporting requirements by merging with a public shell company. This process is called a reverse merger. As with any investment, investors should proceed with caution when considering whether to invest in reverse merger companies.

As mentioned, companies are viewed as public if they are subject to public reporting obligations. There are instances, however, where the securities of a company that does not regularly report business and financial information to the public are nonetheless traded on smaller public markets. Investing in these companies is riskier as there can be little public information to allow investors to make an informed investment decision.

---

The U.S Securities and Exchange Commission (SEC) requires public companies to disclose meaningful financial and other information to the public, which provides a public source for all investors to use to judge for themselves if a company's securities are a good investment.

*(Source: "Researching Public Companies Through EDGAR: A Guide For Investors," U.S. Securities and Exchange Commission (SEC).)*

---

## Transparency And Continuing Disclosures

A public company's disclosure obligations begin with the initial registration statement that it files with the U.S. Securities and Exchange Commission (SEC). But the disclosure requirements don't end there. Public companies must continue to keep their shareholders informed on a regular basis by filing periodic reports and other materials with the SEC. The SEC makes these documents publicly available without charge on its Electronic Data Gathering, Analysis, And Retrieval (EDGAR) website. The filed documents are subject to review by SEC staff for compliance with federal securities laws.

Following are some of the reports that may be filed by U.S.-based public companies. Foreign companies that file reports with the SEC may file different types of reports.

- **Annual reports on Form 10-K**: This report includes the company's audited annual financial statements and a discussion of the company's business results.

- **Quarterly reports on Form 10-Q**: Public companies must file this report for each of the first three quarters of their fiscal year. (After the fourth quarter, public companies file an annual report instead of a quarterly report.) The quarterly report includes unaudited financial statements and information about the company's business and results for the previous three months and for the year to date. The quarterly report compares the company's performance in the current quarter and year to date to the same periods in the previous year.

- **Current reports on Form 8-K**: Companies file this report with the SEC to announce major events that shareholders should know about, including bankruptcy proceedings, a change in corporate leadership (such as a new director or high-level officer), and preliminary earnings announcements.

- **Proxy statements**: Shareholder voting constitutes one of the key rights of shareholders. They may elect members of the board of directors, cast non-binding votes on executive compensation, approve or reject proposed mergers and acquisitions, or vote on other important topics. Proxy statements describe the matters to be voted upon and often disclose information on the company's executive compensation policies and practices.

- **Additional disclosures**: Other federal securities laws and SEC rules require disclosures about a variety of events affecting the company. These include proposed mergers, acquisitions and tender offers; securities transactions by company insiders, and beneficial ownership by a person or group that reaches or exceeds five percent of the company's outstanding shares.

## Public Disclosures Protect Investors

Our federal securities laws are based on public disclosure by companies of meaningful business, financial and other information. Public disclosure by companies serves to advance the mission of the SEC.

# Market Participants

Part of the mission of the SEC is "to maintain standards for fair, orderly, and efficient markets." To do this, the SEC regulates a number of securities market participants. These include:

- **Broker-dealers:** Broker-dealers charge a fee to handle trades between the buyers and sellers of securities. A broker-dealer may buy securities from their customer who is selling or sell from their own inventory to its customer who is buying.

- **Clearing agencies:** Clearing Agencies are Self-Regulatory Organizations (SROs) that are required to register with the SEC. Like all SROs, they are responsible for writing and enforcing their rules and disciplining members. There are two types of clearing agencies—clearing corporations and depositories.

- Clearing corporations, such as the National Securities Clearing Corporation (NSCC) and the Fixed Income Clearing Corporation (FICC), compare member transactions, clear those trades and prepare instructions for automated settlement of those trades. Clearing corporations often act as intermediaries in making securities settlements.

- Depositories, namely The Depository Trust Company (DTC), hold securities certificates for their participants, transfer positions between participants, and maintain ownership records.

- **Credit rating agencies:** Credit Rating Agencies provide opinions on the creditworthiness of a company or security. They indicate the credit quality by means of a grade. Generally, credit ratings distinguish between investment grade and non-investment grade. For example, a credit rating agency may assign a "triple A" credit rating as its top "investment grade" rating, and a "double B" credit rating or below for "non-investment grade" or "high-yield" corporate bonds. Credit rating agencies registered as such with the SEC are known as "Nationally Recognized Statistical Rating Organizations."

- **ECNs/ATSs:** Electronic Communications Networks, or ECNs, are electronic trading systems that automatically match buy and sell orders at specified prices for users of the system. ECNs register with the SEC as broker-dealers and are subject to Regulation ATS. ATSs are Alternative Trading Systems. This term encompasses all systems that perform securities exchange functions and are not registered with the Commission as exchanges.

- **Investment advisers:** Investment advisers are persons or firms that are in the business of providing investment advice to investors or issuing reports or analyses regarding securities. They do these activities for compensation.

- **Securities exchanges:** Securities exchanges are markets where securities are bought and sold. Currently, there are fifteen securities exchanges registered with the SEC as national securities exchanges, including NYSE Euronext, National Association of Securities Dealers Automated Quotations (NASDAQ), The Chicago Board Options Exchange (CBOE), and BATS Exchange. Securities Exchanges are also SROs.

- **Self-Regulatory Organizations (SROs):** An SRO manages its industry through the adoption of rules governing the conduct of its members. SROs also enforce the rules they adopt and discipline members for violating SRO rules. Two well-known SROs are the Financial Industry Regulatory Authority (FINRA) and the Municipal Securities

Rulemaking Board (MSRB). FINRA is the largest SRO in the securities industry. It is the frontline regulator of broker-dealers. MSRB makes rules regulating dealers of municipal securities. The SEC oversees both FINRA and the MSRB. Other SROs include clearing agencies and securities exchanges.

- **Transfer agents:** Transfer agents record changes of security ownership, maintain the issuer's security holder records, cancel and issue certificates, and distribute dividends. Transfer agents stand between issuing companies and security holders. Transfer agents are required to be registered with the SEC, or if the transfer agent is a bank, with a bank regulatory agency. There is no SRO that governs transfer agents. The SEC has announced rules and regulations for all registered transfer agents. The intent is to facilitate the prompt and accurate clearance and settlement of securities transactions and assure the safeguarding of securities and funds.

# Market Indices

A market index tracks the performance of a specific "basket" of stocks considered to represent a particular market or sector of the U.S. stock market or the economy.

There are indices for almost every conceivable sector of the economy and stock market. Many investors are familiar with these indices through index funds and exchange-traded funds whose investment objectives are to track the performance of a particular index.

Here are general descriptions of a few major market indices. (The SEC does not regulate the content of these indices and is not endorsing those described here). You can also find them described on their sponsors' websites and in the available information of the funds that track them.

## Dow Jones Industrial Average (DJIA)

The Dow Jones Industrial Average is an index of 30 "blue chip" stocks of U.S. industrial companies. The Index includes a wide range of companies—from financial services companies, to computer companies, to retail companies—but excludes transportation and utility companies, which are included in separate indices. Unlike many other indices, the DJIA is not a "weighted" index, meaning it does not take market capitalization into account.

## NYSE Composite Index

The NYSE Composite Index tracks the price movements of all common stocks listed on the New York Stock Exchange. The Index is "capitalization-weighted" (that is, each stock's weight in the Index is proportionate to the stock's market capitalization).

## S&P 500 Composite Stock Price Index

The Standard & Poor's 500 Composite Stock Price Index is a capitalization-weighted index of 500 stocks intended to be a representative sample of leading companies in leading industries within the U.S. economy. Stocks in the Index are chosen for market size, liquidity, and industry group representation.

## Wilshire 5000 Total Market Index

The Wilshire 5000 Total Market Index is intended to measure the performance of the entire U.S. stock market. It contains all U.S.-headquartered equity securities with readily available price data. The Index is a capitalization-weighted Index.

## Russell 2000® Index

The Russell 2000® Index is a capitalization-weighted index designed to measure the performance of the 2,000 smallest publicly traded U.S. companies based on in market capitalization. The Index is a subset of the larger Russell 3000® Index.

## Nasdaq-100 Index

The Nasdaq-100 Index is a "modified capitalization-weighted" index designed to track the performance of the 100 largest and most actively traded non-financial domestic and international securities listed on The Nasdaq Stock Market. To be included in the Index, a stock must have a minimum average daily trading volume of 100,000 shares. Generally, companies on the Index also must have traded on Nasdaq, or been listed on another major exchange, for at least two years.

---

National Association of Securities Dealers Automated Quotations (NASDAQ) or the NASDAQ Stock Market, is a national securities exchange that is owned and operated by the NASDAQ OMX Group. The NASDAQ Stock Market comprises three market tiers:

1. the NASDAQ Global Select Market,
2. the NASDAQ Global Market, formerly, the NASDAQ National Market, and
3. the NASDAQ Capital Market, formerly, the NASDAQ SmallCap Market.

For a company to trade on the NASDAQ Stock Market, it must meet the listing requirements of at least one of these three market tiers. Some of these listing requirements include meeting specified minimum thresholds for the number of publicly traded shares, total market value, stock price, and number of shareholders.

The NASDAQ OMX Group also owns and operates two additional national securities exchanges: the NASDAQ OMX PHLX (formerly, the Philadelphia Stock Exchange); and the NASDAQ OMX BX (formerly, the Boston Stock Exchange).

*(Source: "Nasdaq," U.S. Securities and Exchange Commission (SEC).)*

# After-Hours Trading

After-hours trading, also known as extended-hours trading, refers to trading that occurs outside of regular trading hours. Regular trading hours for stocks traded on exchanges and certain other markets are from 9:30 a.m. to 4:00 p.m. Eastern Time. After-hours trading sessions may occur before or after regular trading hours. The duration of after-hours trading sessions varies between markets and trading venues. Investors should contact their brokerage firms to determine if and when after-hours trading sessions are available.

## Overview Of After-Hours Trading

Investors should be aware that the rules governing the various markets and venues that conduct after-hours trading vary and may differ significantly from rules that apply during regular trading hours. Differences may include the types of orders accepted for after-hours trading, the securities that are available to trade, the presence or absence of market makers, and rules designed to protect investors from poor prices. Investors should contact their brokerage firms to determine the specific rules that apply. After-hours trading takes place within computerized trading systems, informally known as "electronic markets," that operate beyond regular trading hours. These "electronic markets" may include, for example, alternative trading systems (ATSs) and electronic communications networks (ECNs) (both operated by broker-dealers), or exchanges and other markets with electronic trading platforms.

## After-Hours Trading Risks

While after-hours trading presents investment opportunities, investors should consider the following risks before engaging in after-hours trading:

- **Order handling:** Some rules that apply to the handling of orders during regular trading hours do not apply to orders in after-hours trading. Investors should check with their brokerage firms to determine how orders placed during afterhours trading are handled, including the markets to which the firm routes orders and whether or not it seeks to route each order to the best displayed price.

- **Lack of liquidity:** Liquidity refers to the existence of buyers and sellers who are willing to trade with incoming orders and the degree of price competition among buyers and sellers. A lack of liquidity can affect an investor's ability to quickly buy or sell stock with a minimal effect on the stock's price. During regular trading hours, buyers and sellers of most stocks rigorously compete on prices to attract trading interest. However, during after-hours trading there generally is less trading interest and less price competition for most stocks, which may raise trading costs, increase uncertainty with respect to prevailing prices, or make it more difficult to execute trades. There may be no market makers actively making markets in most or all stocks. In fact, some stocks may not trade at all during afterhours trading.

- **Larger quote spreads:** The reduced level of trading interest in after-hours trading generally results in wider spreads between the bid and ask prices for a stock or no quotes at all. As a result, investors may find it more difficult to get their orders executed or to get as favorable a price as they could have during regular market hours.

- **Price volatility:** For stocks with limited trading activity, investors may find greater price fluctuations than they typically would see during regular trading hours.

- **Uncertain prices:** The prices of some stocks traded during after-hours trading may not reflect the prices of those stocks during regular hours, either at the end of the regular trading session or upon the opening of regular trading the next business day.

- **Requirement of limit orders:** With respect to after-hours trading, many brokerage firms currently accept only limit orders in order to protect investors from unexpectedly bad prices. Limit orders can be executed only at the limit price or better. If the market moves away from the limit price, the order will not be executed.

- **Order time limit:** Investors should check with their brokerage firms to see whether orders not executed during after-hours trading will be canceled or whether they will be automatically entered when regular trading hours begin. Similarly, investors should also check with their brokerage firms to see if orders placed during regular trading hours will carry over to after-hours trading.

- **Competition with professional traders:** Investors should note that many of the after-hours traders are professional traders who, by nature of their profession, generally have access to more information than individual investors.

# Chapter 32

# Types Of Investment Companies

Investment companies are businesses that market, sell, and manage investments for clients. They pool together the money they receive from individuals, collectively invest it in a variety of securities (stocks, bonds, treasury notes, etc.), and manage the investments for maximum return. Investors then share in the profits and losses of the securities in proportion to the amount of money they put in. Investment companies generally offer a variety of funds and services, including portfolio management, accounting, tax management, and legal services. They can be privately or publicly owned, and in the United States most of them are registered and regulated by the Securities and Exchange Commission (SEC). There are three primary types of investment companies: open-end, closed-end, and unit investment trusts (UITs).

According to the SEC: "Some types of companies that might initially appear to be investment companies may actually be excluded under the federal securities laws. For example, private investment funds with no more than 100 investors and private investment funds whose investors each have a substantial amount of investment assets are not considered to be investment companies—even though they issue securities and are primarily engaged in the business of investing in securities. This may be because of the private nature of their offerings or the financial means and sophistication of their investors." New investors should probably steer clear of these companies.

*(Source: "Investment Companies," U.S. Securities and Exchange Commission (SEC).)*

---

# Open-End Investment Companies

Also known as a mutual fund, an open-end investment company is a business that issues unlimited shares of investments in stocks and/or bonds. It offers the shares on a continuous basis, and these can only be purchased from and sold back to the investment company or a broker designated by the company. So individual investors can't buy the shares from sellers on a secondary market, such as the New York Stock Exchange or the Nasdaq Stock Market.

There are many kinds of open-end investment companies, or mutual funds, including stock funds, bond funds, index funds, and money market funds. They all tend to have different objectives for their investors and different strategies for helping them meet their financial goals. They also have varying degrees of risk, volatility, and fees, all of which should be considered carefully before you invest in one of these funds.

## Advantages Of Open-End Investment Companies

- **Professional management**: Many small investors don't have the time or desire to become knowledgeable about thousands of possible investment opportunities and keep track of their performance. With mutual funds, an experienced portfolio manager handles these tasks in exchange for a fee.

- **Diversification**: With investments, it's never a good idea to put all your eggs in one basket. Better to put your money into a variety of investments, and a variety of types of investments. That way, losses in one area are made up by gains in others. Mutual funds are designed to do exactly that, without you having to make every individual decision.

- **Affordability**: It's not very practical for an individual to build a diversified portfolio with a relatively small initial investment. Some funds allow you to start off with an investment of $500, or even less, making them ideal for new investors.

- **Flexibility**: A lot of open-end investment companies manage several different funds and allow investors to switch between them. So as market conditions or your own circumstances change, you might be able to move between funds with different degrees of risk and types of investments.

- **Liquidity**: Liquidity refers to the ability to convert shares or other holdings into cash easily. And with most mutual funds, you can get out any time you want by informing the company that you want to sell your shares back, and your money could be in your hands within a day or two.

## Disadvantages Of Open-End Investment Companies

- **Fees**: There will be fees for managing your portfolio, and these are almost always charged whether the fund makes money for you or not. These fees vary widely, so they're an important thing to consider as you compare funds and decide where to put your money.

- **Manager performance**: Possibly the most important factor that determines a fund's performance is the skill of the portfolio manager. As you do your research, you'll find comprehensive information on the fund's historical performance, which is very important, but you also need to investigate the person who will be managing the fund. This information is also readily available, and it's just as critical to your decision. A weak manager could lose money for you.

- **Locked-in clauses**: While most funds allow you to sell at any time, some lock in investors for five to seven years. If you need to get your money out earlier, you'll pay a cash penalty. Take this into consideration when choosing a fund.

# Closed-End Investment Companies

Sometimes called a closed-end fund, this type of company does not issue shares on a continuous basis, but rather sells them in a one-time public offering on an exchange. Those shares are then bought and sold on the open market like stock. For that reason, the price of shares in a closed-end fund, after the initial offering, is determined by market demand.

Like open-end investment companies, closed-end funds are managed by professional portfolio managers, and some concentrate on specific industries or types of investments, while others are more generalized. And, like open-end funds, they can have different financial objectives, degrees of risk, and fees, so be sure to do your homework before making a decision.

## Advantages Of Closed-End Investment Companies

- **Professional management**: As with mutual funds, you get the benefit of having your investment managed by an experienced portfolio manager.

- **Profit potential**: Because the price of closed-end funds is determined by market demand, their value could possibly rise significantly above the price you paid, earning you a nice profit. In addition, these funds need to get rid of almost all their interest and dividend income to avoid federal taxes, so they can provide regular dividend income for investors.

- **Trading flexibility**: Although funds are intended to be a long-term investment, the ability to buy and sell closed-end fund shares on a daily basis can allow investors to take advantage of short-term opportunities or sell at the start of a downturn.

- **Liquidity**: Closed-end investment companies are not required to buy back shares from investors as open-end companies are, but the fact that closed-end shares trade on the open market allows you considerable trading flexibility.

## Disadvantages Of Closed-End Investment Companies

- **Fees**: There are management fees associated with closed-end investment companies, and as with open-end funds, these are generally payable whether or not the fund makes money. Shop for the best terms before making a commitment.

- **Volatility**: Where there's profit potential there's also loss potential. Because the price of closed-end funds is determined by market demand, you may need to sell your shares when the value is below what you paid for them.

- **Leverage**: Managers of closed-end funds have more freedom than those of open-end funds when it comes to selecting investments. For example, they may take on short-term debt to increase profits. But if interest rates go up, the return on those leveraged investments can be affected.

- **Trading flexibility**: This can be an advantage if you make smart moves or if you're lucky. But the ability to engage in day-trading can easily work against you through overtrading or making poor decisions.

- **Liquidity**: Again, this can be a plus or minus. If you need money in an emergency, and the current market value of your shares is less than you paid, you can lose money.

> Remember that money invested in open-end companies and UITs is redeemable. Unlike with closed-end companies, that means the fund will buy back your investment at almost any time. Although there may be a penalty for this, it could be important if you need cash in an emergency.

# Unit Investment Trusts (UIT)

A unit investment trust (UIT) is a company that invests in a fixed portfolio of stocks, bonds, and other securities. Investors buy redeemable units (shares) of the trust for a set period of time, during which the trust, if successful, will distribute interest and dividends. At the end of the trust's life, the profits are divided among the investors. The fund is "fixed" in that it buys a portfolio of securities and holds onto them for the life of the UIT with little or no change.

## Advantages Of A UIT

- **Professional management**: Like the other types of investment companies, a major advantage of a UIT is that you have an expert handling your money. In this case, the expertise is primarily applied at the beginning of the UIT when securities are chosen, but there are other duties associated with managing the fund that require professional experience.

- **Diversification**: Investment is spread across stocks, bonds, and other securities that can number from five to hundreds, a strategy that helps protect against losses.

- **Affordability**: Unit Investment Trusts are popular with small investors because you can buy into many of them for a relatively small amount, usually around $1,000.

- **Liquidity**: Like open-end investment funds, UITs are redeemable, which means you can sell all or some of your units back to the fund at any time, although certain restrictions may apply.

## Disadvantages Of A UIT

- **Limited management**: Unlike the other two funds, UITs are fixed, so there's a limit to the moves the fund manager can make. Without active management, the fund really can't respond to market conditions and changes.

- **Fees**: All UITs charge fees. The primary ones are an entry fee, paid when you buy, an exit fee, charged if you cash out early, and a management fee, which is a percentage of your investment that you pay on an ongoing basis to the fund manager for handling the fund. And you pay these fees even if the fund loses money.

- **Limited advice**: Unlike other investments, UITs don't have corporate officers, boards of directors, or investment advisers available to consult with you during the life of the trust.

- **Early termination**: It's rare but a UIT may be able to terminate early, depending on how it's organized. If that happens, you could lose money, depending on the market status at the time of termination.

In addition to the funds discussed here, there are many other pooled-money investments available, including index funds, equity funds, liquid funds, and real estate funds. Do your research, talk to managers or brokers, and consider carefully before making an investment decision.

## References

1. "Advantages and Disadvantages of Mutual Funds," Wallstreetsurvivor.com, n.d.

2. Brown, Jeff. "Pros and Cons of Closed-End Funds," USnews.com, September 7, 2016.

3. "Investment Companies," U.S. Securities and Exchange Commission (SEC), July 9, 2013.

4. "Types of Investment Companies," Investopedia.com, n.d.

5. "Types of Investment Companies," Yourarticlelibrary.com, n.d.

6. Zuckerman, Gregory. "The Pros and Cons of Buying Unit Investment Trusts," Wall Street Journal, November 1, 2015.

# Chapter 33

# Understanding Mutual Funds And Exchange-Traded Funds (ETFs)

## Mutual Funds

### What Are Mutual Funds?

A mutual fund is a company that pools money from many investors and invests the money in securities such as stocks, bonds, and short-term debt. The combined holdings of the mutual fund are known as its portfolio. Investors buy shares in mutual funds. Each share represents an investor's part ownership in the fund and the income it generates.

### Why Do People Buy Mutual Funds?

Mutual funds are a popular choice among investors because they generally offer the following features:

- **Professional management**: The fund managers do the research for you. They select the securities and monitor the performance.

- **Diversification or "Don't put all your eggs in one basket"** Mutual funds typically invest in a range of companies and industries. This helps to lower your risk if one company fails.

- **Affordability**: Most mutual funds set a relatively low dollar amount for initial investment and subsequent purchases.

About This Chapter: Text under the heading "Mutual Funds?" is excerpted from "Mutual Funds," Investor.gov, U.S. Securities and Exchange Commission (SEC), December 27, 2016; Text under the heading "Exchange-Traded Funds (ETF)" is excerpted from "Exchange-Traded Funds (ETFs)," Investor.gov, U.S. Securities and Exchange Commission (SEC), November 23, 2016; Text beginning with the heading "Common Features Of Mutual Funds And ETFS" is excerpted from "Mutual Funds and ETFS," Investor.gov, U.S. Securities and Exchange Commission (SEC), December 28, 2016.

- **Liquidity**: Mutual fund investors can easily redeem their shares at any time, for the current net asset value (NAV) plus any redemption fees.

## What Types Of Mutual Funds Are There?

Most mutual funds fall into one of four main categories—money market funds, bond funds, stock funds, and target date funds. Each type has different features, risks, and rewards.

- **Money market funds** have relatively low risks. By law, they can invest only in certain high-quality, short-term investments issued by U.S. corporations, and federal, state and local governments.

- **Bond funds** have higher risks than money market funds because they typically aim to produce higher returns. Because there are many different types of bonds, the risks and rewards of bond funds can vary dramatically.

- **Stock funds** invest in corporate stocks. Not all stock funds are the same. Some examples are:

  - Growth funds focus on stocks that may not pay a regular dividend but have potential for above-average financial gains.

  - Income funds invest in stocks that pay regular dividends.

  - Index funds track a particular market index such as the Standard & Poor's 500 Index.

  - Sector funds specialize in a particular industry segment.

- **Target date funds** hold a mix of stocks, bonds, and other investments. Over time, the mix gradually shifts according to the fund's strategy. Target date funds, sometimes known as lifecycle funds, are designed for individuals with particular retirement dates in mind.

## What Are The Benefits And Risks Of Mutual Funds?

Mutual funds offer professional investment management and potential diversification. They also offer three ways to earn money:

- **Dividend Payments**: A fund may earn income from dividends on stock or interest on bonds. The fund then pays the shareholders nearly all the income, less expenses.

- **Capital Gains Distributions**: The price of the securities in a fund may increase. When a fund sells a security that has increased in price, the fund has a capital gain. At the end of the year, the fund distributes these capital gains, minus any capital losses, to investors.

- **Increased NAV**: If the market value of a fund's portfolio increases, after deducting expenses, then the value of the fund and its shares increases. The higher NAV reflects the higher value of your investment.

All funds carry some level of risk. With mutual funds, you may lose some or all of the money you invest because the securities held by a fund can go down in value. Dividends or interest payments may also change as market conditions change.

A fund's past performance is not as important as you might think because past performance does not predict future returns. But past performance can tell you how volatile or stable a fund has been over a period of time. The more volatile the fund, the higher the investment risk.

## How To Buy And Sell Mutual Funds

Investors buy mutual fund shares from the fund itself or through a broker for the fund, rather than from other investors. The price that investors pay for the mutual fund is the fund's per share net asset value plus any fees charged at the time of purchase, such as sales loads.

Mutual fund shares are "redeemable," meaning investors can sell the shares back to the fund at any time. The fund usually must send you the payment within seven days.

Before buying shares in a mutual fund, read the prospectus carefully. The prospectus contains information about the mutual fund's investment objectives, risks, performance, and expenses.

## Understanding Fees

As with any business, running a mutual fund involves costs. Funds pass along these costs to investors by charging fees and expenses. Fees and expenses vary from fund to fund. A fund with high costs must perform better than a low-cost fund to generate the same returns for you.

Even small differences in fees can mean large differences in returns over time. For example, if you invested $10,000 in a fund with a 10% annual return, and annual operating expenses of 1.5%, after 20 years you would have roughly $49,725. If you invested in a fund with the same performance and expenses of 0.5%, after 20 years you would end up with $60,858.

It takes only minutes to use a mutual fund cost calculator to compute how the costs of different mutual funds add up over time and eat into your returns.

## Avoiding Fraud

By law, each mutual fund is required to file a prospectus and regular shareholder reports with the SEC. Before you invest, be sure to read the prospectus and the required shareholder reports. Additionally, the investment portfolios of mutual funds are managed by separate entities known as "investment advisers" that are registered with the SEC. Always check that the investment adviser is registered before investing.

---

## Mutual Fund Proxy Voting Records And Policies

Do you want to know how mutual funds vote their proxies? Mutual funds and other registered management investment companies are required to disclose each year how they vote proxies relating to portfolio securities they hold. Not later than August 31st of each year, a mutual fund must file with the SEC a report known as Form N-PX, containing the fund's complete proxy voting record for the most recent 12-month period ended June 30th.

*(Source: "Mutual Fund Proxy Voting Records And Policies," U.S. Securities and Exchange Commission (SEC).)*

---

# Exchange-Traded Funds (ETFs)

## What Is An Exchange-Traded Funds (ETFs)?

Exchange-Traded Funds (ETFs) are a type of exchange-traded investment product that must register with the SEC under the 1940 Act as either an open-end investment company (generally known as "funds") or a unit investment trust.

Like mutual funds, ETFs offer investors a way to pool their money in a fund that makes investments in stocks, bonds, or other assets and, in return, to receive an interest in that investment pool. Unlike mutual funds, however, ETF shares are traded on a national stock exchange and at market prices that may or may not be the same as the net asset value ("NAV") of the shares, that is, the value of the ETF's assets minus its liabilities divided by the number of shares outstanding.

### Things To Consider Before Investing In ETFs

ETFs are not mutual funds. Generally, ETFs combine features of a mutual fund, which can be purchased or redeemed at the end of each trading day at its NAV per share, with the intraday trading feature of a closed-end fund, whose shares trade throughout the trading day at market prices.

Unlike with mutual fund shares, retail investors can only purchase and sell ETF shares in market transactions. That is, unlike mutual funds, ETFs do not sell individual shares directly to, or redeem their individual shares directly from, retail investors. Instead, ETF sponsors enter into contractual relationships with one or more financial institutions known as "Authorized Participants." Authorized Participants typically are large broker-dealers. Only Authorized Participants are permitted to purchase and redeem shares directly from the ETF, and they can do so only in large aggregations or blocks (e.g., 50,000 ETF shares) commonly called "Creation Units."

Other investors purchase and sell ETF shares in market transactions at market prices. An ETF's market price typically will be more or less than the fund's NAV per share. This is because the ETF's market price fluctuates during the trading day as a result of a variety of factors, including the underlying prices of the ETF's assets and the demand for the ETF, while the ETF's NAV is the value of the ETF's assets minus its liabilities, as calculated by the ETF at the end of each business day.

## Types Of ETFs

### Index-Based ETFs

Most ETFs trading in the marketplace are index-based ETFs. These ETFs seek to track a securities index like the S&P 500 stock index and generally invest primarily in the component securities of the index. For example, the SPDR, or "spider" ETF, which seeks to track the S&P 500 stock index, invests in most or all of the equity securities contained in the S&P 500 stock index. Some, but not all, ETFs may post their holdings on their websites on a daily basis.

### Actively Managed ETFs

Actively managed ETFs are not based on an index. Instead, they seek to achieve a stated investment objective by investing in a portfolio of stocks, bonds, and other assets. Unlike with an index-based ETF, an adviser of an actively managed ETF may actively buy or sell components in the portfolio on a daily basis without regard to conformity with an index.

## Making A Decision

Before investing in an ETF, you should read both its summary prospectus and its full prospectus, which provide detailed information on the ETF's investment objective, principal investment strategies, risks, costs, and historical performance (if any). The SEC's EDGAR system, as well as Internet search engines, can help you locate a specific ETF prospectus. You can also find prospectuses on the websites of the financial firms that sponsor a particular ETF, as well as through your broker.

Do not invest in something that you do not understand. If you cannot explain the investment opportunity in a few words and in an understandable way, you may need to reconsider the potential investment.

Finally, you may wish to consider seeking the advice of an investment professional. If you do, be sure to work with someone who understands your investment objectives and tolerance for risk. Your investment professional should understand complex products and be able to explain to your satisfaction whether or how they fit with your objectives.

> For a variety of reasons, an ETF's market price may trade at a premium or a discount to its underlying value. When an Authorized Participant identifies that an ETF's shares are trading at either a premium or discount to their estimated net asset value, it may engage in trading strategies that are expected to result in the market price of an ETF's shares moving back in line with its underlying value. As noted below in more detail, these actions by Authorized Participants, commonly described as "arbitrage opportunities," are designed to keep the market-determined price of an ETF's shares close to its underlying value. The premiums and discounts for specific ETFs may vary over time.
>
> *(Source: "Investor Bulletin: Exchange-Traded Funds (ETFs)," U.S. Securities and Exchange Commission (SEC).)*

# Common Features Of Mutual Funds And ETFs

Some common features of mutual funds and ETFs are described below. Whether any particular feature is an advantage or disadvantage for you will depend on your unique circumstances—always be sure that the investment you are considering has the features that are important to you.

- **Professional management**: Most funds and ETFs are managed by investment advisers who are registered with the SEC.

- **Diversification**: Spreading investments across a wide range of companies or industry sectors can help lower risk if a company or sector fails. Many investors find it less expensive to achieve such diversification through ownership of certain mutual funds or certain ETFs than through ownership of individual stocks or bonds.

- **Low minimum investment**: Some mutual funds accommodate investors who don't have a lot of money to invest by setting relatively low dollar amounts for the initial purchase, subsequent monthly purchases, or both. Similarly, ETF shares can often be purchased on the market for relatively low dollar amounts.

- **Liquidity and trading convenience**: Mutual fund investors can readily redeem their shares at the next calculated NAV—minus any fees and charges assessed on redemption—on any business day. Mutual funds must send investors payment for the shares within seven days, but many funds provide payment sooner. ETF investors can trade their shares on the market at any time the market is open at the market price—minus any fees and charges incurred at the time of sale. ETF and mutual fund shares traded through a broker are required to settle in three business days.

- **Costs despite negative returns**: Investors in mutual funds must pay sales charges, annual fees, management fees and other expenses, regardless of how the mutual fund performs. Investors may also have to pay taxes on any capital gains distribution they receive. Investors in ETFs must pay brokerage commissions, annual fees, management fees and other expenses, regardless of how the ETF performs. ETF investors may also have to pay taxes on any capital gains distributions; however, because of the structure of certain ETFs that redeem proceeds in kind, taxes on ETF investments have historically been lower than those for mutual fund investments. It is important to note that the tax efficiency of ETFs is not relevant if an investor holds the mutual fund or ETF investment in a tax-advantaged account, such as an IRA or a 401(k).

- **Lack of control**: Investors in both mutual funds and ETFs cannot directly influence which securities are included in the funds' portfolios.

- **Potential price uncertainty**: With an individual stock or an ETF, an investor can obtain real-time (or close to real-time) pricing information with relative ease by checking financial websites or by calling a broker. By contrast, with a mutual fund, the price at which an investor purchases or redeems shares will depend on the fund's NAV, which the fund might not calculate until many hours after an order has been placed.

# Factors To Consider

Before Investing in Mutual Funds or ETFs:

- **Determine your financial goals and risk tolerance.** When it comes to investing in mutual funds and ETFs, investors have thousands of choices. Before you invest in any mutual fund or ETF, you must decide whether the investment strategy and risks are a good fit for you. You should also consider more generally whether the unique style of investing of the mutual fund's or ETF's sponsor is a good fit for you. The first step to successful investing is to figure out your current financial goals and risk tolerance—either on your own or with the help of an investment professional.

- **Beware of risk.** All investments carry some level of risk. An investor can lose some or all of the money he or she invests—the principal—because securities held by a fund go up and down in value. Dividend payments may also fluctuate as market conditions change. Mutual funds and ETFs have different risks and rewards. Generally, the higher the potential return, the higher the risk of loss.

- **Consider the sponsor's investing style.** Before you invest, you may want to research the sponsor of the mutual fund or ETF you are considering. The sponsor's website is often a good place to begin, and it is helpful to spend some time browsing through the website to get a better understanding of the sponsor's underlying philosophy on investing. Each sponsor has its own style of investing that will affect how it manages its mutual funds and ETFs. It is helpful to understand each sponsor's style of investing, so you can better choose the right investment for you.

- **Ask and check.** Before you engage an investment professional or purchase shares of a mutual fund or ETF, make sure you research and verify relevant information to determine which option is best suited for you.

- **Investment professionals**: Details on an investment professional's background and qualifications are available on the SEC's Investment Adviser Public Disclosure (IAPD) website (www.adviserinfo.sec.gov/) or on the SEC's website for individual investors, Investor.gov. If you have any questions about checking the background of an investment professional, you can call the SEC's toll-free investor assistance line at 800-732-0330 for help.

- **Mutual funds and ETFs**: You can research a mutual fund or ETF by reading its prospectus carefully to learn about its investment strategy and the potential risks. You can find the prospectus on the mutual fund's or ETF's website or on the SEC's Electronic Data Gathering, Analysis, and Retrieval (EDGAR) database.

# How Mutual Funds And ETFs Can Provide Returns To Investors

Investors can make money from their investments in three ways:

1. **Dividend payments**: Depending on the underlying securities, a mutual fund or ETF may earn income in the form of dividends on the securities in its portfolio. The mutual fund or ETF then pays its shareholders nearly all of the income (minus disclosed expenses) it has earned.

2. **Capital gains distributions**: The price of the securities a mutual fund or ETF owns may increase. When a mutual fund or ETF sells a security that has increased in price, the mutual fund or ETF has a capital gain. At the end of the year, most mutual funds and ETFs distribute these capital gains (minus any capital losses) to shareholders. ETFs seek to minimize these capital gains by making in-kind exchanges to redeeming Authorized Participants instead of selling portfolio securities.

3. **Increased NAV/Increased market price**: If the market value of a mutual fund's portfolio increases, after deduction of expenses and liabilities, then the net asset value of the mutual fund and its shares increases. If the market value of an ETF's portfolio increases, after deduction of expenses and liabilities, then the net asset value of the ETF increases, and the market price of its shares may also increase.

With respect to dividend payments and capital gains distributions, mutual funds usually will give investors a choice: the mutual fund can send the investor a check or other form of payment, or the investor can have the dividends or distributions reinvested in the mutual fund to buy more shares (often without paying an additional sales load). If an ETF investor wants to reinvest a dividend payment or capital gains distribution, the process can be more complicated and the investor may have to pay additional brokerage commissions. Investors should check with their ETF or investment professional.

# Things That Could Reduce Mutual Funds' And ETFs' Returns

Investors should consider the effect that fees, expenses, and taxes will have on their returns over time. They can significantly reduce the returns on mutual funds and ETFs.

## Fees And Expenses

As with any business, running a mutual fund or ETF involves costs. Funds pass along these costs to investors by imposing fees and expenses.

**Shareholder fees** are fees charged directly to mutual fund investors in connection with transactions such as buying, selling, or exchanging shares, or on a periodic basis with respect to account fees. An investor can find these fees and charges listed in the "Fee Table" section of a mutual fund's prospectus or summary prospectus under the heading, "Shareholder Fees." ETFs don't charge these fees directly to investors, but they may have several types of transaction fees and costs, which are described below.

271

**Operating expenses** are ongoing mutual fund and ETF costs such as investment advisory fees for managing the fund's holdings, marketing and distribution expenses, as well as custodial, transfer agency, legal, and accountant's fees. Operating expenses are regular and recurring fund-wide expenses that are typically paid out of fund assets, which means that investors indirectly pay these costs. These expenses are identified in the "Fee Table" section of a mutual fund's or ETF's prospectus or summary prospectus under the heading, "Annual Fund Operating Expenses." Although these fees and expenses may not be listed individually as specific line items on an account statement, they can have a substantial impact on an investment over time.

Fees and expenses vary from fund to fund. If the funds are otherwise the same, a fund with lower fees will outperform a fund with higher fees. Remember, the more investors pay in fees and expenses, the less money they will have in their investment portfolio. As noted above, index funds typically have lower fees than actively managed funds.

# Chapter 34

# Types Of Mutual Funds: Index Funds, Stock Funds, Bond Funds, And Money Market Funds

A mutual fund is an investment company that pools money from many individuals and invests it in different kinds of securities, such as stocks, bonds, and treasury notes. These combined assets are called the fund's portfolio, and it is managed by a professional investment adviser who is registered by the U.S. Securities and Exchange Commission (SEC). Investors purchase shares in the fund, and each investor's number of shares represents his or her proportion of ownership of the portfolio and its income or losses. Mutual fund shares are sometimes purchased from the fund itself and sometimes from investment professionals, such as brokers. In either case, the shares are redeemable, which means the fund will buy back the shares whenever investors want to sell them.

Mutual funds are designed for people who don't want to pick and choose their own investments but would rather leave the details of managing their portfolio to professionals. Although some mutual funds concentrate on one specific type of investment, most invest in a variety of financial instruments. There are about 10,000 individual mutual funds in North America, and many different kinds of funds, so you should be able to find one that meets your needs. Let's look at some of the common types.

> Before investing in a mutual fund, request a copy of the fund's prospectus. There are two kinds, the statutory prospectus and the shorter summary prospectus, if the fund issues one. Either prospectus will contain the most important information you need, including the fund's investment objectives, strategies, principal risks, fees and expenses, and past performance.

# Index Funds

A market index is a measure of the value a selected group of stocks or bonds that is used to track changes in market performance over a long period of time. There are a lot of them, but some of the best known are the Dow Jones Industrial Average, the Standard & Poor's 500, the Nasdaq 100, and the Wilshire 5000. Index funds are designed to mimic the performance of one specific index. Some invest in all the companies in a particular index, while others choose a representative sample of those companies. Either way, the value of index funds rises and falls along with the index.

Why invest in an index fund? Since the well-known indexes tend to reflect the overall performance of the stock market over a long period, index funds are considered to be relatively low-risk investments for people seeking steady growth. And by definition they include a diversified portfolio—some more than others—which can help protect you against losses in any one area by offsetting them with gains in other areas. Also, index funds tend to have lower fees because they include a fairly static group of securities, unlike other funds that require more time on the part of a manager.

> You may hear the terms "active funds" and "passive funds." Active funds are those in which the manager uses research and experience to identify investments that he or she thinks will perform the best. Most funds are active funds. Passive funds, also called index funds, are those that try to replicate the performance of one of the market indexes.
>
> *(Source: "Mutual Funds and Exchange-Traded Funds (ETFs): A Guide for Investors," U.S. Securities and Exchange Commission (SEC).)*

There are only a couple of downsides to index funds. For one thing, their managers have less flexibility than those of other funds. Since the fund is tied to an index, if that group of stocks performs poorly, the manager can only look so widely to find new stocks to offset the losses. And with index funds being designed for steady, long-term growth, they're not a good investment for anyone hoping to make a big gain in a short period of time.

# Equity Funds

Also called stock funds, this is the largest category of mutual funds. Equity funds invest in stocks, most often with the goal of long-term growth combined with some income, called dividends, that is paid to investors on a regular basis. Unlike an index fund, an equity fund is not tied to a pre-selected group of securities, so the manager can buy and sell stocks periodically based on research and his or her own experience, as long as the portfolio continues to conform to the stated objectives of the fund.

There is a wide variety of equity funds designed to meet the financial needs, goals, and risk tolerance of practically any investor. For example, large-cap funds invest in many of the world's largest companies, while mid-cap funds and small-cap funds concentrate on smaller companies. There are also growth equity funds for investors hoping to get a larger return than the stock market as a whole, global equity funds that concentrate on international stocks, private equity funds that invest in privately owned companies, and many others.

Investing in equity funds can be more risky than putting money into an index fund, but a lot depends on both the manager and the type of fund. Managers have more freedom with an equity fund, so their research methods, abilities, and track record are major factors in the fund's performance. And growth funds, for example, tend to be more risky than ones designed for steadier, more modest returns. So it's important to research the historical performance and details of both the manager and the fund itself before deciding to invest.

## Bond Funds

As the name implies, these funds invest in bonds, rather than stocks. Types of bonds include U.S. Treasury Bonds and municipal bonds, which are issued by governments, and corporate bonds, issued by companies. In all cases, when you invest in bonds you are loaning money for a set period of time, during which you are paid interest on a regular basis. Then, when the bond matures at the end of that period, you get back your principal.

Bonds are considered an important part of any properly diversified portfolio, because even during times of poor market conditions they remain a relatively safe investment and provide interest income. And, like any fund, allowing a professional adviser to handle the management relieves you of the burden of doing daily research and making detailed decisions. Plus, managers tend to get better bond prices than most individual investors.

On the other hand, bond funds carry some interest rate risk. If interest rates rise, the value of the portfolio will decrease, and if you need to sell at that time you could get less than your initial investment. Also, regular income from bond funds fluctuates as the value of the individual bonds changes, so you can't predict how much income you'll get at any given time. There are also fees associated with bond funds that may be higher than with a stock fund.

# Money Market Funds

Money market funds invest in short-term, fixed-income, securities like U.S. Treasury Bills, government bonds, and certificates of deposit. Their goal is to retain stable value while paying regular dividends to investors. Money market funds are highly liquid, making them a good investment for people close to retirement or others seeking modest returns with low risk.

The biggest advantages of money market funds are security and stability. Since your money goes into low-risk investments, often backed by government agencies, they're considered one of the safest places to invest. In addition, their objective of paying regular interest at a moderate rate can help protect investors at times of stock market downturns. And since these funds are very liquid, they can be used as a source of emergency cash while still giving you a better return than savings account interest.

The downside is that you pay for safety and stability. Money market funds generally pay less interest than other investments, and it's possible that the rate of inflation could outpace the dividends you get from the fund. Also, there are fees associated with managing money market funds, and with the low rate of interest, at times of high inflation those fees could significantly reduce your return.

# Other Funds

There are many other types of funds available to investors. Depending on your individual circumstances and preferences, you might find that some of these will meet your financial needs:

- **Balanced funds**: These funds invest in a mix of stocks, bonds, and some money market vehicles in an attempt to reduce risk while still providing both income and gains in value.

- **Fixed income funds**: Fixed income funds are designed for conservative investors who want to receive regular payments with little risk. They most often invest in government bonds and some high-yield corporate bonds.

- **Global or international funds**: These funds concentrate on stock issued by companies in many different countries, sometimes including the United States. Depending on their mix of investments, they can be riskier than other funds due to the possibility of political instability in some regions or economic uncertainty in developing countries.

- **Real estate funds**: These primarily focus on publicly traded stocks issued by companies associated with the commercial and residential real estate markets, such as builders, mortgage companies, and property managers. They may also invest in vacant property, agricultural land, and apartment complexes.

- **Fund of funds**: These are funds that invest in other funds. Their goal is to simplify asset allocation for investors and provide a highly diversified portfolio.

- **Specialty funds**: Some of these include sector funds, which concentrate on particular segments of the economy, like technology, health, and automotive; commodity-focused funds that buy stock in companies involved with such products as crude oil, natural gas, and cattle; and regional funds, which specialize in a particular area of the world. There are also socially responsible funds that try to get a healthy return for investors while meeting certain ethical guidelines. For example, most of these funds don't invest in businesses involved with tobacco, weapons, or certain types of power generation.

> Beware of the tax consequences. When you purchase an individual stock, you pay income tax each year on the dividends you receive, but you don't pay capital gains tax (a tax on the increase in value of the stock from the time you bought it) until you sell the stock. However, with a mutual fund, you may have to pay taxes each year on the fund's capital gains, even if there were no dividends and you didn't sell any shares. That's because the law requires mutual funds to distribute any net capital gains from the sale of portfolio securities to shareholders.

There's such a huge variety of mutual funds that it's critical, especially for new investors, to do your homework before deciding where to put your money. A lot of funds are ideal for those new to investing, with low minimum initial buy-ins and easy-to-understand objectives and reports. Others are really best for more experienced investors, either because of risk or complexity or both. Be sure not only to research a fund's historical performance but also the fund manager's track record. And find an adviser who understands your particular financial situation and is willing to work closely with you to help you meet your goals.

## References

1. "7 Common Types of Mutual Funds," Getsmarteraboutmoney.ca, n.d.

2. Coleman, Hank. "Benefits and Drawbacks of Money Market Funds," Moneyq&a. com, n.d.

3. Dumont, Chris. "A Guide to the Different Types of Mutual Funds," Mutualfunds. com, September 17, 2014.

4. Kennon, Joshua. "What Is an Equity Fund?" Thebalance.com, September 24, 2016.

5. "Mutual Funds and Exchange-Traded Funds (ETFs): A Guide for Investors," U.S. Securities and Exchange Commission, January 26, 2017.

6. Prosser, Mark. "Should You Invest in Individual Bonds or Bond Funds?" Forbes.com, June 13, 2012.

7. Rodgers, David S. "Advantages and Disadvantages to Index Funds," LinkedIn.com, December 19, 2015.

# Chapter 35

# What Is A Hedge Fund?

Hedge funds pool investors' money and invest the money in an effort to make a positive return. Hedge funds typically have more flexible investment strategies than, for example, mutual funds. Many hedge funds seek to profit in all kinds of markets by using leverage (in other words, borrowing to increase investment exposure as well as risk), short-selling and other speculative investment practices that are not often used by mutual funds.

You generally must be an accredited investor, which means having a minimum level of income or assets, to invest in hedge funds. Typical investors include institutional investors, such as pension funds and insurance companies, and wealthy individuals. Hedge funds are not subject to some of the regulations that are designed to protect investors. Depending on the amount of assets in the hedge funds advised by a manager, some hedge fund managers may not be required to register or to file public reports with the U.S. Securities and Exchange Commission (SEC). Hedge funds, however, are subject to the same prohibitions against fraud as are other market participants, and their managers owe a fiduciary duty to the funds that they manage.

## What Information Should I Seek If I Am Considering Investing In A Hedge Fund?

- Read a fund's offering memorandum and related materials. The hedge fund's offering documents and agreements contain important information about investing in the fund, including the investment strategies of the fund, whether the fund is based in the United

About This Chapter: This chapter includes text excerpted from "Hedge Funds," U.S. Securities and Exchange Commission (SEC), October 5, 2016.

States or abroad, the risks of the investment, fees earned by the hedge fund manager, expenses charged to the hedge fund and the hedge fund manager's potential conflicts of interest. It is important that you read all the documents before making your decision to invest in a hedge fund. You should consider consulting an independent financial advisor before investing in a hedge fund.

- Understand the fund's investment strategy. There are a wide variety of hedge funds with many different investment strategies. Some hedge funds will be diversified among many strategies, managers and investments, while others may take highly concentrated positions or may only use a single strategy. Make sure you understand the level of risk involved in the fund's investment strategies and ensure that they are suitable to your personal investing goals, time horizons and risk tolerance. As with any investment, generally the higher the potential returns, the higher the risks you must assume.

- Determine if the fund is using leverage or other speculative investment techniques. Leverage is the use of borrowed money to make an investment. A hedge fund using leverage will typically invest both the investors' capital and the borrowed money to make investments in an effort to increase the potential returns of the fund. The use of leverage will magnify both the potential gain and the potential loss from an investment. The use of leverage can turn an otherwise conservative investment into an extremely risky investment. A hedge fund may also invest in derivatives (such as options and futures) and use short-selling (selling a security it does not own) to increase its potential returns, which could likewise increase the potential gain or loss from an investment.

- Evaluate potential conflicts of interest disclosed by hedge fund managers. For example, if your investment adviser recommends that you invest in a fund that the adviser manages, there may be a conflict of interest because your adviser may earn higher fees from your investments in the hedge fund than the adviser might earn from other potential investments.

- Understand how a fund's assets are valued. Hedge funds may invest in highly illiquid securities that may be difficult to value. Moreover, many hedge funds give themselves significant discretion in valuing illiquid securities. You should understand a fund's valuation process and know the extent to which a fund's securities are valued by independent sources. Valuations of fund assets will affect the fees that the manager charges.

- Understand how a fund's performance is determined. Hedge funds do not need to follow any standard methodology when calculating performance, and they may invest in securities that are relatively illiquid and difficult to value. By contrast, federal securities laws dictate how mutual funds can advertise their performance by requiring specific ways to calculate current yield, tax equivalent yield, average annual total return and after-tax return, as well as having detailed requirements for the types of disclosure that must accompany any performance data. If you are provided with performance data for the hedge fund, ask whether it reflects cash or assets actually received by the fund as opposed to the manager's estimate of the change in value of fund assets and whether the data includes deductions for fees.

- Understand any limitations on your right to redeem your shares. Unlike mutual funds where you can elect to sell your shares on any given day, hedge funds typically limit opportunities to redeem, or cash in, your shares (e.g., monthly, quarterly or annually), and often impose a "lock-up" period of one year or more, during which you cannot cash in your shares. In the time it takes for you to redeem your shares, their value could diminish and you will not have use of the money invested in those shares. Furthermore, hedge funds may charge you a redemption fee before you are allowed to cash in your shares. Hedge funds may also have authority to suspend redemptions under certain circumstances, including in times of market distress or when their investments are not able to be quickly or easily liquidated.

- Research the backgrounds of hedge fund managers. Before entrusting your money to anyone, research their background and qualifications. Make sure hedge fund managers are qualified to manage your money, and find out whether they have a disciplinary history within the securities industry. If the manager is registered with the SEC, you can get this information (and more) by reviewing the manager's Form ADV. Form ADV is the uniform form used by investment advisers to register with both the SEC and state securities regulators. You can search for and view a firm's Form ADV using the SEC's Investment Adviser Public Disclosure (IAPD) website. You also can get copies of Form ADV for individual advisers and firms from the investment adviser, the SEC's Public Reference Room or the state securities regulator where the adviser's principal place of business is located. If you don't find the investment adviser firm in the SEC's IAPD database, be sure to call your state securities regulator or search FINRA's BrokerCheck database for any information they may have.

> **Disciplinary history**: In a recent action, *SEC v. GEI Financial Services, Inc.,* the SEC alleged that a hedge fund manager failed to disclose to his advisory clients that the State of Illinois had barred him from acting as an investment adviser.

# What Questions Should I Ask The Hedge Fund Manager Before Investing?

- Ask about fees and expenses. Fees and expenses affect your return on investment. Hedge funds typically charge an annual asset management fee of 1 percent to 2 percent of assets as well as a "performance fee" of 20 percent of a hedge fund's profit. These fees are typically higher than the fees charged by a mutual fund. A performance fee could motivate a hedge fund manager to take greater risks in the hope of generating a larger return.

> **Excessive fees**: In SEC v. GEI Financial Services, Inc., the SEC alleged that the hedge fund manager withdrew excessive fees from the hedge fund he managed. The amounts withdrawn allegedly were based on fee calculations that substantially differed from what the manager initially told investors about how the fees were to be calculated.
>
> A fund of hedge funds is an investment company that invests in hedge funds—rather than investing in individual securities. Funds of hedge funds typically charge a fee for managing your assets, and some may also include a performance fee based on profits. These fees are charged in addition to any fees paid to the underlying hedge funds and, therefore, you will be paying two layers of fees. You may wish to read FINRA's investor alert, which describes some of the costs and risks of investing in funds of hedge funds.

- Ask about how a fund's assets are safeguarded. A hedge fund's manager generally has authority to access and transfer the fund's assets. This authority can potentially be misused. To guard against this, many hedge funds undergo an annual financial audit by an independent auditor that includes verification of the existence of the fund assets. You should inquire about where a fund's assets are held (e.g., whether they are held in custodial accounts at a reputable bank or broker) and whether an independent third party confirms or otherwise verifies the existence of the fund's assets.

- Ask about others that perform services for the fund. A hedge fund typically has third parties who provide various services to the fund, including a prime broker, an administrator, an outside accountant that audits the fund's financial statements, and possibly a valuation agent. You should consider contacting these third party service providers to check the accuracy of information provided to you by the hedge fund and its manager.

- Don't be afraid to ask questions. You are entrusting your money to someone else. You should know where your money is going, who is managing it, how it is being invested, how you can get it back, what protections apply to your investment and what your rights are as an investor.

---

**Manager malfeasance**: In a recent action, *In the Matter of Gerasimowicz,* the SEC's Enforcement Division alleged that, unbeknownst to investors, a hedge fund manager over the course of several years invested the majority of a fund's assets into a private business owned by the manager's affiliated company. The fund was marketed as being invested primarily in public equity securities with the aim of constructing a "diversified portfolio" and employing "controlled risk diversification." The manager allegedly failed to inform investors of this substantial investment in a private business or the conflict of interest resulting from the manager's substantial personal investments in the business. The business ultimately filed for bankruptcy, and a distribution to the fund to recover its investment in the business is uncertain and could be very small. Audited financial statements that were months late in being prepared and delivered to investors, if delivered at all, allegedly failed to timely alert investors to the investment.

In another recent action, *SEC v. Lion Capital Management, LLC,* the SEC alleged that a manager used his hedge fund as a ruse to misappropriate over $550,000 from a retired schoolteacher. The schoolteacher considered the manager a close family friend and believed him to be a successful money manager. Instead of investing as he represented, the manager allegedly used the funds for personal and office expenses, including his residential mortgage, office rent and staff salaries. The manager allegedly provided false account statements to the schoolteacher reflecting nonexistent gains on her investment.

---

What protections do I have if I purchase a hedge fund? Hedge fund investors do not receive all of the federal and state law protections that commonly apply to most mutual funds. For example, hedge funds are not required to provide the same level of disclosure as you would receive from mutual funds. Without the disclosure that the securities laws require for most mutual funds, it can be more difficult to fully evaluate the terms of an investment in a hedge fund. It may also be difficult to verify representations you receive from a hedge fund.

The SEC can take action against a hedge fund or a manager that defrauds investors, and the SEC has brought a number of fraud cases involving hedge funds. For example, a number of these cases involved hedge fund managers misrepresenting their experience and the fund's track record. Other cases involved "Ponzi schemes," where returns to existing investors were paid with funds contributed by new investors. In some of the cases the SEC has brought, the hedge funds sent phony account statements to investors to cover up the fact that their money had been stolen. That's why it is extremely important to thoroughly check out every aspect of any hedge fund you might consider as an investment.

**Ponzi schemes**: In a recent action, *SEC v. Jawed*, the SEC alleged that a hedge fund manager operated a long-running, $37 million Ponzi scheme. Instead of investing in securities as he represented to investors, the manager allegedly used most of his investors' money to pay back old investors, to pay himself, to travel and to create an illusion of achievement by hiring professionals and educated personnel. The manager allegedly hid the Ponzi scheme by creating fake, illiquid investments. With increasing redemption requests, the manager and others he hired manufactured a sham buyout of the funds to make investors think their hedge fund interests would soon be redeemed. In another recent action, *SEC v. Alleca,* the SEC alleged that a hedge fund manager caused investor losses of $17 million as he engaged in a Ponzi scheme to cover-up losses from his undisclosed trading. The manager created a fund of hedge funds—a hedge fund that would be invested in other hedge funds. Instead of investing in other hedge funds, the manager allegedly engaged in active securities trading and incurred substantial losses. To satisfy redemption requests and conceal losses, the manager created two additional funds and allegedly siphoned investors' money from these funds to satisfy redemptions on the first fund.

# Chapter 36

# What To Expect When You Invest In Stocks

## Understand What It Means To Invest

When investing, you have a greater chance of losing your money than when you save. Unlike Federal Deposit Insurance Corporation (FDIC)-insured deposits, the money you invest in securities, mutual funds, and other similar investments are not federally insured. You could lose your "principal," which is the amount you've invested. That's true even if you purchase your investments through a bank. But when you invest, you also have the opportunity to earn more money. On the other hand, investing involves taking on some degree of risk.

## Learn About Investment Options

While the U.S. Securities and Exchange Commission (SEC) cannot recommend any particular investment product, a vast array of investment products exists, including stocks and stock mutual funds, corporate and municipal bonds, annuities, exchange-traded funds, money market funds, and U.S. Treasury securities.

Stocks, bonds, and mutual funds are the most common asset categories. These are among the asset categories you would likely choose from when investing in a retirement savings program or a college savings plan. Other asset categories include real estate, precious metals

About This Chapter: Text under the heading "Understand What It Means To Invest" is excerpted from "Understand What It Means To Invest," Investor.gov, U.S. Securities and Exchange Commission (SEC), November 23, 2016; Text under the heading "Learn About Investment Options" is excerpted from "Learn About Investment Options," Investor.gov, U.S. Securities and Exchange Commission (SEC), November 23, 2016; Text under the heading "Investing On Your Own" is excerpted from "Investing On Your Own," Investor.gov, U.S. Securities and Exchange Commission (SEC), December 3, 2016; Text under the heading "Assessing Your Risk Tolerance" is excerpted from "Assessing Your Risk Tolerance," Investor.gov, U.S. Securities and Exchange Commission (SEC), December 3, 2016; Text under the heading "Risk And Return On Savings And Investment Products" is excerpted from "Risk And Return," Investor.gov, U.S. Securities and Exchange Commission (SEC), December 24, 2016.

and other commodities, and private equity. Some investors may include these asset categories within a portfolio. Investments in these asset categories typically have category-specific risks.

Before you make any investment, understand the risks of the investment and make sure the risks are appropriate for you. You'll also want to understand the fees associated with the buying, selling, and holding the investment.

# Investing On Your Own

The first step to investing, especially investing on your own, is to make sure you have a financial plan. How much are you going to invest? For how long? What are your financial goals? Do you understand your tolerance for risk? All investments carry some risk.

The next step is research, research, research. When investing on your own, you are responsible for your decisions. How will you select one stock, bond, or mutual fund over others? Always make sure that all securities are registered with the SEC, using the SEC's Electronic Data Gathering, Analysis, and Retrieval System (EDGAR) database. Don't purchase solely on stock tips from others.

There are several ways you can invest on your own, including Online Investing, Direct Investing, and Dividend Reinvestment Plans.

# Assessing Your Risk Tolerance

When it comes to investing, risk and reward go hand in hand. The phrase "no pain, no gain"—comes close to summing up the relationship between risk and reward. Don't let anyone tell you otherwise: all investments involve some degree of risk. If you plan to buy securities—such as stocks, bonds, or mutual funds—it's important that you understand that you could lose some or all of the money you invest.

The reward for taking on risk is the potential for a greater investment return. If you have a financial goal with a long time horizon, you may make more money by carefully investing in higher risk assets, such as stocks or bonds, than if limit yourself to less risky assets. On the other hand, lower risk cash investments may be appropriate for short-term financial goals.

An aggressive investor, or one with a high risk tolerance, is willing to risk losing money to get potentially better results. A conservative investor, or one with a low risk tolerance, favors investments that maintain his or her original investment.

Many investment websites offer free online questionnaires to help you assess your risk tolerance. Some of the websites will even estimate asset allocations based on responses to the questionnaires. While the suggested asset allocations may be a useful starting point, keep in mind that the results may be biased towards financial products or services sold by companies or individuals sponsoring the websites.

# Risk And Return On Savings And Investment Products

Students should understand that every saving and investment product has different risks and returns. Differences include how readily investors can get their money when they need it, how fast their money will grow, and how safe their money will be.

## Savings Products

Savings accounts, insured money market accounts, and certificate of deposits (CDs) are viewed as very safe because they are federally insured. You can easily get to money in savings if you need it for any reason. But there's a tradeoff for security and ready availability. The interest rate on savings generally is lower compared with investments.

While safe, savings are not risk-free: the risk is that the low interest rate you receive will not keep pace with inflation. For example, with inflation, a candy bar that costs a dollar today could cost two dollars ten years from now. If your money doesn't grow as fast as inflation does, it's like losing money, because while a dollar buys a candy bar today, in ten years it might only buy half of one.

## Investment Products

Stocks, bonds, and mutual funds are the most common investment products. All have higher risks and potentially higher returns than savings products. Over many decades, the investment that has provided the highest average rate of return has been stocks. But there are no guarantees of profits when you buy stock, which makes stock one of the most risky investments. If a company doesn't do well or falls out of favor with investors, its stock can fall in price, and investors could lose money.

You can make money in two ways from owning stock. First, the price of the stock may rise if the company does well; the increase is called a capital gain or appreciation. Second, companies sometimes pay out a part of profits to stockholders, with a payment that's called a dividend.

Bonds generally provide higher returns with higher risk than savings, and lower returns than stocks. But the bond issuer's promise to repay principal generally makes bonds less risky than stocks. Unlike stockholders, bondholders know how much money they expect to receive, unless the bond issuer declares bankruptcy or goes out of business. In that event, bondholders may lose money. But if there is any money left, corporate bondholders will get it before stockholders.

The risk of investing in mutual funds is determined by the underlying risks of the stocks, bonds, and other investments held by the fund. No mutual fund can guarantee its returns, and no mutual fund is risk-free.

Always remember: the greater the potential return, the greater the risk. One protection against risk is time, and that's what young people have. On any day the stock market can go up or down. Sometimes it goes down for months or years. But over the years, investors who've adopted a "buy and hold" approach to investing tend to come out ahead of those who try to time the market.

# Chapter 37

# Placing An Order To Buy Or Sell A Stock

## Executing An Order

When you place an order to buy or sell stock, you might not think about where or how your broker will execute the trade. But where and how your order is executed can impact the overall cost of the transaction, including the price you pay for the stock. Here's what you should know about trade execution:

### Trade Execution Isn't Instantaneous

Many investors who trade through online brokerage accounts assume they have a direct connection to the securities markets, but they don't. When you push that enter key, your order is sent over the Internet to your broker—who in turn decides which market to send it to for execution. A similar process occurs when you call your broker to place a trade.

While trade execution is usually seamless and quick, it does take time. And prices can change quickly, especially in fast-moving markets. Because price quotes are only for a specific number of shares, investors may not always receive the price they saw on their screen or the price their broker quoted over the phone. By the time your order reaches the market, the price of the stock could be slightly—or very—different.

SEC regulations do not require a trade to be executed within a set period of time. But if firms advertise their speed of execution, they must not exaggerate or fail to tell investors about the possibility of significant delays.

About This Chapter: Text beginning with the heading "Executing An Order" is excerpted from "Executing An Order," Investor.gov, U.S. Securities and Exchange Commission (SEC), November 23, 2016; Text beginning with the heading "Market And Limit Orders" is excerpted from "Trading Basics: Understanding The Different Ways To Buy And Sell Stock," Investor.gov, U.S. Securities and Exchange Commission (SEC), December 28, 2016.

# Your Broker Has Options For Executing Your Trade

Just as you have a choice of brokers, your broker generally has a choice of markets to execute your trade.

- For a stock that is listed on an exchange, your broker may direct the order to that exchange, to another exchange, or to a firm called a "market maker."

- A "market maker" is a firm that stands ready to buy or sell a stock listed on an exchange at publicly quoted prices. As a way to attract orders from brokers, some market makers will pay your broker for routing your order to them—perhaps a penny or more per share. This is called "payment for order flow."

- For a stock that trades in an over-the-counter (OTC) market, your broker may send the order to an "OTC market maker." Many OTC market makers also pay brokers for order flow.

- Your broker may route your order—especially a limit order—to an electronic communications network (ECN) that automatically matches buy and sell orders at specified prices.

- Your broker may decide to send your order to another division of your broker's firm to be filled out of the firm's own inventory. This is called "internalization." In this way, your broker's firm may make money on the "spread"—which is the difference between the price the firm paid for the security and the price at which the firm sells it to you.

# Your Broker Has A Duty Of "Best Execution"

Many firms use automated systems to handle the orders they receive from their customers. In deciding how to execute orders, your broker has a duty to seek the best execution that is reasonably available for its customers' orders. That means your broker must evaluate the orders it receives from all customers in the aggregate and periodically assess which competing markets, market makers, or ECNs offer the most favorable terms of execution.

The opportunity for "price improvement" is an important factor a broker should consider in executing its customers' orders. "Price improvement" is the opportunity, but not the guarantee, for an order to be executed at a better price than the current quote.

Of course, the additional time it takes some markets to execute orders may result in your getting a worse price than the current quote—especially in a fast-moving market. So, your broker is required to consider whether there is a trade-off between providing its customers' orders with the possibility, but not the guarantee, of better prices and the extra time it may take to do so.

# You Have Options For Directing Trades

If for any reason you want to direct your trade to a particular exchange, market maker, or ECN, you may be able to call your broker and ask him or her to do this. But some brokers may charge for that service. Some brokers offer active traders the ability to direct orders to the market maker or ECN of their choice.

# Market And Limit Orders

## Orders

Investors have several options when it comes to placing an order to buy or sell securities. For example, whether you place an order directly with your broker or trade online, you can instruct your broker to buy or sell at a specified price. Or you can place an order that is good for one day only or for an extended period.

Understanding how different types of orders work may make a difference in whether your trade gets executed and at what price.

*(Source: "Orders," U.S. Securities and Exchange Commission (SEC).)*

The two most common order types are the market order and the limit order.

## Market Order

A market order is an order to buy or sell a stock at the best available price. Generally, this type of order will be executed immediately. However, the price at which a market order will be executed is not guaranteed. It is important for investors to remember that the last-traded price is not necessarily the price at which a market order will be executed. In fast-moving markets, the price at which a market order will execute often deviates from the last-traded price or "real time" quote.

**Example:** An investor places a market order to buy 1000 shares of XYZ stock when the best offer price is $3.00 per share. If other orders are executed first, the investor's market order may be executed at a higher price.

In addition, a fast-moving market may cause parts of a large market order to execute at different prices.

**Example:** An investor places a market order to buy 1000 shares of XYZ stock at $3.00 per share. In a fast-moving market, 500 shares of the order could execute at $3.00 per share and the other 500 shares execute at a higher price.

## Limit Order

A limit order is an order to buy or sell a stock at a specific price or better. A buy limit order can only be executed at the limit price or lower, and a sell limit order can only be executed at the limit price or higher. A limit order is not guaranteed to execute. A limit order can only be filled if the stock's market price reaches the limit price. While limit orders do not guarantee execution, they help ensure that an investor does not pay more than a predetermined price for a stock.

**Example:** An investor wants to purchase shares of ABC stock for no more than $10. The investor could place a limit order for this amount that will only execute if the price of ABC stock is $10 or lower.

# Special Orders And Trading Instructions

In addition to market and limit orders, brokerage firms may allow investors to use special orders and trading instructions to buy and sell stocks. The following are descriptions of some of the most common special orders and trading instructions.

## Stop Order

A stop order, also referred to as a stop-loss order, is an order to buy or sell a stock once the price of the stock reaches a specified price, known as the stop price. When the stop price is reached, a stop order becomes a market order. A buy stop order is entered at a stop price above the current market price. Investors generally use a buy stop order to limit a loss or to protect a profit on a stock that they have sold short. A sell stop order is entered at a stop price below the current market price. Investors generally use a sell stop order to limit a loss or to protect a profit on a stock that they own. Before using a stop order, investors should consider the following:

- Short-term market fluctuations in a stock's price can activate a stop order, so a stop price should be selected carefully.

- The stop price is not the guaranteed execution price for a stop order. The stop price is a trigger that causes the stop order to become a market order. The execution price an investor receives for this market order can deviate significantly from the stop price in a fast-moving market where prices change rapidly. An investor can avoid the risk of a stop order executing at an unexpected price by placing a stop-limit order, but the limit price may prevent the order from being executed.

- For certain types of stocks, some brokerage firms have different standards for determining whether a stop price has been reached. For these stocks, some brokerage firms use only last-sale prices to trigger a stop order, while other firms use quotation prices. Investors should check with their brokerage firms to determine the specific rules that will apply to stop orders.

## Stop-Limit Order

A stop-limit order is an order to buy or sell a stock that combines the features of a stop order and a limit order. once the stop price is reached, a stop-limit order becomes a limit order that will be executed at a specified price (or better). The benefit of a stop-limit order is that the investor can control the price at which the order can be executed.

Before using a stop-limit order, investors should consider the following:

- As with all limit orders, a stop-limit order may not be executed if the stock's price moves away from the specified limit price, which may occur in a fast-moving market.

- Short-term market fluctuations in a stock's price can activate a stop-limit order, so stop and limit prices should be selected carefully.

- The stop price and the limit price for a stop-limit order do not have to be the same price. For example, a sell stop limit order with a stop price of $3.00 may have a limit price of $2.50. such an order would become an active limit order if market prices reach $3.00, although the order could only be executed at a price of $2.50 or better.

- For certain types of stocks, some brokerage firms have different standards for determining whether the stop price of a stop-limit order has been reached. For these stocks, some brokerage firms use only last-sale prices to trigger a stop-limit order, while other firms use quotation prices. Investors should check with their brokerage firms to determine the specific rules that will apply to stop-limit orders.

## Day Orders, Good-'til-Canceled Orders, And Immediate-Or-Cancel Orders

Day orders, Good-'til-Canceled (GTC) orders, and Immediate-or-Cancel (IOC) orders represent timing instructions for an order and may be applied to either market or limit orders.

unless an investor specifies a time frame for the expiration of an order, orders to buy and sell a stock are Day orders, meaning they are good only during that trading day.

A GTC order is an order to buy or sell a stock that lasts until the order is completed or canceled. Brokerage firms typically limit the length of time an investor can leave a GtC order open. This time frame may vary from broker to broker. Investors should contact their brokerage firms to determine what time limit would apply to GtC orders. An IOC order is an order to buy or sell a stock that must be executed immediately. Any portion of the order that cannot be filled immediately will be canceled.

## Fill-Or-Kill And All-Or-None Orders

Two other common special order types are Fill-Or-Kill (FOK) and All-Or-None (AON) orders. An FoK order is an order to buy or sell a stock that must be executed immediately in its entirety; otherwise, the entire order will be canceled (i.e., no partial execution of the order is allowed). An Aon order is an order to buy or sell a stock that must be executed in its entirety, or not executed at all. However, unlike the FoK orders, Aon orders that cannot be executed immediately remain active until they are executed or canceled.

# Opening Transactions

Investors should be aware that any order placed outside of regular trading hours and designated for trading only during regular hours will usually be eligible to execute at an opening price. Investors should contact their brokerage firms to find out their broker's policies regarding opening transactions.

---

**Online trading is quick and easy, online investing takes time**

With a click of mouse, you can buy and sell stocks from more than 100 online brokers offering executions as low as $5 per transaction. Although online trading saves investors time and money, it does not take the homework out of making investment decisions. You may be able to make a trade in a nanosecond, but making wise investment decisions takes time. Before you trade, know why you are buying or selling, and the risk of your investment.

**Online trading is not always instantaneous**

Investors may find that technological "choke points" can slow or prevent their orders from reaching an online firm. For example, problems can occur where:

- an investor's modem, computer, or Internet Service Provider is slow or faulty;

- a broker-dealer has inadequate hardware or its Internet Service Provider is slow or delayed; or
- traffic on the Internet is heavy, slowing down overall usage.

A capacity problem or limitation at any of these choke points can cause a delay or failure in an investor's attempt to access an online firm's automated trading system.

*(Source: "Tips For Online Trading," U.S. Securities and Exchange Commission (SEC).)*

# Chapter 38
# Day Trading

## What Is Day Trading?

Day trading is the practice of buying and selling stocks, commodities, securities, or options very quickly, usually by making many buy/sell transactions in a single day. Day traders are people who make their living by rapidly trading stocks with the goal of earning small profits on each one of a large number of trades. Because the value of individual stocks tends to change throughout a single day, day traders try to maximize their stock purchases by selling stocks at a higher price than they paid to buy the stocks. Day traders closely watch the fluctuating prices of stocks they own, and sell their stocks when the price reaches a certain value. As a result, day traders often hold the stocks they buy for very short periods of time, sometimes selling stocks a few seconds or minutes after they bought them. Day traders rarely hold stocks for long periods of time.

> **Quick Note**
> Day trading is extremely risky and can result in substantial financial losses in a very short period of time. Day traders must be able to tolerate this risk without losing confidence in their ability to make successful trades.

## Who Are Day Traders?

In general, there are two kinds of day traders: those who work alone and those who work for a large financial institution. Day traders who work for a financial institution usually have

"Day Trading," © 2017 Omnigraphics.

extensive resources at their disposal, including the most advanced trading technology and software, access to large amounts of money for making stock purchases, and support staff that may assist with analysis of financial news in real time. Day traders who work alone sometimes manage money on behalf of other people and/or use their own money for trading. Individual day traders often do not have access to the robust resources and support that are available to institutional day traders. All day traders are typically well-educated and informed about the trading markets so that they can leverage information to maximize numerous transactions in a very short amount of time.

Day trading is a high-stress, fast-paced business that requires patience, intense focus, dedication, and quick reaction time. Each day trader will likely have a different approach or personal style when making short-term trades, but there are some characteristics that are generally shared by all successful day traders. The most successful day traders have extensive in-depth knowledge of the trading marketplace. Day trading requires a deep level of understanding of financial basics and stock market fundamental concepts. Day traders also need money that they can afford to lose, which is called capital. The use of capital for day trades helps to ensure that day traders minimize their risk. Every successful trader also works with a strategy that guides each of their trading decisions. A good strategy, informed by thorough analysis and plenty of real-time information, helps day traders achieve consistent profits and limit losses to acceptable levels. Perhaps the most important characteristic of a successful day trader is discipline. Adhering to a strategy and not allowing oneself to become overwhelmed by excitement or emotion requires an exceptional amount of discipline.

> The most common factor that causes day traders to quickly lose large amounts of money is failure to follow a strategy. A well-planned trading strategy typically outlines specific trading criteria and the discipline to follow the strategy. Most people simply do not have the money, time, or personality to become successful day traders.

# How Does Day Trading Work?

Like all stock market transactions, day trading is governed by the U.S. Securities and Exchange Commission (SEC). The SEC defines day trading and publishes certain rules and guidelines that apply to short-term transactions. In general, day traders are defined as anyone who executes four or more buy/sell transactions within five business days, where the number of day trades exceeds six percent of that person's total number of trades for that same five-day period.

The SEC's definition is a minimum requirement, and some brokerage firms use a definition that is either more restrictive or broader in its view of day trading. Many brokerages require day traders to maintain $25,000 worth of minimum equity with which to execute rapid buy/sell transactions. This minimum equity deposit is usually required to be maintained at all times. If a trader's equity account falls below the minimum amount, they will not be allowed to make any more trades until the minimum deposit is restored.

Conversely, some brokerages place limits on the amount of trades each day trader can make. For example, some brokerages limit trades to a maximum of four times the value of the equity amount. If a day trader exceeds this limitation, their ability to execute day trades will be restricted for a period of time during which the trader must meet certain requirements. This practice is known as a margin call.

# Pros And Cons Of Day Trading

Day trading is considered a somewhat controversial activity. Some financial experts believe that day trading provides important benefits to the stock market in that day trades help the market operate with more efficiency while also providing a necessary amount of liquidity in stock values. (The term liquidity refers to money that is easily accessible or easily converted to cash.)

By contrast, some other financial experts find fault with day trading because it can be easily used to cheat vulnerable stock market investors. Critics of day trading typically view the practice as a suspicious get-rich-quick scheme that does more harm than good. For this reason, many professional money managers and financial advisors do not participate in or recommend day trading to their clients.

> **Did You Know?**
>
> Day trading is highly controversial but it is neither illegal nor unethical. Questioned by critics and praised by practitioners, day trading is one of the most hotly debated topics on Wall Street.

# Day Trading Tools

Like most other professions, day trading requires access to and knowledge of specific tools and technology. Some common tools required for day trading include:

- Stock screening software programs that help traders focus on specific stocks and compare them against a set of criteria. The software performs the analysis based on criteria chosen by the trader, and produces a list of potential stocks that meet the specified goal.

- Streaming quote software that acts as an important analytic tools for day traders. Real-time information on stock values and other criteria help traders quickly react to changing market conditions.

- Watch lists that allow traders to constantly and automatically monitor the performance and value of specific stocks.

- Trading strategy building software that helps traders define the most appropriate criteria for buy/sell transactions in order to meet specific trading goals. Strategy building software typically includes functions such as market forecasting, risk prioritizing, market simulations, and advanced analysis.

- Multiple news sources that help day traders maximize real-time information that is related to the stock market. Successful day traders strive to be among the first to know when something happens in the world that will ultimately affect stock values. This requires constant monitoring and analysis of various sources of financial and current events news. Many different software programs exist to help traders keep up with the constant flow of information.

## References

1. "An Introduction to Day Trading," Investopedia, January 10, 2017.

2. "What is Day Trading?" Dummies.com, n.d.

3. "Margin Rules for Day Trading," U.S. Securities and Exchange Commission Office of Investor Education and Assistance, February 2011.

4. "Day Trading: Your Dollars at Risk," U.S. Securities and Exchange Commission, April 20, 2005.

5. "Pros & Cons of Day Trading vs Swing Trading," Investopedia, September 27, 2016.

6. "What Are the Pros and Cons of Day Trading?" Fox Business, March 28, 2012.

7. "The Four Best Tools for Day Trading," Day Trade Warrior Blog, February 27, 2017.

8. "Top Day Trading Tools," Advisory HQ, n.d.

# Chapter 39

# What Are Direct Investment Plans?

Direct Investment Plan is a term that covers two types of investments:

1. Direct Stock Purchase Plans (sometimes called DSPs)

2. Dividend Reinvestment Plans (called DRIPs).

Both of them allow you to purchase stock directly from a company without going through a broker or other investment professional. And you don't necessarily need to buy in one-share increments; some companies allow you to buy portions of shares with a monthly commitment of a specified amount of dollars. Although they've been around since the 1960s, these plans were largely ignored for many years. But recently they've become more popular as small investors discovered them and began taking advantage of their benefits. Now, more than 1,000 major companies offer direct investment plans.

DSPs and DRIPs are virtually the same, with only a couple of noteworthy differences: With a DRIP, you may be required to already own at least one share of the company's stock before you can enroll in its program. So if you don't currently own that stock, you'll need to go through a broker and pay a brokerage fee. Once you're in the company's program, your dividends are automatically used to buy more shares or portions of shares—that's the "dividend reinvestment" part of the plan.

With DSPs, on the other hand, you aren't required to own a share of the company's stock in order to get into the plan. You simply open an account with the company of your choice and begin buying shares or portions of shares. After that, you continue to purchase more stock on a regular basis, perhaps by having a set amount of money deducted from your checking account each month.

Other than those differences, the two types of plans operate very much the same. For example, most don't allow you to buy or sell shares at a specific market price any time you want. Instead, they usually set times (daily, weekly, monthly, or quarterly) when they will sell or buy back shares at an average market price. However, the details will vary considerably from company to company. Some charge a very small per-share fee when you buy, while others charge you sell. And some don't charge any fees. So it's important to research the plan thoroughly, compare features of different plans, and ask a lot of questions before deciding to enroll.

# Advantages Of Direct Investment Plans

Companies benefit from direct investment plans in a couple ways. They build customer loyalty (if you own Coca-Cola stock, you're likely to drink Coke rather than Pepsi), and they make it easier for more people to buy stock. But there are advantages for investors as well, including:

- **Convenience**: Most of these plans allow investors to set up recurring monthly payments, using automatic deductions from a checking or savings account.

- **No brokerage fees**: Although there may be setup fees or buy and sell fees, they're usually very small compared to what you'd pay a broker.

- **Fractional purchases**: A major benefit for new investors is that you don't need to buy in one-share increments. You can buy portions of shares. So if shares cost $200 and you invest $50 per month, you buy one share every four months.

- **Low buy-in and commitment**: With a DRIP, you usually do need to own one full share to get started, but with some DSPs you can begin by buying just a portion of a share. And some plans then let you contribute as little as $25 per month.

- **Dollar-cost averaging**: Because you're investing a set amount of money each month, you're getting more shares when the per-share price is low and fewer when the price is high. That way, over a long period of time, you're likely to pay a lower average cost per share.

> Of more than 1,000 major companies with direct investment plans, about one-third of them do not charge fees for investing or reinvesting, although there may be other charges, such as fees when you sell stock. So it pays to do your homework and compare plans carefully.

# Disadvantages Of Direct Investment Plans

Although there are a number of very good reasons for consumers to consider enrolling in a direct investment plan, there are some negative factors to consider before you make a final decision, such as:

- **Fees**: Direct investment plans may allow you to avoid expensive brokerage charges, and some don't charge any fees at all. But some could charge fees that include initial setup fees for opening your account (usually $10 to $25), a small purchase fee every time money is transferred to buy more stock (as little as $1), and a sell fee when you sell shares (around $15 per batch, plus a few cents per share).

- **DRIP expense**: Don't forget that if the plan you're interested in is a DRIP, you may need to be a shareholder before you enroll in the plan. That means you'll need to work with a broker to buy your first share.

- **Commitment**: Some companies offer low-commitment amounts, and some are higher, but either way you are committing to regular investments of a set amount of money. For this reason, some investors are more comfortable saving their money until they can make a one-time stock purchase, rather than enrolling in a plan.

- **Lack of diversity**: Depending on how many direct investment plans you enroll in, and how you choose them, you could be tied to the rise and fall of one particular company or a single industry. That's why many people prefer mutual funds, which are diversified by nature.

- **Record keeping**: When you invest with a broker, you receive a regular statement that lists all your investments. But if you put your money into several direct investment plans, you'll get statements from each of them, leaving it to you to compile the information for your own records, as well as for tax preparation.

A few of the companies with direct investment plans that might interest young investors include Cisco Systems, Coca-Cola, Domino's Pizza, Ford Motor Company, Harley-Davidson, Hershey, Intel, Macy's, Mattel, Microsoft, Nike, Nokia, PepsiCo, Sony, and Yahoo. But even though owning shares in a favorite company can make investing more fun and interesting, be sure to research your chosen company thoroughly, just as would before making any other financial decision.

# How To Get Started With Direct Investment Plans

If you've weighed the pluses and minuses and decided that direct investment plans are for you, here are some steps to help you begin investing:

- **Pick a company**: Many people want to enroll in the direct investment plan of a company they like, while others may just like the idea of direct investment. For the latter group, lists of companies that offer such plans are available online.

- **Research**: Once you have a company in mind, the first order of business is to determine whether it has a direct investment plan. This information can usually be found on the company's website under a link titled "Investors" or "Investor Information."

- **More research**: Even if you're already interested in a particular company, it's smart to check online for the recent performance of the company's stock. This can also usually be found in the Investor section of the website, as well as through a Google search. If you have several companies in mind, research each of them and make comparisons. Unless you're an experienced investor, be wary of any company whose stock has been struggling. As a new investor, you're looking for a degree of stability.

- **Still more research**: Once you decide on a company, go back to its website page where you learned that it offers direct investment plans. There you'll find the name of the company's transfer agent and possibly a link to the agent's website. (The transfer agent is a third party who will transfer the stock into your name.) And that site will have even more details about the plan, such as the minimum monthly investment and various fees involved, including a fee that might be charged by the transfer agent.

- **Open your account**: Once you've decided that the company and its plan meet your needs, you'll find instructions for enrolling in the company's direct investment plan on the transfer agent's website. Follow the instructions for entering your personal information—including name, social security number, bank account details, amount you want to invest monthly—and you will have an account.

- **Shareholder note**: If you're already a shareholder in a company, there may be a method for you to enroll in its direct investment plan by dealing directly with the company, rather than going through the transfer agent. This information should be on the company's website.

---

For new investors, one of the biggest attractions of many direct investment plans is that you don't have to buy entire shares of stock, which might be out of your price range. Instead, you can specify an amount—perhaps as little as $25—to be deducted from your checking account on a regular basis to begin accumulating shares.

---

Clearly, direct investment plans offer many advantages for investors who want to buy stock in a particular company but don't want to work through a broker. The biggest pluses, for new investors in particular, are convenience and avoiding those high brokerage fees. But the advent of the Internet changed the world of investing significantly. There are now online brokers who make investing easier and also charge lower fees than traditional brokerage houses. If your primary goal is to buy stock in a single company, and you want to do it by investing small amounts on a monthly basis, then a direct investment plan may be perfect for you. But if you're main objection to working with a broker is the amount of fees charged, you might want to investigate some of the online alternatives—as well as compare fees charged by several brokers—before making a final decision.

## References

1. "Direct Investment Plan Basics," Teenvestor.com, n.d.

2. "Direct Investment Plans: Buying Stock Directly from the Company," U.S. Securities and Exchange Commission (SEC), March 1, 2002.

3. "Direct Investment Plans (DRIPs)," Directinvesting.com, n.d.

4. "How to Enroll in Direct Investment Plans (DRIPs)," Directinvesting.com, n.d.

5. "Introducing Direct Investment Plans (DRIPs)," Directinvesting.com, n.d.

6. Miller, G.E. "Direct Stock Purchase Plans (DSPP) & DRIPs: An Overview," 20somethingfinance.com, January 11, 2017.

# Chapter 40
# Investing In Foreign Stocks

Individual investors in the United States have access to a wide selection of investment opportunities. These opportunities include international investments and domestic investments that give investors international exposure, such as U.S.-registered mutual funds that invest in foreign assets and the other examples described below. The U.S. Securities and Exchange Commission's (SEC) Office of Investor Education and Advocacy is issuing this Investor Bulletin to help educate investors about certain aspects of international investing by describing ways individual investors may obtain information about international investments and investments that offer international exposure—including special issues and risks to consider with these investments.

## International Investing

More Americans are investing in international investments or in domestic investments that give them an international exposure than ever before. Although most foreign stocks trade in the U.S. markets as American depositary receipts (ADRs), some foreign companies list their stock directly here as well as in their local market. Many foreign companies are registered and file reports with the SEC, and many more are unregistered and trade in the over-the-counter market. Investors also can purchase stock directly on foreign markets. In addition, Americans can also gain international exposure by investing in U.S.-registered mutual funds or ETFs that hold international investments in their portfolio.

*(Source: "International Investing," U.S. Securities and Exchange Commission (SEC).)*

---

About This Chapter: This chapter includes text excerpted from "International Investing," U.S. Securities and Exchange Commission (SEC), December 8, 2016.

# Should I Consider International Investments?

Two of the chief reasons individual investors invest in international investments and investments with international exposure are:

- **Diversification** (spreading investment risk among foreign companies and markets in addition to U.S. companies and markets); and

- **Growth** (taking advantage of the potential for growth in some foreign economies, particularly in emerging markets).

Investors should consider various factors when assessing potential investments, whether domestic or international.

International investment returns may move in a different direction, or at a different pace, than U.S. investment returns. In that case, including exposure to both domestic and foreign securities in a portfolio may reduce the risk that an investor will lose money if there is a drop in U.S. investment returns and a portfolio's overall investment returns over time may have less volatility. Keep in mind, though, that this is not always true and that with globalization, markets are increasingly intertwined across borders.

Investors should balance these considerations along with issues and risks unique to international investing, including those described below.

# How Can I Invest Internationally?

There are a number of ways individual investors may gain exposure to international investments. As with all investments, investors should first learn as much as they can about an investment before investing.

**U.S.-registered mutual funds.** There are different kinds of U.S.-registered mutual funds that invest in foreign securities, including: global funds (that invest primarily in foreign companies, but may also invest in U.S. companies); international funds (that invest in companies outside of the United States); regional or country funds (that invest primarily in a particular region or country); or international index funds (that seek to track the results of a particular foreign market or international index). Investing through U.S.-registered mutual funds may reduce some of the potential risks of investing internationally because mutual funds may provide more diversification than most investors could achieve on their own and they are subject to U.S. regulations protecting investors.

**U.S.-registered exchange-traded funds (ETFs).** U.S.-registered exchange-traded funds can offer similar benefits as U.S.-registered mutual funds. A share in an ETF that tracks an international index seeks to give an investor exposure to the performance of the underlying international or foreign stock or bond portfolio along with the ability to trade the ETF shares like any other exchange-traded security. An actively managed ETF that invests in non-U.S. assets can also give an investor international exposure along with the same ability to trade the ETF shares like any other exchange-traded security.

**American depositary receipts.** The stocks of most foreign companies that trade in U.S. markets are traded as American depositary receipts (ADRs). Each ADR represents one or more shares of a foreign stock or a fraction of a share. If investors own an ADR they have the right to obtain the foreign stock it represents, but U.S. investors usually find it more convenient and cost-effective to own the ADR. The price of an ADR generally corresponds to the price of the foreign stock in its home market, adjusted for the ratio of ADRs to foreign company shares. Investors can purchase ADRs through a U.S. broker.

**U.S.-traded foreign stocks.** Although most foreign stocks trade in the U.S. markets as ADRs, some foreign companies list their stock directly here as well as in their local market. For example, some Canadian stocks that are listed and traded on Canadian markets are also listed and trade directly in U.S. markets, rather than as ADRs. Some foreign companies list their securities in multiple markets, which may include U.S. markets. Investors can purchase U.S.-listed foreign stocks that trade in the United States through a U.S. broker.

**Trading on foreign markets.** A U.S. broker may be able to process an order for shares of a company that only trades on a foreign securities market. These foreign companies are not likely to file reports with the SEC. The information available about these companies may be different than the information available about companies that file reports with the SEC. Moreover, the information may not be available in English.

# Where Can I Find Information About Investing Internationally?

Investors should learn as much as they can about an investment, and about a broker-dealer or an investment adviser, before they invest. Tracking down information on international investments may require extra effort, but it will make investors more informed. One of the most important things to remember is to read and understand the information about an investment before investing. Here are some sources of information to consider:

**SEC reports.** Foreign companies listed on U.S. stock exchanges or that publicly offer their securities in the United States must file reports with the SEC. The SEC requires these foreign companies to file electronically, so their reports are available through the SEC's Electronic

Data Gathering, Analysis, and Retrieval (EDGAR) website at no charge. However, if the company's securities trade on the over-the-counter markets in the United States rather than on a stock exchange, the company may not be required to file reports with the SEC.

**U.S.-registered mutual funds and ETFs.** Investors can get the prospectus for a particular U.S.-registered mutual fund or ETF directly from the mutual fund or ETF. Many of these funds also have websites and phone lines to assist investors that may provide helpful information about international investing. In addition, prospectuses of U.S.-registered mutual funds and ETFs are also available through the SEC's EDGAR website at no charge.

**U.S.-registered broker-dealers and investment advisers.** A broker or investment adviser may have research reports on particular foreign companies, individual countries or geographic regions. Ask whether updated reports are available on a regular basis. A broker or investment adviser also may be able to provide investors with copies of SEC reports and other information.

**Foreign companies.** Foreign companies often prepare annual reports, and some companies also publish an English language version of their annual report. Ask a broker for copies of the company's reports or check to see if they are available from the SEC. Some foreign companies post their annual reports and other financial information on their websites.

**Foreign regulators.** Investors may be able to learn more about a particular foreign public company by contacting or searching the website of the foreign securities regulator that oversees the markets in which that company's securities trade. Many foreign securities regulators post information about issuers and registrants on their websites, including audited financial statements. Foreign regulators sometimes post warnings about investment scams and information about their enforcement actions that can be useful to investors.

The International Organization of Securities Commissions (IOSCO) includes a list of foreign securities regulators that are members of IOSCO on its website. IOSCO also publishes investor alerts that it receives from its securities regulator members on the Investor Protection page on its website.

**Publications.** Many financial publications and international business newspapers provide extensive news coverage of foreign companies and markets.

**Internet Resources.** Various government, commercial, and media websites offer information about foreign companies and markets. However, as with any investment opportunity, investors should be extremely wary of "hot tips," overblown statements, and information posted on the Internet from unfamiliar sources. For tips on how to spot and avoid Internet fraud, please visit Investor.gov or the "Investor Information" section of SEC's website.

U.S. investors may already have investments that provide international exposure. In the United States, we have access to information and products from all over the world. Foreign companies can achieve the status of household names in the United States without public awareness that these companies are domiciled outside of the United States, or they may conduct a majority of their business operations abroad. In addition, many U.S. companies are multinational corporations or have substantial foreign operations. Investors should conduct a review of their holdings, including any U.S.-registered mutual funds and ETFs, to determine whether the securities they own or are considering for purchase already provide them with international exposure.

# What Issues And Risks Should I Consider When Investing Internationally?

While investing in any security requires careful consideration, international investing raises some special issues and risks. These include:

**Access to different information.** In some jurisdictions, the information provided by foreign companies is different than information provided by U.S. companies. The nature, amount and frequency of disclosures required under foreign law may also be different from that required of U.S. companies. In addition, foreign companies' financial statements may be prepared using a different set of accounting standards than companies use in the United States. Information foreign companies publish may not be in English.

Moreover, the financial statements of publicly listed companies in the United States, whether based in the United States or abroad, must be audited by an independent public accounting firm subject to oversight by the Public Company Accounting Oversight Board (PCAOB). The financial statements of a foreign company that is not publicly listed in the United States may or may not be subject to analogous auditing and auditor oversight arrangements.

**Costs of international investments.** International investing can be more expensive than investing in U.S. companies. In some countries there may be unexpected taxes, such as withholding taxes on dividends. In addition, transaction costs such as fees, broker's commissions and taxes may be higher than in U.S. markets. Investors also should be aware of the potential risks and effects of currency conversion costs on an investment. U.S.-registered mutual funds and ETFs that invest abroad may have higher fees and expenses than funds and ETFs that invest in U.S. securities, in part because of the extra expense of trading in foreign markets.

**Working with a broker or investment adviser.** If investors are working with a broker or investment adviser, they should make sure the investment professional is registered with the SEC or (for some investment advisers) with the appropriate state regulatory entity. It is generally against the law for a broker, foreign or domestic, to contact a U.S. investor and solicit an investment unless the broker is registered with the SEC. If U.S. investors directly contact and work with a foreign broker not registered with the SEC, they may not have the same protections as they would if the broker were registered with the SEC and subject to the laws of the United States. Investment advisers advising U.S. persons on investments in securities must register in the U.S. or must be eligible for an exemption to registration.

Details on a U.S.-registered broker's or investment adviser's background and qualifications are available on the SEC's Investment Adviser Public Disclosure (IAPD) website which is also available through the SEC's website for individual investors, Investor.gov. If investors have any questions about checking the background of an investment professional, they can call the SEC's toll-free investor assistance line at (800) 732-0330 for help.

**Changes in currency exchange rates and currency controls.** A foreign investment also has foreign currency exchange risks. When the exchange rate between the foreign currency and the U.S. dollar changes, it can increase or reduce an investment return in a foreign security. In fact, it is possible that a foreign investment may increase in value in its home market but, because of changing exchange rates, the value of that investment in U.S. dollars is actually lower. In addition to exchange rates, investors should be aware that some countries may impose foreign currency controls that restrict or delay investors or the company invested in from moving currency out of a country. These controls could affect the value and liquidity of an investment.

**Changes in market value.** All securities markets can experience dramatic changes in market value. One way to attempt to reduce the impact of these price changes is to be prepared to hold investments through adverse times and sharp downturns in domestic or foreign markets, which may be long lasting.

**Political, economic, and social events.** Depending on the country or region, it can be more difficult for individual investors to obtain information about and comprehensively analyze all the political, economic and social factors that influence a particular foreign market. These factors may provide diversification from a domestically-focused portfolio, but they may also contribute to the risk of international investing.

**Different levels of liquidity.** Some foreign markets may have lower trading volumes for securities or fewer listed companies than U.S. markets. Some foreign markets are open for shorter periods than U.S. markets. In addition, some countries may restrict the amount or type of securities that foreign investors may purchase. Where these factors exist, a market may have less liquidity, which may make it more difficult to find a buyer when investors want to sell their securities.

**Legal remedies.** Where investors purchase a security can affect whether they have, and where they can pursue, legal remedies against the foreign company or any other foreign-based entities involved in a transaction. Investors should be mindful of this when either buying or selling securities on foreign securities exchanges or otherwise outside the United States or entering into securities transactions with parties located outside the United States. In these situations, investors may not have the ability to seek certain legal remedies in U.S. courts as private plaintiffs. Moreover, even if investors sue successfully in a U.S. court, they may not be able to collect on a U.S. judgment against a foreign company, entity or person. Investors may have to rely on legal remedies that are available in the home country, if any.

The SEC's law enforcement authority with respect to fraudulent conduct protects investors and markets within the United States and protects against fraudulent conduct outside the United States that has a foreseeable substantial effect within the United States. SEC action, however, may or may not lead to the investor receiving funds to redress any fraud. In addition, the SEC may face legal and other obstacles to obtaining information that it would need for investigations or litigation if the information is located in a foreign country.

Investors who would like to provide information about fraud or wrongdoing involving potential violations of the U.S. securities laws may contact the SEC using the SEC's Tips, Complaints and Referrals Portal.

**Different market operations.** Foreign markets may operate differently from the major U.S. trading markets. For example, there may be different time periods for clearance and settlement of securities transactions. Some foreign markets may not report securities trades within the same period as U.S. markets. Rules providing for the safekeeping of shares held by foreign custodian banks or depositories may differ from those in the United States. If a foreign custodian has credit problems or fails, shares purchased in a foreign market may have different levels of protection than provided under the laws of the United States.

# Chapter 41

# Microcap Stocks: Among The Most Risky

## What Is A Microcap Stock?

The term "microcap stock" (sometimes referred to as "penny stock") applies to companies with low or micro market capitalizations. Companies with a market capitalization of less than $250 or $300 million are often called "microcap stocks"—although many have market capitalizations of far less than those amounts. The smallest public companies, with market capitalizations of less than $50 million, are sometimes referred to as "nanocap stocks."

## Where Do Microcap Stocks Trade?

Many microcap stocks trade in the "over-the-counter" (OTC) market. Quotes for microcap stocks may be available directly from a broker-dealer or on OTC systems such as the OTC Bulletin Board (OTCBB), OTC Link LLC (OTC Link), or Global OTC.

- **OTC Bulletin Board** is an electronic inter-dealer quotation system that displays quotes, last-sale prices, and volume information for many OTC equity securities that are not listed on a national securities exchange. The OTCBB is operated by the Financial Industry Regulatory Authority, Inc. (FINRA).

About This Chapter: Text beginning with the heading "What Is A Microcap Stock?" is excerpted from "Investor Bulletin: Microcap Stock Basics (Part 1 of 3: General Information)," Investor.gov, U.S. Securities and Exchange Commission (SEC), November 23, 2016; Text beginning with the heading "Risks You Should Consider Before Investing In Microcap Stocks" is excerpted from "Investor Bulletin: Microcap Stock Basics (Part 3 of 3: Risk)," Investor.gov, U.S. Securities and Exchange Commission (SEC), December 3, 2016; Text beginning with the heading "How Do I Get Information About Microcap Companies?" is excerpted from "Investor Bulletin: Microcap Stock Basics (Part 2 of 3: Research)," Investor.gov, U.S. Securities and Exchange Commission (SEC), November 23, 2016.

- **OTC Link LLC** is an electronic inter-dealer quotation system that displays quotes, last-sale prices, and volume information in exchange-listed securities, OTC equity securities, foreign equity securities and certain corporate debt securities. In addition to publishing quotes, OTC Link provides, among other things, broker-dealer subscribers the ability to send and receive trade messages, allowing them to negotiate trades. OTC Link is registered with the U.S. Securities and Exchange Commission (SEC) as a broker-dealer and operates an Alternative Trading System (ATS) pursuant to Regulation ATS, and is a member of FINRA. OTC Link organizes stocks into three marketplaces based, in part, on the amount and quality of available information about the particular stock.

- **Global OTC** is an electronic inter-dealer quotation system that displays quotes, last-sale prices, and volume information in OTC equity securities. Archipelago Trading Services, Inc., a broker-dealer registered with the SEC, operates Global OTC as an Alternative Trading System pursuant to Regulation ATS.

# How Are Microcap Stocks Different From Other Stocks?

**Lack of public information**. Often, the biggest difference between a microcap stock and other stocks is the amount of reliable publicly-available information about the company. Most large public companies file reports with the SEC that any investor can get for free from the SEC's website. Professional stock analysts regularly research and write about larger public companies, and it is easy to find their stock prices on the Internet or in newspapers and other publications. In contrast, the same information about microcap companies can be extremely difficult to find, making them more vulnerable to investment fraud schemes and making it less likely that quoted prices will be based on full and accurate information about the company.

**No minimum listing standards**. Companies that list their stocks on exchanges must meet minimum listing standards. For example, they must have minimum amounts of net assets and minimum numbers of shareholders. In contrast, companies quoted on the OTC Bulletin Board (OTCBB), OTC Link LLC (OTC Link) or Global OTC generally do not have to meet any minimum listing standards, but are typically subject to some initial and ongoing requirements.

**Risk**. While all investments involve risk, microcap stocks are among the most risky. Many microcap companies are new and have no proven track record. Some of these companies have no assets, operations, or revenues. Others have products and services that are still in development or have yet to be tested in the market. Another risk that pertains to microcap stocks involves the low volumes of trades, which may make it difficult for you to sell your shares when you want to do so. Because many microcap stocks trade in low volumes, any size trade can have a large percentage impact on the price of the stock. Microcap stocks may also be susceptible to fraud and manipulation.

# Risks You Should Consider Before Investing In Microcap Stocks

**Lack of liquidity**. A stock's liquidity generally refers to how rapidly a stock can be bought or sold without substantially impacting its price. Stocks with low liquidity may be difficult to sell, increasing the possibility that you may sustain a more substantial loss if you cannot sell the shares when you want to. Historically, microcap stocks have been less liquid than the stocks of larger companies. Before investing in a microcap company, you should carefully consider that you may have difficulty later selling the stock or that the sale will have a noticeable impact on the stock's selling price.

**High volatility**. A stock's volatility generally refers to how much its price may change in a short period time. Stocks with high volatility generally experience large price changes in a very short period of time. While all stocks experience volatility to some degree, microcap stocks have historically been more volatile than stocks of larger companies. Before investing in microcap stocks, you should carefully consider the possibility that these stocks may be susceptible to sudden large price changes; particularly in light of the potential difficulty you may have selling these stocks, as noted above.

**Fraud**. Reliable publicly-available information about microcap stocks is often limited. Also, the stocks of microcap companies are historically less liquid and more thinly traded (lower volume) than the stocks of larger companies. These factors make it easier for fraudsters to manipulate the stock price or trading volume of microcap stocks.

## What The Frauds Look Like

Many of the new frauds target investors worldwide who purchase "microcap" stocks, the low-priced and thinly traded stocks issued by the smallest of U.S. companies. If the stock price falls, the fraudsters swoop in, falsely claiming that they can help investors recover their losses—for a substantial fee disguised as some type of tax, deposit, or refundable insurance bond. Here's how some of the most common schemes work:

- **Aggressive Sales**: Dishonest brokers purchase large blocks of stock from U.S. issuers at a deep discount. They then use high-pressure sales tactics to persuade non-U.S. investors to buy, often at extremely inflated prices. Once the brokers have finished selling the stock, the price typically collapses, leaving investors vulnerable to substantial losses.

- **Absentee Brokers**: For many investors, the scam ends here. When they attempt to contact the individuals who sold the worthless stock, the investors discover that the brokers have disappeared.

- **Advanced Fee Schemes:** For other investors, the fraud takes on a new twist. Fraudsters posing as legitimate U.S. brokers or firms offer to help the investors recover their losses by exchanging the worthless stock for an established, blue chip stock or by purchasing the stock outright. But investors must first pay an upfront "security deposit" or post an "insurance" or "performance bond."

- **Further Demands for Money**: As long as an investor appears willing to make payments, the fraudsters will keep asking for more—falsely claiming that the payments will cover additional fees, taxes, bonds for the courier service, or other similar expenses.

*(Source: "The Fleecing of Foreign Investors: Avoid Getting Burned By "Hot" U.S. Stocks," U.S. Securities and Exchange Commission (SEC).)*

# Microcap Company "Red Flags"

- **SEC trading suspensions.** The SEC has the power to suspend trading in any stock for up to 10 days if, in the SEC's opinion, it is in the public interest and will protect investors. This can occur if it appears to the SEC that there is a lack of current and accurate information concerning the company and its stock. Before investing, determine whether a company's stock has been the subject of a SEC trading suspension. You can find information about trading suspensions on the SEC's website.

- **Stock promotions (including email, text messages, and social media sites recommending a stock).** Carefully consider whether a company's stock seems to be more heavily promoted than its products or services. Microcap stocks are particularly vulnerable to "pump-and-dump" schemes. These can occur when paid promoters or company insiders make false and misleading statements to create a buying frenzy and then quickly sell their shares before the hype ends. After the promoters profit from their sales, the stock price typically drops and investors lose money.

- **Unexplained increases or decreases in stock price or trading volume.** Carefully consider whether you should invest in a company's stock if the historical price or trading volume of the stock shows dramatic increases or decreases for no apparent reason, as this may suggest manipulation.

- **No history of operational success.** Use caution before investing in a company's stock if the company has no history of operational success; yet still projects large future revenues, especially if the projections appear based solely on information about the company's industry rather than on the company itself.

- **Insiders own large amounts of the stock.** In many microcap fraud cases—especially "pump and dump" schemes—the company's officers and promoters own significant amounts of the stock. When one person or group controls most of the stock, they can more easily attempt to manipulate the stock's price. You can ask your broker or the company whether one person or group controls most of the company's stock; however, accurate information may not be available. You also should consider whether a company issues financial instruments that are convertible into equity/stock positions, as this could mask control over large portions of a company's stock.

- **No real business operations.** Frequent or unexplained changes in company name or type of business, little or no assets, minimal revenues, or implausible press releases may suggest no real business operations.

## How To Avoid Getting Burned

The best way to protect against investment fraud is to ask tough questions about the opportunity and the people promoting it—before you invest. For example, you'll want to know:

**Are the Broker and the Firm Licensed?** Contact your securities regulator to find out. The International Organization of Securities Commissioners (IOSCO) provides contact information for most securities regulators on its website. Be sure to ask whether the broker or the firm has a history of complaints. If the person claims to work with a U.S. brokerage firm, call the FINRA's public disclosure hotline at (800) 289-9999, or visit its website.

**Is the Investment Registered with SEC?** Check the SEC's EDGAR database to find out. But always remember the fact that a company has registered its securities or has filed reports with the SEC doesn't guarantee that the company will be a good investment. Likewise, the fact that a company hasn't registered and doesn't file reports with SEC doesn't mean the company is a fraud.

**Where Does the Stock Trade?** Many frauds involve microcap companies whose stocks are quoted in the "pink sheets" or on the OTC Bulletin Board. These companies generally do not meet the minimum listing requirements for trading on a national exchange, such as the New York Stock Exchange or the Nasdaq Stock Market. And companies quoted in the pink sheets generally do not file reports or audited financial statements with the SEC. It can be very difficult for investors to find reliable, unbiased information about microcap companies. For that reason, microcap stocks can be among the most risky investments.

*(Source: "The Fleecing Of Foreign Investors: Avoid Getting Burned By "Hot" U.S. Stocks," U.S. Securities and Exchange Commission (SEC).)*

# Other Considerations

- Be aware that dormant shell companies that continue to trade may be aggressively promoted and are susceptible to market manipulation.

- Look closely at a company that became public through a reverse merger.

- Look closely at a company that has recently undergone a reverse stock split (reducing the number of shares and increasing the share price proportionately), particularly when the reverse stock split also accompanies a reverse merger in a short time frame.

- Review independent information about the company's management and its directors. Consider whether these individuals have background or expertise in the business of the company.

- Cautiously examine any unsolicited (you didn't ask for it and don't know the sender) stock recommendation.

- Never deal with brokers who refuse to provide you with written information about the investments they're promoting.

- Unless you are accessing an account that you established, do not provide bank or brokerage account numbers, passwords, PINs, credit card information, Social Security numbers (SSN), or other personally identifiable information online or over the phone.

Before investing your money, take these simple steps:

- Check the background and registration status of anyone recommending or selling an investment by using the SEC's Investment Adviser Public Disclosure (IAPD) database, which is available on Investor.gov.

- Find out whether the SEC has suspended public trading of the company's stock by reviewing this list of recent trading suspensions. Also, just because the SEC has not suspended trading a company's stock does not mean that the investment is safe.

- Determine whether the securities offering is registered with the SEC by using the SEC's Electronic Data Gathering, Analysis, and Retrieval (EDGAR) database. If an offering is not registered with the SEC, check if it is registered with your state securities regulator. Registration has important legal consequences impacting your ability to purchase the stock or sell the stock after you have purchased it.

Make sure you understand the company's business and its products or services. Carefully review all materials you are given and verify every statement you are told about the investment.

Pay attention to the company's financial statements, particularly if they are not audited by a certified public accountant (CPA). If there are no financial statements or other company reports, ask your broker to provide any information they can about the company. If your broker has solicited you to purchase this stock and cannot provide you basic information regarding the company (for example, the company's financials), carefully consider whether this is an appropriate investment for you. To report possible securities fraud to the SEC, submit a tip or complaint.

# How Do I Get Information About Microcap Companies?

Investors may have difficulty finding accurate, complete and current information about microcap companies. Many microcap companies do not file reports with the SEC, so it's hard for investors to get the facts about the company's management, products, services, and finances. Before you consider investing in a microcap company, make sure you carefully research the company.

If you are working with a broker or an investment adviser, you can ask your investment professional if the company files reports with the SEC and to provide you written information about the company and its business, finances, and management. Be sure to carefully read any prospectus and the company's latest financial reports. Check to see if the financial reports have been audited. Also, remember you should never use unsolicited e-mails, message board postings and company news releases as the sole basis for your investment decisions. Unfortunately, some of the information you receive may be false or misleading, or may be distributed by persons with an undisclosed interest in causing investors to buy stock for more than it is worth. You can also get information on your own from these sources:

- **From the company.** Ask the company if it is registered with the SEC and files reports with the SEC. If the company is small and not subject to SEC reporting requirements, you could also call your state securities regulator to try to get information about the company, its management, and the brokers or promoters who've encouraged you to invest in the company. Consider whether the management has the background or expertise needed to execute its business plan. Consider whether the company has the resources or any competitive advantage indicating that it will succeed. Carefully review the company's website. You may also consider searching for company information on the OTC Markets website at www.otcmarkets.com.

- **From the SEC.** Many companies must file reports with the SEC. Using the SEC's EDGAR database, you can find out whether a company files with the SEC and get any reports that the company has filed. For companies that file reports with the SEC but do not file them on EDGAR, use the SEC's online form or email the SEC's Public Information Office.

- **From your state securities regulator.** If you have difficulty finding information on a microcap company through the company itself, your broker-dealer, or the SEC, you should contact your state securities regulator to find out whether they have information about the company and the people behind it. Even though the company may not have registered its securities with the SEC, it may have registered them with your state. Your regulator will tell you whether the company has been legally cleared to sell securities in your state.

- **From other government regulators.** Many companies, such as certain banks, do not have to file reports with the SEC. But banks must file updated financial information with their banking regulators.

- **From reference books, websites, and commercial databases.** Visit your local public library or the nearest law or business school library. You'll find many reference materials containing information about companies. You can also access commercial databases that may have more information about the company's history, management, products or services, revenues, and credit ratings. The SEC cannot recommend or endorse any particular research firm, its personnel, or its products. But there are a number of commercial resources you may consult, including: Bloomberg, Dun & Bradstreet, Hoover's Profiles, Lexis-Nexis, and Standard & Poor's Corporate Profiles. Ask your librarian about additional resources.

- **The Secretary of State where the company is incorporated.** Contact the secretary of state where the company is incorporated to find out whether the company is a corporation in good standing. You may also be able to obtain copies of the company's incorporation papers and any annual reports it files with the state.

Just because a company appears to have readily available company information or files reports with a regulator, does not mean it's safe to invest in that company. You should always carefully consider any investment decision.

# Part Five
## If You Need More Information

# Chapter 42

# Directory Of Savings And Investment Organizations

## Information For Savers And Investors

### *America Saves*

Consumer Federation of America (CFA)
1620 Eye St. N.W.
Ste. 200
Washington, DC 20006
Phone: 202-387-6121
Fax: 202-265-7989
Website: www.americasaves.org
E-mail: information@americasaves.org

### *American Association of Individual Investors (AAII)*

625 N. Michigan Ave.
Chicago, IL 60611
Toll-Free: 800-428-2244
Phone: 312-280-0170
Fax: 312-280-9883
Website: www.aaii.com

---

About This Chapter: Resources in this chapter were compiled from several sources deemed reliable; all contact information was verified and updated in March 2017.

### American Financial Services Association (AFSA)

AFSA Education Foundation
919 18th St. N.W.
Ste. 300
Washington, DC 20006
Website: www.afsaonline.org
E-mail: info@afsamail.org

### American Institute of Certified Public Accountants (AICPA)

Professional Ethics Division
220 Leigh Farm Rd.
Durham, NC 27707-8110
Toll-Free: 888-777-7077
Phone: 919-402-4500
Fax: 919-402-4505
Website: www.aicpa.org
E-mail: service@aicpa.org

### Bankrate, Inc.

11760 U.S. Hwy 1
Ste. 200
North Palm Beach, FL 33408
Toll-Free: 855-733-0700
Phone: 561-630-2400
Fax: 561-625-4540
Website: www.bankrate.com

### Better Investing Community

National Association of Investors Corp. (NAIC)
711 W. 13 Mile Rd.
Ste. 900
Madison Heights, MI 48071
Toll-Free: 877-275-6242
Phone: 248-583-6242
Fax: 248-583-4880
Website: www.betterinvesting.org
E-mail: service@betterinvesting.org

## Choose to Save®

Employee Benefit Research Institute's Education and Research Fund (EBRI-ERF)
1100 13th St. N.W.
Ste. 878
Washington, DC 20005
Website: www.choosetosave.org

## Council for Economic Education (CEE)

122 E. 42nd St.
Ste. 2600
New York, NY 10168
Phone: 212-730-7007
Fax: 212-730-1793
Website: www.councilforeconed.org

## Dominion Bond Rating Service (DBRS)

DBRS Tower
181 University Ave.
Ste. 700
Toronto, ON M5H 3M7
Phone: 416-593-5577
Fax: 416-593-8432
Website: www.dbrs.com
E-mail: info@dbrs.com

## Federal Citizen Information Center (FCIC)

General Services Administration's Office of Citizen Services and Innovative Technologies
Toll-Free: 888-8-PUEBLO (888-878-3256)
Phone: 719-295-2675
Website: www.publications.usa.gov
E-mail: Pueblo@gpo.gov

## Federal Deposit Insurance Corporation (FDIC)

Division of Finance
3501 N. Fairfax Dr. Bldg. E
Fifth Fl.
Arlington, VA 22226
Toll-Free: 877-ASK-FDIC (877-275-3342)
Phone: 703-562-2222
TDD Toll-Free: 800-925-4618
Website: www.fdic.gov

### Financial Planning Association (FPA)

7535 E. Hampden Ave.
Ste. 600
Denver, CO 80231
Toll-Free: 800-322-4237
Phone: 303-759-4900
Website: www.plannersearch.org
E-mail: Info@OneFPA.org

### InCharge Debt Solutions

5750 Major Blvd.
Ste. 300
Orlando, FL 32819
Toll-Free: 800-565-8953
Phone: 407-291-7770
Website: www.incharge.org/foundation

### Institute for Financial Literacy (IFL)

P.O. Box 1842
Portland, ME 04102
Toll-Free: 866-662-4932
Phone: 207-873-0068
TTY: 866-662-4937
Fax: 207-873-0118
E-mail: Help@FinancialLit.org

### Insurance Information Institute (III)

110 William St.
New York, NY 10038
Phone: 212-346-5500
Website: www.iii.org

### Investment Company Institute (ICI)

1401 H St. N.W.
Ste. 1200
Washington, DC 20005
Phone: 202-326-5800
Website: www.ici.org

## Investor Protection Trust (IPT)
1020 19th St. N.W.
Ste. 890
Washington, DC 20036-6123
Phone: 202-775-2111
Website: www.investorprotection.org
E-mail: iptinfo@investorprotection.org

## Iowa State University (ISU) Cooperative Extension
2150 Beardshear Hall
Ames, IA 50011-2031
Toll-Free: 800-447-1985
Website: www.extension.iastate.edu

## Jump$tart Coalition for Personal Financial Literacy (JCPFL)
1001 Connecticut Ave. N.W.
Ste. 640
Washington, DC 20036
Phone: 202-846-6780
Fax: 202-223-0321
Website: www.jumpstart.org
E-mail: info@jumpstartcoalition.org

## MarketWatch, Inc.
201 California St.
13th Fl.
San Francisco, CA 94111
Website: www.marketwatch.com

## Nasdaq
1 Liberty Plaza
165 Bdwy.
New York, NY 10006
Phone: 212-401-8700
Website: www.nasdaq.com

### National Association of Real Estate Investment Trusts (NAREIT)
1875 I St. N.W.
Ste. 600
Washington, DC 20006
Toll-Free: 800-3-NAREIT (800-362-7348)
Phone: 202-739-9400
Fax: 202-739-9401
Website: www.reit.com

### National Endowment for Financial Education (NEFE)
1331 17th St.
Ste. 1200
Denver, CO 80202
Phone: 303-741-6333
Website: www.nefe.org

### National Futures Association (NFA)
300 S. Riverside Plaza
Ste. 1800
Chicago, IL 60606-6615
Toll-Free: 800-621-3570
Phone: 312-781-1300
Fax: 312-781-1467
Website: www.nfa.futures.org
E-mail: information@nfa.futures.org

### Native Financial Education Coalition (NFEC)
National Congress of American Indians (NCAI)
Embassy of Tribal Nations
1516 P St. N.W.
Washington, DC 20005
Phone: 202-466-7767
Fax: 202-466-7797
Website: www.ncai.org/initiatives/nativefinancial-ed/nfec
E-mail: nfec@ncai.org

### New York Stock Exchange, Inc. (NYSE)
11 Wall St.
New York, NY 10005
Phone: 212-656-3000
Website: www.nyse.com

## North American Securities Administrators Association (NASAA)

750 First St. N.E.
Ste. 1140
Washington, DC 20002
Phone: 202-737-0900
Fax: 202-783-3571
Website: www.nasaa.org
E-mail: info@nasaa.org

## OTC Markets Group Inc.

304 Hudson St.
Third Fl.
New York, NY 10013
Phone: 212-896-4400
Fax: 212-868-3848
Website: www.otcmarkets.com
E-mail: info@otcmarkets.com

## Securities Industry and Financial Markets Association Foundation for Investor Education (SIFMA)

120 Bdwy.
35th Fl.
New York, NY 10271
Phone: 212-313-1200
Fax: 212-313-1301
Website: www.sifma.org

## TSX Inc.

TMX Group Limited
The Exchange Tower
130 King St. W.
Toronto, ON M5X 1J2
Toll-Free: 888-873-8392
Phone: 416-947-4670
Website: www.tmx.com
E-mail: info@tsx.com

## U.S. Commodity Futures Trading Commission (CFTC)

3 Lafayette Centre
1155 21st St. N.W.
Washington, DC 20581
Toll-Free: 866-FON-CFTC (866-366-2382)
Phone: 202-418-5000
TTY: 202-418-5428
Fax: 202-418-5521
Website: www.cftc.gov
E-mail: Questions@cftc.gov

## U.S. Department of the Treasury

1500 Pennsylvania Ave. N.W.
Washington, DC 20220
Phone: 202-622-2000
TTY: 877-304-9709
Fax: 202-622-6415
Website: www.treasury.gov; www.treas.gov

## USAA Educational Foundation (USAAEF)

9800 Fredericksburg Rd.
San Antonio, TX 78288-0026
Website: www.usaaef.org
E-mail: edfoundation_info@usaa.com

## Wi$eUp

Financial Planning for Generation X & Y Women
200 Constitution Ave. N.W. Rm. S-3002
Washington, DC 20210
Toll-Free: 800-827-5335
Website: wiseupwomen.tamu.edu
E-mail: wiseupwomen@wiseupwomen.org

# Help And Protection For Savers And Investors

### Alliance Against Fraud Alliance Against Fraud (AAF) in Telemarketing

National Consumers League (NCL)
1701 K St. N.W.
Ste. 1200
Washington, DC 20006
Phone: 202-835-3323
Fax: 202-835-0747
Website: www.nclnet.org/tags/alliance_against_fraud
E-mail: info@nclnet.org

### Board of Governors of the Federal Reserve System

20th St. and Constitution Ave. N.W.
Washington, DC 20551
Toll-Free: 800-827-3340
Phone: 202-974-7008
Website: www.federalreserve.gov

### Coalition Against Insurance Fraud (CAIF)

1012 14th St. N.W.
Ste. 200
Washington, DC 20005
Phone: 202-393-7330
Website: www.insurancefraud.org
E-mail: info@insurancefraud.org

### Consumer Federation of America (CFA)

1620 I St. N.W.
Ste. 200
Washington, DC 20006
Phone: 202-387-6121
Fax: 202-265-7989
Website: www.consumerfed.org
E-mail: cfa@consumerfed.org

### Federal Financial Institutions Examination Council (FFIEC)

3501 Fairfax Dr.
Rm. D8073a
Arlington, VA 22226
Website: www.ffiec.gov

### Federal Trade Commission (FTC)

600 Pennsylvania Ave. N.W.
Washington, DC 20580
Toll-Free: 877-FTC-HELP (877-382-4357)
Phone: 202-326-2222
TDD/TTY: 866-653-4261
Website: www.ftc.gov

### Financial Industry Regulatory Authority (FINRA)

1735 K St.
Washington, DC 20006
Toll-Free: 844-57-HELPS (844-574-3577)
Phone: 301-590-6500
Website: www.finra.org

### Municipal Securities Rulemaking Board (MSRB)

1300 I St. N.W.
Ste. 1000
Washington, DC 20005
Phone: 202-838-1500
Fax: 202-898-1500
Website: www.msrb.org
E-mail: MSRBsupport@msrb.org

### National Association of Insurance Commissioners (NAIC)

1100 Walnut St.
Ste. 1500
Kansas City, MO 64106-2197
Phone: 816-842-3600
Fax: 816-783-8175
Website: www.naic.org

## National Credit Union Administration (NCUA)

Consumer Complaints Specialist
1775 Duke St.
Alexandria, VA 22314
Phone: 703-518-6300
Website: www.ncua.gov

## National Fraud Information Center/Internet Fraud Watch

National Consumers League (NCL)
1701 K St. N.W.
Ste. 1200
Washington, DC 20006
Toll-Free: 800-876-7060
TDD/TTY: 202-835-0778
Fax: 202-835-0767
Website: www.fraud.org

## Office of the Comptroller of the Currency (OCC)

Office of Enterprise Governance and the Ombudsman
400 Seventh St. S.W.
Washington, DC 20219
Toll-Free: 800-613-6743
Phone: 202-649-6800
TDD: 713-658-0340
Website: www.occ.treas.gov

## Securities Investor Protection Corporation (SIPC)

1667 K St. N.W., Ste. 1000
Washington, DC 20006-1620
Phone: 202-371-8300
Fax: 202-223-1679
Website: www.sipc.org
E-mail: asksipc@sipc.org

## U.S. Securities and Exchange Commission (SEC)

100 F St. N.E.
Washington, DC 20549
Phone: 202-942-8088
Fax: 202-772-9295
Website: www.sec.gov
E-mail: help@sec.gov

# Chapter 43
# Additional Resources For Saving And Investing

## Other Teen Finance Books from Omnigraphics

### Cash and Credit Information for Teens, *Third Edition*

Tips For A Successful Financial Life, Including Facts About Earning Money, Paying Taxes, Budgeting, Banking, Shopping, Online And Mobile Payments, Using Credit, And Avoiding Financial Pitfalls

### College Financing Information For Teens, *Third Edition*

Tips For A Successful Financial Life, Including Facts About Planning, Saving, And Paying For Postsecondary Education. With Information About College Savings Plans, Grants, Loans, Scholarships, Community And Military Service, And More

## Online Investment Games

### *HowTheMarketWorks*

HowTheMarketWorks.com is owned by Stock-Trak Inc., the leading provider of educational stock market games and stock market contests. It focuses on how the market works rather than giving advice on which stocks to buy.
Website: www.howthemarketworks.com

### *Investopedia Simulator*

The Investopedia Stock Simulator uses real data from the markets, the trading occurs in context of a game, which can involve joining an existing game or the creation of a custom game that allows the user to configure the rules. Options, margin trading, adjustable commission rates and other choices provide a variety of ways to customize the games.
Website: www.investopedia.com/simulator

---

About This Chapter: Resources in this chapter were compiled from several sources deemed reliable; all website information was verified and updated in March 2017.

### Stock Market Game

The Stock Market Game will help you develop positive money habits and prepare you for your future.
Website: www.stockmarketgame.org

### UpDown

UPDOWN is a financial social media that provides users with a virtual investment platform. Its full-fledged trading simulation with a virtual portfolio function allows investors to test and improve their skills through collaboration, competition, and aggregated wisdom.
Website: www.updown.com

### Virtual Stock Exchange (VSE)

V-S-E is the World's #1 Free Global Stock Market Game, with stocks, currencies, and commodities from over 30 different countries around the world. It's trading platform is used by over 20,000 teachers and 200,000 students every year to learn about personal finance, investing, economics, mathematics, and social studies.
Website: www.virtual-stock-exchange.com

### Wall Street Survivor

Wall Street Survivor allows you to get in the driver's seat and manage your own fantasy stock portfolio while competing risk-free against friends and strangers.
Website: www.wallstreetsurvivor.com

## Online Financial Journals And Publications

### Barron's Online

Barron's is America's premier financial magazine providing in-depth analysis and commentary on the markets, updated every business day online.
Website: www.barrons.com

### Business Week

Bloomberg delivers business and markets news, data, analysis, and video to the world, featuring stories from Businessweek and Bloomberg News.
Website: www.bloomberg.com/businessweek

### Forbes

Forbes provides latest business and financial news and analysis covering personal finance, lifestyle, technology, and stock markets.
Website: www.forbes.com

### Investor's Business Daily

Investor's Business Daily provides exclusive stock lists, investing data, stock market research, education, and the latest financial and business news to help investors make more money in the stock market.
Website: www.investors.com

### Kiplinger Personal Finance Magazine

Kiplinger publishes business forecasts and personal finance advice, available in print and online.
Website: www.kiplinger.com

### Wall Street Journal

Wall Street Journal is a daily newspaper providing business, economic, and current headlines from the United States and around the world.
Website: www.wsj.com

### YoungMoney

Articles, surveys, and information about money management for young adults.
Website: www.youngmoney.com

# Web-Based Financial Sources

### CNN Money

CNNMoney is a business site with business, markets, technology, media, luxury, and personal finance information.
Website: money.cnn.com

### Federal Reserve Education

Instructional information about the Federal Reserve, economics, and financial education.
Website: www.federalreserveeducation.org

### Financial Literacy and Education Commission (FLEC)

This website is a product of the Congressionally chartered Federal Financial Literacy and Education Commission, which is made up of more than 20 Federal entities that are coordinating and collaborating to strengthen financial capability and increase access to financial services for all Americans.
Website: www.mymoney.gov

### Financial Planning Association (FPA)

The Financial Planning Association® (FPA®) is the principal professional organization for CERTIFIED FINANCIAL PLANNER™ (CFP®) professionals, educators, financial services providers, and students who seek advancement in a growing, dynamic profession.
Website: www.onefpa.org

### Gainskeeper, Wolters Kluwer Financial Services

GainsKeeper, a part of Wolters Kluwer Financial Services, provides automated tax-based financial tools and services to the investment community.
Website: www.gainskeeper.com

### Investing for Your Future, Rutgers Cooperative Extension

Improve Cooperative Extension System communities' ability to co-create and disseminate programs and knowledge for their publics.
Website: www.investing.rutgers.edu

### Investopedia

Investopedia is the world's leading source of financial content on the web, with more than 20 million unique visitors and 60 million page views each month.
Website: www.investopedia.com

### Investor Protection Trust (IPT)

The Investor Protection Trust (IPT) is a non-profit organization devoted to investor education. The IPT provides independent, objective information needed by consumers to make informed investment decisions.
Website: www.investorprotection.org

### Investor Words

InvestorWords is an online financial glossary and contains over 15,000 definitions, helping millions of individuals understand important concepts required to succeed in today's financial world.
Website: www.investorwords.com

### Investor's Business Daily, Inc.

Investor's Business Daily, Inc. delivers actionable investing content, comprehensive tools, and educational resources to help you make smarter trading decisions.
Website: www.investors.com/ibd-university

### Investor's Clearinghouse, Alliance for Investor Education

The Alliance for Investor Education provides services for investing, investments, and the financial markets among current and prospective investors of all ages.
Website: www.investoreducation.org

## Investorguide.com

InvestorGuide.com is an online guide to investing with thousands of categorized links to financial and investing news, research, tools, and other finance based resources.
Website: www.investorguide.com

## MarketWatch

MarketWatch, published by Dow Jones & Co., is a provider of business news, personal finance information, real-time commentary, and investment tools and data, with dedicated journalists generating hundreds of headlines, stories, videos, and market briefs a day from 10 bureaus in the U.S., Europe, and Asia.
Website: www.marketwatch.com

## MoneyWi$e

MoneyWi$e offers multilingual financial education materials, curricula, and teaching aids with regional meetings and roundtables to train community-based organization staff so that consumers at all income levels and walks of life can be reached.
Website: www.money-wise.org

## MotleyFool.com

The Motley Fool helps millions of people attain financial freedom through its website, podcasts, books, newspaper column, radio show, mutual funds, and premium investing services.
Website: www.motleyfool.com

## NEFE High School Financial Planning Program (HSFPP), National Endowment for Financial Education (NEFE)

The National Endowment for Financial Education (NEFE) empowers financial decision making for individuals and families through every stage of life.
Website: hsfpp.nefe.org

## Seeking Alpha

Seeking Alpha is a platform for investment research, with broad coverage of stocks, asset classes, ETFs, and investment strategy.
Website: seekingalpha.com

## TheStreet, Inc.

TheStreet is a leading digital financial media company whose network of digital services provides users, subscribers, and advertisers with a variety of content and tools through a range of online, social media, tablet, and mobile channels.
Website: www.thestreet.com

# Other Resources For Investors

## TeenBusiness Media, LLC

TeenVestor.com is a comprehensive news and information portal for young investors and their parents/educators. It provides in-depth information about investing, starting your own business, the stock market, and the economy.
Website: www.teenvestor.com

## TreasuryDirect, U.S. Department of the Treasury

TreasuryDirect is a financial services website that lets you buy and redeem securities directly from the U.S. Department of the Treasury in paperless electronic form. You enjoy the flexibility of managing your savings portfolio online as your needs and financial circumstances change—all the time knowing your money is backed by the full faith of the U.S. government.
Website: www.treasurydirect.gov

## U.S. Securities and Exchange Commission (SEC)

The U.S. Securities and Exchange Commission (SEC) protects investors, maintain fair, orderly, and efficient markets, and facilitate capital formation.
Website: www.sec.gov

# Mobile Investment Apps

## Acorns

Acorns is an app that rounds up the spare change from your credit or debit card and helps you to invest it.
Website: www.acorns.com

## Betterment

Betterment is an app that uses screenshots to give you reports on account balances and overall performance.
Website: www.betterment.com

## BlackGold

The BlackGold app gives you all the up-to-date information you could possible need to invest in oil.
Website: itunes.apple.com

## Digit

Digit checks your spending habits and moves money from your checking account if you can afford it. Easily withdraw your money any time.
Website: www.digit.co

## FinMason

FinMason is a free app that gives you unbiased views of investing and the market without actually selling stock advice.
Website: www.finmason.com

## Kapitall

Kapitall treats investing as the game it's so often compared to.
Website: www.kapitall.com

## Mint

Manage your money, pay your bills, and track your credit score with Mint.
Website: www.mint.com

## Openfolio

Openfolio is an app that leverages the influencing power of social media networks.
Website: www.openfolio.com

## Robinhood

Robinhood is a simple brokerage service geared towards those who are just dipping their toes into the investment water.
Website: www.robinhood.com

## Wealthfront

Wealthfront is a simple investment app that bases investments on a portfolio you create, letting their automated algorithms do the rest.
Website: www.wealthfront.com

# Index

# Index

Page numbers that appear in *Italics* refer to tables or illustrations. Page numbers that have a small 'n' after the page number refer to citation information shown as Notes. Page numbers that appear in **Bold** refer to information contained in boxes within the chapters.

347

# D

# G

# H

# I